PSYCHIC CLOSE ENCOUNTERS

D1439891

THE
UFO
FILES

PSYCHIC CLOSE ENCOUNTERS

ALBERT BUDDEN

BLANDFORD

First published in the UK 1999 by Blandford
A Member of the Orion Publishing Group

Cassell & Co.
Wellington House
125 Strand
London WC2R 0BB

Previously published by Blandford as
Psychic Close Encounters – The Electronic Indictment

Distributed in the United States by Sterling Publishing Co., Inc.,
387 Park Avenue South, New York, NY 10016-8810

A Cataloguing-in-Publication Data entry for this title is available and may be
obtained from the British Library

ISBN 0-7137-2799-3

Printed in Great Britain by Cox & Wyman Ltd, Reading, Berks.

Contents

For Marilyn, my long-suffering wife

Acknowledgements

A very limited number of people have been involved in the production of this book. First and foremost, I must express my heartfelt thanks to Anne Silk FADO (Hons), FFDO, FRSA of Great Missenden in Buckinghamshire, UK. At times she has verged on becoming co-author, because of her rare and erudite knowledge of electronic pollution and electromagnetics generally.

Thanks also to Michael Buhler, artist and art-lecturer for his unique speciality of illustrating specific cases with a ufologist's understanding of the significance of imagery to the UFO phenomenon; and for his sensitive drawings that appear in these pages.

Philip Mantle generously provided case material from his own investigations and case-files.

Preface

This book is the culmination of 12 years of involvement in the study of the close-encounter experience. It is the presentation of a theory that is a synthesis of several areas of understanding; a fusion of approaches, each of which explains some, but not all, of the characteristics of the UFO experience with the two unifying and mutual factors of human psychology and electromagnetics.

Because it is an argument that progresses in stages, each level building on the preceding one, there is a structure to the theory that is comparable to the spiral curriculum; that is to say, aspects that are outlined at one point are returned to later, but at a higher level, making for a series of repeated visits with incremental repetition. This expressive technique is appropriate because of the number of across-category concepts that need supporting explanations to clarify them which cannot be set out all at once.

Over the past few years, the ruthless surgery of scepticism has removed much ufological dead wood. In the process, it has elevated the subject, somewhat painfully, to an area of study that contains a scientific approach. Such a clear-out of the muddling jumble of fantasy – largely based on the extraterrestrial hypothesis or other alien intelligence concepts – can only benefit the subject and allow scientists to look upon it without embarrassment. However, these redundant theories arose in the first place because it is so difficult to examine the close-encounter experience and not come away with an overwhelming feeling, if not conviction, that there *is* an intelligence at work.

In its enthusiasm for truth, scepticism can leave the subject stripped of interest without replacing it with new questions and new enigmas. It reveals not only the folly of fantasy, but it tells us that there is no mystery. This is as nonsensical as the faith-based ideas that it rejects, as it implies that everything is known and that there are no further questions to be asked; all is misperception and illusion. Yet, such dismissal is not applied to the chemistry of the cell or the nature of mind; there is a depth and an enigma in both of them which is applicable to the ill-explored, close-encounter experience.

The theory expounded in this book is called the electro-staging hypothesis. Rather than merely causing the phenomenon to evaporate, as scepticism tends to, it redirects the mystery in other directions, one of which explores how the intelligence involved in close-encounters – the human unconscious or, more descriptively, the unconscious intelligence – is able to create the appearance and conviction of an alien intelligence that visits us from the stars. Before it does this, however, it has to cut away the ufological dead wood.

The cases presented have, where required, the identities of the witnesses protected. Most, however, are quite willing to allow their real names to be used. In a few cases, their experiences have already been made public, and they have since regretted this exposure. In such instances, to avoid opening up old wounds so to speak, pseudonyms and initials have been employed.

Some of the cases discussed are illustrated because the language of imagery can say things that words cannot. The intelligence behind the phenomenon knows the power of pictures and primarily expresses itself in imagery. This intelligence, in its quest to manipulate belief and establish an identity for itself in the social world, constantly uses the language of imagery, and actually obtains the raw material for it from similar illustrations in a type of image-recycling process. Cryptic as it may sound, images from some close-encounters have been reproduced as paintings, drawings and statues which have become sacred icons, e.g. the Blessed Virgin Mary or Jesus. Such entities seem to originate from another dimension. The image is important.

Sometimes, the personal evolution of researchers' conclusions is as fascinating as the phenomenon itself. I used to believe in aliens. Over the years, those who became fascinated by the UFO phenomenon typically went through a number of attitude changes – or *should* have done, if they had really approached the subject with a truly enquiring outlook. These evolutionary stages could be mapped out with a certain predictability. They began with the extraterrestrial hypothesis (ETH), moved through conspiracy theories, psychic manipulation, and so on. For example, I was once appalled to realize how my own clever detection of psychic manipulation by 'the Unnamed' was plotted within a sociological study of ufologists' beliefs as a stage of development that many others had shared!

I was equally dismayed by the painful dismantling of much of the evidence for alien activity, even though I always felt uncomfortable with the identification of aliens from another world. They were not alien enough for my liking. They did not seem to be bothered by our different gravity, atmospheric pressure or its gases for breathing, although a few were reported with helmets and breathing apparatus etc. Also, the aliens looked too much like us and, when they did speak, often used the language of the witness. Three final nails in the coffin came in the form of a growing sense of absurdity and in reading two books.

As an investigator, and one working in the UK, I had always preferred to look into a few cases in depth rather than documenting many to lesser extents. I came across the Rowley Regis case in the West Midlands which provided uncontentious evidence of electromagnetic exposure. It was also extremely absurd. It involved aliens who visited an uneducated lady and her dog, spoke in gruff voices of Jesus and Tommy Steele and left in a tiny craft with ski-runners underneath, taking a mince pie each. I became aware for the need of a scale to measure the absurdities that 'contaminated' many other cases: an absurdity quotient.

Then 'The Pennine UFO Mystery' occurred. Jenny Randles relayed Persinger's ideas about the orange ball-of-light phenomenon (BOL) association with close-encounter experiences and expounded her own unidentified atmospheric phenomenon concept. This linked exactly with the Rowley Regis case, where the witness confronted a huge orange ball-of-light before encountering three 'aliens'. Could the electromagnetic fields have triggered her experience just as Persinger suggested? I looked into it, and realized that it was a prime example of just what Persinger had proposed, and it provided an excellent, detailed description of the effects that before were just an idea.

Then I read a publication produced by the Society for Psychical Research (SPR), written by Andrew MacKenzie and called *Hauntings and Apparitions*. I was surprised to learn that apparitions behaved in exactly the same way as UFO-related entities. The cases involving ghosts and entities also had the same infrastructure as close-encounters. From these broad strokes I focused on to detailed aspects that overlapped all the way down the line. From then on, the boundaries between the two areas of study dissolved and the two fused with an exciting ease. The trouble was, however, what seemed obvious to me was ignored by everyone else, or so it seemed.

I plunged into writing a book on how alien intelligences were influencing the human mind from another dimension (after getting the scientific okay from quantum theorist Paul Davies's book *Other Worlds*) and how they were using the mechanisms by which individuals saw ghosts etc. to do this. I even gave a lecture to the British UFO Research

Association (BUFORA), which expounded these ideas. Nobody took a blind bit of notice. Nor should they have, as the speech was full of buzzwords from scientific psi research and was a rush of undigested psychic overlap discoveries.

Then came a quiet period where I suspended any real theorizing and just absorbed the discoveries from researchers, for example Paul Devereux, Jacques Vallée and Jenny Randles. Of course, this list is not exhaustive. I already had a scientific background and read around the subject of UFOs, especially in psychological areas. I collected more and more material on the Rowley Regis case and visited the area itself. This was definitely a turning-point. During my investigations, and from reading other case reports, various features of the landscape such as proximity to quarries, hills, minerals, faults, open bodies of water and radio masts had been linked with high-strangeness cases. When I got to Rowley Regis, there they all were. I was stunned. I felt that I was closing in on a 'final theory', although a huge piece was still missing.

A detailed account of what happened over the next few years would constitute a book in itself, so let me jump to the point when I met Anne Silk. Anne is involved in the wide field of electromagnetics and she gave a lecture to BUFORA, where, to my surprise, she began to quote from an article I had written on the Rowley Regis case. Her views were refreshingly outside of the UFO study 'culture' and after a rapid exchange of material over the following few months, I realized that electromagnetics was the common thread that linked all my ideas so far. It also dawned on me that there is no chance of understanding the UFO phenomenon by only reading books about it; it has to be related to scientific areas outside of UFO study, such as the epic *Electromagnetic Man* by C. W. Smith.

My present position embodied in the electro-staging hypothesis appears to satisfy all of the characteristics of the close-encounter experience that have been identified as such, and it is open-ended in its approach; that is to say, it is a method of practical enquiry that can be developed and tested. I offer a piece of advice – as a parting shot – for anyone developing any theory about close-encounters: remove the concept of an alien intelligence; it has stopped me from getting anywhere in the past, for unfortunately, it does not exist on planet Earth.

Albert Budden

MIDDLESEX

1 The Electro-staging Hypothesis (ESH) – Perspectives and Approach

This section represents a guided tour of the contents of an opening chapter on a collection of interrelating ideas. It is as if you had entered an exhibition called the electro-staging hypothesis, and you have been met at the door by your guide, who then proceeds to give you an introductory talk, followed by a tour of the exhibits.

An efficient guide, who wishes to keep the job, will pause longer over key aspects and explain them up to a point; but, being aware of the size and complexity of the exhibition, and not wishing to confuse anyone with too much, too soon, he or she makes the salient points and presses on. This is the structure of this chapter. Its function is to communicate a way of looking at and making sense of the close-encounter (CE) experience at the same time as describing it. To a large extent, it is a programme of events:

> From the early days of ufology up to and including the Warminster era, researchers' 'filters' for testing for errors and fraud were totally open. This left ufologists open to ridicule. Orthodox scientists have been using closed filters for UFOs. However, it must be possible to set the size of the filter properly, as appropriate measuring instruments have been found to measure what was once regarded as paranormal. Science is therefore, denying itself a lot of information by not accepting the challenge.[1]

During the past 40 years or more, there have been thousands of reports of experiences involving UFOs. The sheer variety of these reports is staggering, and closer scrutiny of them has revealed that 90 per cent of them are misperceptions of mundane objects, such as planes, balloons, meteors, fireballs, birds and astronomical bodies. However, in addition to aerial sightings, there have also been reports of human interaction with 'aliens'.

This apparent contact has evolved over the decades to become increasingly complex. In the 1950s, these close-encounters, as they came to be known, were identified generally as physical confrontations with extraterrestrials and their technology by most of those involved in UFO study at the time. Eventually, a number of alternative theories were put forward, suggesting such origins as underground civilizations, time-travellers, visitors from other dimensions, and combinations of these. The search for an overall explanation has preoccupied many in this field, and it continues, of course, today.

As an investigator of UFO-related events (URE), it has dawned on me that the phenomenon is a *mixture* of different occurrences; some related directly and others quite separate. Therefore, as the stimuli responsible for UFO reports *are* a mixture, it is impossible to formulate a theory that will account for everything reported; it would be like trying to find a common cause for rainbows, coffee, snakes and toffee; it is just not possible. UFO experiences, which include sighting reports, include a *variety* of unrelated identified flying objects (known as IFOs), a *variety* of unknown or scarcely known natural phenomena (such as ball-lightning), a *variety* of hoaxes, plus a *variety* of stories based partly or entirely on fantasy. Therefore, *it is just not possible to construct a theory that would account for everything reported in the UFO study field*. Instead, I have taken representative samples of certain types of URE, and I have constructed a hypothesis to render them understandable, with the secondary aim of wider application.

Such raw data has been analysed and subjected to selective processes by experienced investigators and researchers over the years, and I believe that we are now able to identify the signal among the noise. This rigorous and somewhat sceptical approach has revealed a range of hallmarks and patterns which *do* seem to be associated with genuinely mysterious events that science, if it is to be truly enquiring, should investigate.

In almost all countries of the world there are UFO study groups of amateur or semi-professional status. There are also some countries with official counterparts; notably America, France, Australia and, more covertly, England. Each individual has their own ideas about the nature of the UFO phenomenon, and, of course, those of similar outlook group together. In the early 1990s positions have become so polarized and entrenched that the situation has taken on the feeling of a religious war, where individuals' beliefs are set against others in unyielding opposition. It is against this backdrop of a Cold War in ufology that I write a book, so long overdue. In broad terms, its aim is to outline and develop the *hypothesis that the UFO close-encounter (CE) experience consists of dramatically staged events produced by the human mind in altered states of consciousness.* In many cases, these UREs have physical aspects that are similar to, and are of the same order as, those displayed by what are commonly referred to as poltergeists. The psychic explanation for URE is not a new one, but it has not been adequately formulated. This may be due partly to the fact of specialization; most people outside psychical study often assume that anything psychic is merely 'all in the mind', without physical aspects. Such an assumption does not adequately explain an 'obviously' physical phenomenon involving ground traces, radar returns, photographic evidence, military jet chases and multiple witnessing. Those in psychical research, with few exceptions, retain the popularist view of UFOs as extraterrestrial (ET) in nature and dismiss them as outside their field of interest. This book aims to redress these misconceptions.

To be more exact, my approach states that it is the activity of the human unconscious *in combination* with a variety of natural and artificial energies that produces staged realities identified as the CE experience. This is still to state my approach broadly. It is *the unconscious – or more descriptively, the unconscious intelligence (UI) – that utilizes its reality-defying abilities (including psychokinesis, or 'mind over matter') to produce the effects of an advanced, magical technology in these 'staged productions', its motivating purpose being to establish and maintain an external social identity.* This latter aspect is the key to this approach.

For the most part, it is our conscious mind that governs our behaviour. In our routine, daily lives, we are preoccupied with problem-solving, function-based, survival-orientated consciousness. Most of the time, the expression of the unconscious is secondary, despite having a number of subliminal functions to play as an undercurrent to our conscious selves. This constant hidden activity of the unconscious directs our thoughts and actions. The deeper spiritual levels are those that Jung referred to when he stated that humankind had a natural religious function.[2] It is a part of the mind that all religions have their own name for, and it is an intelligence that is aware that the impressions we have of the world (that we call reality) is really a stable illusion. It includes areas of the mind that communicate with our conscious selves through dreams, art, religion and, of course, insanity.[3] It is the intelligence behind visionary experiences and it is also the intelligence behind UFO CEs. It is a function that is largely 'frustrated'; as a natural state of affairs, there is an imbalance between the two 'selves' that is quite normal, if not actually desirable, in order for us to cope with life. There is, therefore, psychological 'background pressure' to *integrate* the unconscious into the conscious: the intrusion of visionary, psychic and spiritual experiences *is* this integration taking place spontaneously.[4] It is clear that some people are more prone to these experiences than others, and that at the other extreme, there are some individuals whose unconscious content is so latent and repressed that it would take a particularly violent 'psychic explosion' to release it into consciousness!

Although such psychic expressions are usually thought of as 'all in the mind', it is clear that this part of the mind in conjunction with altered states of *body* can actually manipulate physical reality. Under certain conditions, it will use this ability to produce realities with a temporary, upgraded physical aspect, that make those who see them absolutely convinced that they really exist. These realities include the UFO CE experience; the physical manipulation is called psychokinesis (PK); other examples of this process at work are called poltergeists. It is precisely this order of perceptions that brings into question the relationship between our minds and what we conventionally call reality – as it is clear that our mental processes are involved with its production and maintenance at some fundamental level.[5] I have referred to reality as a stable illusion; under certain conditions, this illusion breaks down and it is manipulated by the UI for its own ends. What 'ends' could these possibly be? What would motivate the human unconscious to produce the reality of a flying saucer and alien occupants? As mentioned, the UI *wants* existence and expression in the conscious 'world'; rather like a genie that is cooped up within the confines of a bottle, there is motivating 'pressure' from within to carve out an important piece of the 'real world' for itself.

The reality-status of dreams or even hallucinations is not always enough for the unconscious: it wants to become externalized in a way that dreams do not satisfy. Nor does it only settle for the identity of an extraterrestrial; there is a range to select from, including the Blessed Virgin Mary; spirits of the dead and the living; time and interdimensional travellers; angels, fairies, demons, etc.; or just visitors from 'elsewhere'.[6] Why a particular identity is chosen by the unconscious depends largely on the raw material in the 'picture library' of the individual. Memory-banks are raided by the unconscious and material collected from a variety of sources (such as film, television, books, paintings and icons) is swiftly brought together to produce the close-encounter realities individuals perceive. Sometimes, the job is so hurried it would seem that the different identities are mixed up. It is then that witnesses report such absurdities as trolls piloting spaceships, or the ghost of their dead father cropping up during a confrontation with aliens.

Also, it is evident on close examination of these entity types that the unconscious has delved inwards to produce representations of parts of the central nervous system. Such a strategy provides an entity that appears to be a consistent type, no matter who perceives it, as we all have the same neural structures. In order to explain this, a digression into areas of human biology is required.

In the study of the nervous system, a notional model is constructed (called a homunculus) which is human-like in form, to show the uneven distribution of nerves throughout the human body.[7] It is a figure whose proportions are dictated by nerve density; the more nerves there are in a particular feature, the larger it is depicted in the homunculus. Consequently, we end up with a creature that has huge hands, feet, tongue, genitals and lips, as these are the most sensitive areas. (See the plate section)

Adopting a similar approach, if we take the form of an entity that has been consistently reported and described, such as the UFO-associated 'grey', and work backwards, its appearance, rather than being based on nerve distribution as in the homunculus, seems to correspond to an optically dominant consciousness, at the expense of a reduced representation of the other auditory, olfactory and tactile senses. This reflects the fact that the close-encounter experience predominantly expresses itself visually, that is, through imagery. (See the plate section)

Sociological and religious aspects

The CE is sometimes so dramatic that it amounts to a religious experience which can form the basis for a spiritual movement. Such encounters frequently transform the witness's personality and outlook, causing them, typically, to become more creative, open to new ideas, sensitive, 'Green', diet-conscious (sometimes leading to vegetarianism), psychically aware and, especially, spiritual; in fact, an outlook where the unconscious plays a greater part in daily life in a more overt way. It is exactly this social activity, as a quasi-religious movement, that is sought after by the unconscious as it is a channel for it to become externalized. To an extent, UFO witnesses are modern-day visionaries.

Natural radiation

This is a key aspect in the understanding of UREs, and it is an integral aspect of the ESH. The ability of the unconscious to manipulate the perceptions and, therefore, the reality of the witness, is facilitated by its interaction with electromagnetic radiation. This may originate from natural sources: for example, fault-lines in geological strata, where the physical movement of the rocks creates piezo-electrical charges that build up and are released by earth-tremors or general tectonic strain.[8] Individuals at these locations are subjected to seismic electricity, radio waves and other electromagnetic fields which, although largely invisible, can induce altered states of consciousness that give rise to the CE experience. These 'places of power' often gain a reputation for strange occurrences which is reflected in the folklore of the area. The term 'geopathic stress' is sometimes used for such earth energy.

Unidentified atmospheric phenomena (UAP)

Possibly the most important aspect in the understanding of the UFO phenomenon, and central to the ESH, is the unidentified atmospheric phenomenon, or UAP. This is a general term for a variety of phenomena characterized as luminous spheres (or other shapes) of radiating electro-magnetic energy. Two examples of UAPs are ball-lightning and earth-lights. The former occurs frequently, but not exclusively, in a water-laden, thundery or charged atmosphere, and it has been well documented over the years.

The earthlight, however, has only really been identified and described since 1982 by Paul Devereux. He has presented conclusive evidence that they are produced, like seismic electricity, at fault-lines in geological strata. Although the precise geophysical mechanism for their production is still being investigated, it is evident that powerful piezo-electrical effects in subterranean areas of tectonic strain contribute to the production of this phenomenon. The mechanism of triboluminescence has also been proposed.[9]

The earthlight varies in its appearance, but it is mainly observed as a large sphere of orange light which can irradiate witnesses who get too close, sometimes causing thermal and sunburn effects.[10] The limits to the radiation types that earthlights can emit are not known, but they seem to include ionizing as well as non-ionizing fields at times.

Earthlights are an important part of the ESH because proximity to them not only causes systemic effects, but altered states of consciousness during which the unconscious produces hallucinatory perceptions of the CE experience. It is also evident that they can alter the physiology and electrical emissions from the witness's system, causing a breakdown of the subjective/objective classifications of reality for a short period. This is, in fact, the classical CE event, where the witness or witnesses report seeing a light in the sky and then proceed to an apparent confrontation with aliens. The radical mistake that many researchers make is to fail to identify such CE experiences as two (at least) distinct sections: the confrontation with the UAP and the subsequent encounter experience. A good example of this is the following case:

The Stonehenge incident
Location: On the approach road to, and at, the Stonehenge Monument
Witnesses: Dorne and Lee
Date: On or about 18 November 1990

This case can be summarized as a dual-witness encounter with an earthlight UAP which precipitated reality distortions, including, for one of the witnesses, the hallucination of a humanoid entity.

Both witnesses were in their mid-twenties and they could be described as young professionals – Dorne being a graduate art teacher at a state school.

They were driving back to London after visiting friends and they decided to take in Stonehenge to make their journey more interesting. Both had visited the monument a few weeks previously. On a small approach road to the site, they noticed an orange glow behind a copse to their right, about a hundred feet away. As they approached a road junction, a huge orange globe of light rose up from the trees and hovered in front of the windscreen, keeping pace with the car as they neared Stonehenge proper. They then drove through a band of fog, about waist high and 3 foot (1 m) thick, which spanned the road; after which everything went strangely silent.

Dorne and Lee parked next to the heel-stone, beside the fence, and got out to look at the orange globe, leaving the engine running. For some reason Lee would not look at it, but gazed instead at the full moon above the Stones. During this time, the globe performed aerial acrobatics in a regular pattern which engaged Dorne's attention, while Lee continued his moon-watching. At times, the brilliant orange ball dived behind a small hill nearby or vanished and then reappeared.

All of a sudden, Lee screamed to Dorne to get into the car because security guards were approaching, which she did without looking back and they sped away. The globe followed them as they drove through another band of fog. They stopped in a lay-by after five minutes and Lee recounted what had frightened him so much. Apparently, a dark figure had suddenly appeared beside the monument and approached menacingly and noisily by stamping through the thick leaves. When it got to the fence, Lee saw that it was about 7 foot (2 m) tall and correspondingly broad, and totally black and featureless. It was at this point that he screamed to Dorne to get into the car, although it was behind the security fence surrounding the monument. As they climbed into the car, the figure appeared mysteriously on their side of the fence, and at the moment that they had sped away, it was beside the driver's door.

Still in the lay-by recovering from this getaway, Dorne and Lee noticed that a fresh banana on the dashboard had turned to brown syrup, so they threw it out. The orange globe followed them further, until they reached the motorway, where it vanished.

Comment

This illustrates how close proximity to a radiating UAP can produce a CE reality. The field exposure also 'cooked' the banana, it would seem, accelerating the ripening process.

Artificial radiation

Artificial electromagnetic and/or electrical fields that emanate from radio-wave transmitting antennae, microwave repeaters and television transmitting masts, high-tension cables mounted on pylons (or buried) and a variety of other communication and electrical systems can also induce CE experiences. It is evident that these electromagnetic fields register in the human body, and are then represented by it as hallucinatory or apparitional phenomena, including UFOs and aliens. The effect is intermittent and requires a specific combination of EM-sensitive subjects (a condition described later) and frequency type. The accompanying physical effects on the body and the environment of such an irradiated subject are taken as 'proof' of their alien nature; but, in fact, such symptoms and effects can be found extensively in the literature of biological electromagnetics.[11] The part of the brain or body so affected by such field exposure dictates the *content* of the hallucinatory or visionary experience. For example, if the optical nerves are affected, aliens using a bright ray of light on the eye of the witness may be depicted. This is how the unconscious represents such unnatural radiation in the human system.

These 'places of power' are referred to as 'hot spots', and particularly potent ones, in terms of affecting subjects, are created by a *combination* of natural and artificial radiation.

The psychic/close-encounter overlap

As mentioned above, the altered states induced by radiation from the sources just described give rise to strange realities for the witness and, in many cases, for others too. These realities can be traditional psychic events, such as ghosts and 'guardian angels', poltergeists and coincidences.

They are also mixed and matched with themes of extraterrestrials, which have been added by the unconscious, to produce a very bizarre mixture of perceptions indeed. Setting aside the question of the 'reality-status' or how 'real' these perceptions are, it is clear that the people who perceive these things are an important area of study. This is not to imply that they are unstable in any way, but for anyone who investigates UFO CEs at first hand for any length of time, it quickly becomes almost a cliché to report that these witnesses have a history of psychic experiences. These may include apparitions, precognition, out-of-body experiences (OBEs), 'spirit contact', and dream/waking threshold experiences, sometimes reaching back to childhood. Their UFO encounter is just one more strange event in a catalogue of associated and overlapping experiences.

To an investigator faced with a witness with just such a history, it becomes almost arbitrary as to which experience to focus on to document in a case report. One realizes how meaningless it would be to take their UFO encounter out of this context and to ignore the psychic events. However, this is precisely what those who subscribe to the ETH do.

Such across-category experiences are indicative that the unconscious is responsible for both apparitions and 'aliens' as perceptual realities. This ghost/alien overlap is mirrored in the blurred distinctions between the witness's identification of extraterrestrial encounters and mental contact with disembodied, spirit-like alien intelligences. The two frequently merge and examples of hybrid 'ghost-spacemen' in the case-studies in Chapter Seven is indicative of a cultural merging and the unconscious catering for all shades of propensity to believe.

Why the themes of an advanced alien technology should grow out of, or match, ghostly or spiritual contexts is partly due to the way that the special effects in the realities produced by the unconscious are interpreted. For example: 'The ghost of the ancient mariner fades away to rejoin his dead ship-mates in the ether of the souls'; but 'a spaceman is beamed back to the mothership by an advanced teleportation device, then the signal fades . . .'. This suggests that there are differing interpretations of basically the same perceptual effect, depending on the cultural viewpoint.

Consider the following characteristics of UFO-related 'aliens', each of which is followed by examples taken from the UFO-study literature.

Characteristic one
Their visibility is erratic in that they are likely to appear or disappear suddenly and inexplicably; they fade in or out and are self-luminous.

EXAMPLES:

1 (of an entity) 'He approached the figure, reached out to put his hand on

21

the being's shoulder and, when his hand was about three inches away, the being vanished in front of his eyes . . .' (*FSR*, Vol. 27, No. 1, p. 8)

2 'On November 18th 1957, Cynthia Appleton was in her home at Aston near Birmingham . . . Suddenly there appeared the figure of a spaceman standing on her left by the fireplace. She said he appeared "just like a TV picture, a blurred image and then suddenly everything is clear" . . .' (*Operation Earth*, Brinsley Le Poer Trench) (See the plate section between pages 112 and 113.)

3 'Then, as Bob was standing in the garden, a human-shaped form of some six feet tall materialized in front of him and this was in the form of strips of light, horizontal and one on top of the other. Although startled, Bob put his hand through it but felt nothing, and the image faded away.' (*Earthlink*, Spring 1979, p. 18)

Characteristic two
They may pass through solid walls or locked doors.

EXAMPLE:

1 'It had a head, two arms and two legs, but the arms seemed to be coming from the chest and not the shoulders. There were two beams of light for eyes. I can't believe it but I saw it walk through the fence of the nuclear research place.' (The Ken Edwards case in *The Welsh Triangle*, Peter Paget)

Characteristic three
They may rise into the air without physical support, and may glide instead of walk.

EXAMPLES:

1 'To the boy's amazement, the little creature flew over the hill to a saucer-shaped craft which was about fifty feet in diameter and hovering about five feet off the ground. The object opened, the creature floated in and the craft flew away.' (*Situation Red: The UFO Siege*, Leonard Stringfield)

2 (of entities below a mirror-like UFO) 'After a conversation with him that lasted a few moments they turned and glided away apparently suffering no impedance from the rough grass.' (*Northern UFO News*, Autumn 1983)

Characteristic four
They may communicate ideas without words, gestures or other symbols (i.e., telepathically).

EXAMPLES:

1 (of an entity) 'And the eyes were like eggs, egg-shaped, very round and penetrating. When you heard this voice in your head, what did it sound like? He only said, "please don't be afraid"; and it sounded very mellow and warm'. (*The UFOnauts*, Hans Holzer, 1976)

2 'He was floated into a room and given a medical examination on a table or bed. There was a tall human-like being in a white cloak . . . the examining was done by smaller beings, about 3½ feet tall "with heads shaped like lamps" . . . the aliens also told Alan by telepathy that they knew him.' (The Alan Godfrey case in *Abduction*, Jenny Randles, 1988)

3 'During the initial establishment of what seemed to have been mental telepathy, Betty misconceived a mental impression generated by Quazgaa. The leader stretched out his hand, and she asked, "Do you want something to eat?" They merely nodded.' (*The Andreasson Affair*, Raymond Fowler, 1979)

Characteristic five

They are often perceived tactually and audibly as well as visibly, and these three kinds of perception are consistent with one another.

EXAMPLE:

1 'The next thing Schirmer remembered was rolling down the window of his car. One of the strangers grabbed him and pressed against the side of his neck. Schirmer got out of the car. The alien asked him, "Are you the watchman over this place?" . . . Officer Schirmer asked whether the stranger was for real. In answer he squeezed his shoulder.' (*The UFOnauts*, Hans Holzer, 1976)

From the above, it does seem that the characteristics given before the corresponding examples are an accurate summary of the nature of UFO-related entities. However, the only trouble is that it is actually a list of characteristics of *apparitions* compiled by the Society for Psychical Research from their case reports and published in Andrew MacKenzie's book, *Hauntings and Apparitions* (1982). One of the things that surprised me when I began my research into apparitions was the fact that they display selective physical characteristics.[12] Witnesses have felt their touch; they obscure objects, such as furniture; they reflect in mirrors; they are seen by groups of witnesses; they negotiate around objects and use doorways (in addition to appearing transparent and ephemeral in other cases). These modes of apparent physical substance are obviously, from this comparison, shared by UFO-related entities. The point is: the unconscious has a repertoire of effects that are repeated in both contexts.

Nor is this ability to produce these perceptions confined to entities.

There are reports of flying discs and planes that could not have been there in a mundane sense, but played their part in the 'staging' of a CE experience for the witness, as their own personalized reality. Similarly, phantom stage-coaches and even buses have been reported, which somewhat negates the 'spirits of the dead' interpretation of ghostly realities.

The scientific status of the electro-staging hypothesis

If a theory is to be regarded as scientific, it must be able to be tested. The experiments used for testing must be repeatable by others to get the same results or otherwise as the case may be. The theory must also be able to be disproved if it is incorrect.

There are various interrelating aspects of the ESH, one of the most important of which is the influence of UAPs. This is the name given to centres of radiating energy that travel through the atmosphere. They are usually luminous (but not always) and include, as stated above, ball-lightning and earthlights. Furthermore, it will be argued that there are artificially created UAPs (albeit accidentally), called 'electroforms' that can also irradiate the witness. However, whatever the type, each radiates electromagnetic energy.

While we may not have a UAP to test, the radiation that they give out can be produced under controlled conditions, and the conclusions that we have come to regarding their effects on the human system have been through reports from those who have encountered them. There has been quite a lot of work carried out on this aspect and a good deal of it will be presented in the relevant chapters. In particular, studies published in the *Journal of Bioelectricity* by Dr M. A. Persinger, Dr A. Ruttan and Dr Stanley Koren describe experimental findings which confirm the effects of electromagnetic fields on the human system mentioned so far. Basically, what they say is that subjects *do* hallucinate and develop altered states of consciousness (ASCs) when exposed to such fields.

The ESH argues that the unconscious frequently responds to these fields during altered states, and presents perceptions and/or realities that are dramatic representations of interaction with aliens and their technology, the purpose of which is to establish an acceptance of the unconscious in society. Let us split this into its elements to examine its scientific aspects. One of the ways that dreams are expressed is by dramatization. Dream sequences portray aspects of the psyche that reflect inner wishes and anxieties. It is this expressive form of the unconscious, recognized by psychoanalysis, that is utilized during CEs. However, the encounter medium is not always an internal cinema but what could be called external 'field-boosted' realities, which is as good a term as any at this stage of the argument. The point is, whatever the reality-status of these perceptions (which have transient physical properties), they *could* be reproduced under controlled conditions; or, to be more exact, the conditions proposed for their production could be reproduced in a controlled way. From the examination of numerous reports, they obviously have been reproduced under 'accidental' or uncontrolled conditions. The closest to a controlled situation is an authentic seance, where undoubtedly fields are involved.

It would be only too easy to subject individuals to artificial fields without their knowledge to see if they produce strange realities and perceptions around which they weave a belief system, but would it be ethical? Moreover, just what type of experiment would it take to test if the unconscious *is* actually trying to integrate into society under these circumstances? The point being made is that this aspect of the ESH *could* be tested, and the problems of experimental design overcome, but it would involve an infringement of human rights. Experiments on people are frowned upon in official circles, at least in public.

A far better way would be to find such conditions and individuals 'in place' and determine their belief systems. A good example of this is provided by the 'Jane Murphy' case examined in the final chapter. However, in my investigations it is equally clear that not every encounter experience has this belief-inducing effect, and some are more successful than others, and some are completely unsuccessful. In the 'Terror in the House of Dolls' case, for example, the sudden appearance of groups of little androgynous cloaked beings in the house of the family concerned terrified them. Perhaps this reaction is incidental and some of the family members *do* now recognize the possibility of an alien race. In some cases, the witness does not develop a change of outlook or a belief system until it is triggered at a much later date when they come into contact with someone who provides an 'identification' of their experience, or puts it into a context to which they can relate. In these cases, the strange, anomalous event remains just that, and it exists in their memory as a perceptual island, unrelated to anything that they have experienced before or since. However, if the phenomenon (this actually means anything that is apprehended by the senses) had *any* effect on their *Weltanschauung* (or 'world-view'), then to some extent the unconsicous has accomplished something in the social world. It is obvious, however, that not *all* psychic or CE experiences lead to a belief system. Just as humankind's sex drive is ultimately to ensure the survival of the species, it has many forms and outlets that do not necessarily result in a birth. In the same way, a religion or belief is not always born out of a psychic or CE experience, and it is the generalized psycho-social processes associated with CE experiences that are induced by the unconscious. It makes use of the social pressures of consensus that 'make real' social structures. This process is known as reification in sociology. This can be a very vigorous process, as folklorists will testify. The 'folklore effect' is a strange phenomenon propagated, ultimately, subliminally. It is where an idea catches the public imagination so strongly that even people in authority will conspire in a double-think way to propagate a belief in something that really does not exist. This is precisely the social effect referred to earlier regarding the aim of the unconscious in producing the CE experience.

Tracing the genesis of a belief system, however, is a sociological activity, and sociology is not an exact science; indeed, in the opinion of most sociologists, it is not a science at all. Generally speaking, there are inherent problematical aspects in terms of objectivity.[13] That is to say, man studying social man is very different from man studying the natural world. In the latter, man is part of a separate system. He is distinct from nature and he is 'culture-bound'. This means that he brings with him an internal set of values, norms, assumptions, etc., to the study of another human group which affect his interpretation of the data and the design of the experiments themselves. There is nothing intrinsically wrong with this approach, as long as such value-judgements are recognized. However, sociology cannot be regarded as scientific in the same way as, say, testing crystal formation or the behaviour of light waves. It is a fundamental error to regard social realities as having the same objective status as nature.[14] So, with these reservations in mind, it would be *possible* to set up a social experiment to test the hypothesis that CEs have a tendency to create belief systems, and that such systems become the basis for social coherence in the same manner that religion does.

The Subud connection

There is extensive sociological literature on the social reality of religion, where groups have developed out of an individual's visionary experience.[15] A good example of this is the development of the Subud faith, where such an experience was triggered by what can only be described as an unidentified atmospheric phenomenon (UAP). An understanding of the function that a close-encounter experience can fulfil is an important issue, as it adds to the evidence regarding its nature.

In the 1950s, Pak Subud, who had no particular religious background, encountered a large sphere of blinding light that came down and enveloped him while he was walking through an open rural area. It transformed him into what J. G. Bennett, the person who brought Subud to England, called a 'meditative ecstatic state', where he felt that he had contacted his unconscious, or 'soul'.[16]

After this experience, Pak only had to be in the presence of someone for this state to be passed on to them, and he appeared actually to emanate light. He felt that he should pass on to others this power which created a channel from the conscious mind to the unconscious. As a result, Subud meetings developed. The initiation of individuals into Subud can be very dramatic, and even traumatic. It takes place at a gathering of established Subud members. They simply meet in a room and the initiate joins them. Men and women are segregated into different rooms.

There is no formal dogma or structure whatsoever; neither is there any teaching. The initiation ceremony for new members is called the Latihan, or the 'Opening'. When all are assembled, somebody simply says, 'Begin.' The session ends with someone saying 'Finish.' This may seem rather empty, but an ex-Subud member relates that when she was present for her Latihan, it was far from that. At first, nothing happened apart from people around her chanting, crying and praying. Eventually, feeling bored, she knelt down and immediately found that a force descended upon her and whirled her around so hard that she was repeatedly flung bodily across the room. This was repeated on subsequent meetings. Nothing else happened, so she left Subud.

A little later, she had a complete mental and physical breakdown and became unbearably sensitive. She developed multiple allergies and had to revise her diet, eating and drinking only pure, fresh food. She did not smoke or drink, and she could not take sugar without becoming ill. Electrical equipment malfunctioned in her presence and she developed an intolerance to fluorescent light. She developed psychic sensitivities and began to experience apparitions and other entities at night which took on a strong spiritual significance for her. These visitations continue to this day, nearly 15 years after her Latihan. Encounters with UAPs can produce exactly the *same* effect, as will be described later. The Subud example demonstrates a number of aspects of the ESH, which are:

1 It is a good example from relatively recent times of a religious movement that developed directly from an ostensibly visionary experience, which is indistinguishable from a CE experience with a UAP – a type which has been described in thousands of cases in the UFO-study literature.

2 It shows how the original experience gave rise to a 'contagion effect', both in terms of social grouping and the stimulation of the unconscious, to

produce psychic effects (i.e., the initial energy and the subsequent entity perceptions).

3 It demonstrates how stimulation of the unconscious can bring about a permanent change in outlook, as well as alterations to the physiology, perceptions and sensitivity of an individual. *It is precisely this order of change that can occur as a result of a CE experience, as a result of which the witness effectively functions as a 'medium', 'sensitive' or focus-person would in a haunting or poltergeist outbreak.* Typically, like this woman after the Latihan, witnesses report a range of psychic phenomena in the post-encounter period. These include poltergeist effects and apparitions, and also extra-sensory abilities as a result of their increased sensitivity due to the 'opening', or stimulation, of their unconscious. During the CE, their nervous system is exposed to EM radiation (from sources already mentioned). The Latihan produces a similar effect by group activation, and this suggests that there is an overlap between the action involved in both cases; *that is to say, there seems to be a 'matching' and similarity between such human group influences and electromagnetic fields in relation to their effects upon the human system.* This is not, of course, the only evidence of this that shall be presented, but it is mentioned here to introduce the concept.

4 It is common for close-encounter witnesses to suffer some type of disabling or debilitating effects as a result of their experience, just as this woman found that her general health collapsed. Such effects are usually much less dramatic.

5 The violent effects underline the extremely physical aspects of certain psychic phenomena, in contradiction to the generally held assumption that they are 'all in the head' – mental, subjective effects, or insubstantial apparitions.

6 It has strong parallels with the induction of PK effects by group effort in the 'Phillip' experiment conducted by A. R. G. Owen in Toronto in the 1970s. This involved concentrated group-will to produce the effects and communication of an imaginary entity. The Latihan does not use directed group-will as such, but as mentioned, a contagion effect originating from an initial close-encounter experience, created by the personal energetic emissions from the members in a group.

7 If a group of 'activated unconscious minds' can produce psychic effects in an individual (as we saw with the Latihan), then it follows that such effects may be possible 'naturally', without the conscious organization of such groups as Subud, and the concept of a network of unconscious minds producing or contributing to the precipitation of a CE experience is an interesting idea. This is certainly in accord with apparitional theory:

This may lead us to wonder whether a ghostly presence could be created unconsciously by a person with strong psychic abilities, and whether this presence could be perceived by others. The line of speculation suggests that, if poltergeist phenomena may be created by a living person's repressed hostility, apparitions may be created by other repressed needs of a living individual.[17]

The ability of the unconscious

In the previous section it has been argued that the unconscious presents purposefully 'staged' events to give the appearance of the existence of a range of identities. Before we even look at any of the mechanisms that are used to accomplish this, it is obvious that the unconscious is in a very advantageous position for this task. It is in touch with the inner store of imagery, experiences and beliefs of the individual; it has 'insider' knowledge of the operations of the perceptual system and, therefore, what would be required to satisfy and convince that system of the reality of something.

In addition to this, it can also manipulate physical reality in a variety of remarkable ways – psychokinesis. So, the human unconscious is in a very powerful position to be able to create realities not only for its owner, but also, to some extent, for others too.

Interaction with these realities also varies in complexity, from a simple brief perception to reoccurring exchanges over an extended period. In any particular case, what merits a private hallucination and what involves extended group perceptions depends not only on the internal potential of individuals, but also on the ambient conditions that affect the altered state of consciousness (ASC). It is this ASC, where the unconscious is dominant, that is transitory in nature, and has to be both triggered and maintained.[18]

The unconscious in any one individual scans the immediate environment around it on a more or less permanent basis, and when it detects such an energy, it uses it to create an apparition, vision or CE experience. This is why electronic equipment frequently malfunctions during such experiences (i.e., there are redirected electromagnetic energies involved).

Individual outlets for the unconscious vary. In some instances, psychological pressure from latent trauma can intrude into consciousness in the form of irrational behaviour, nightmares, apparitions, visions, or close-encounters. Art therapy enables individuals to externalize their repressed, painful feelings in a more controlled manner as graphic symbols, thereby making them easier to perceive and, therefore, to cope with. A considerably more dynamic approach is the theraputic concept of 'psychodrama'. This group-therapy approach entails endowing chosen actors with the identity of those in the patient's family that have been the cause of, or were instrumental in creating, unresolved conflicts in their earlier life. This 'let's pretend' approach encourages the projection of the identity of these 'guilty' parties on to proxy individuals, which provides a substitute confrontation with those who have injured the subject. The aim is for the emotional impetus to override the fact of pretence, and the expression of real 'connected' and directed emotions from a previously frustrated position.[19]

Similarly, 'alien abduction' experiences can function on the 'trauma pressure' that is harnessed by the unconscious as an expressive vehicle for inner pain. The 'abduction' scenario is a symbolic 'acting out' and is, therefore, a form of psychodrama. The implication is, therefore, that such encounters are internally perceived visions, and it will be shown that the physical aspects are the product of an exposure to electromagnetic fields, which produces the altered state facilitating the experience in the first place.

Primal therapy

This was developed by psychiatrist Dr Arthur Janov in the 1970s. Basically, what Janov says is that people become neurotic in adult life due to traumatic events that happened to them in their early years that they have repressed and forgotten. Then they forget that they have forgotten. These deeply buried traumas remain in the personal unconscious and create irrational anxieties. Over a period of time, this develops into a state of stress which undermines the performance of the individual's rational functions when any generalized anxiety occurs. This repressed stress in itself can act as a trigger to perceive apparitions, hallucinations, etc., just as it gives rise to the vivid imagery in nightmares. It will be shown later how this stress-related unconscious state is triggered by the additional stress of excessive sound and light, which is harnessed by the unconscious purposefully, as part of the stage management of CEs.

Janov's method allows the person to feel the original non-symbolized pain created by trauma. This 'pain-connection' is a 'primal', and it is healing in itself. During neurotic stress, the individual deals with it by symbolizing it, and because of the impairment of the rational functions during this, the unconscious can become dominant over the conscious mind and throw up (an analogy with vomiting to clear the system of unwanted material) imagery that enters conscious perception. Janov presents an example of this as someone who had developed a particular belief system:

> And then they came. One night I lay down and fell asleep. While sleeping, I became aware that I was floating about the house from room to room. I flew into the kitchen and there they were, two lads from the spaceship, dressed in uniform. Each one lightly grabbed one of my arms and escorted me through the window into our backyard, and we started ascending. I was afraid to say anything to them, but I heard that rumbling sound again, sort of like a huge diesel engine. It was the sound of the saucer. I struggled to be free of them, and the next thing I knew that I was awake, shaking in fear. They had made their move. Never have I had a dream so vivid; never had I been so aware. That was no ordinary dream – they had made actual contact with me. They had complete control of the astral plane.[20]

There are a number of relevant issues here for the 'alien abduction' experience, or CE4:

1 This 'abductee' as a patient of Janov symbolized early trauma, as the experience described.

2 This experience is entirely indistinguishable from other CE4 experiences, and suggests that they too share this aspect of externalized trauma. Comparison with 'actual' reports reveals an overlap with even the subsidiary details, such as the time-lapse-like scene change, where the percipient suddenly finds himself back at home with no sense of transition.

3 This condition of repressed trauma builds up in all stable individuals who use 'normal' defence mechanisms to cope with these early precipitations of stress, or 'Pain', as Janov terms them. Consider this extract from his book:

> I have pointed out that early events register in our systems even when there has been no consciousness of them. Thus our systems register 'trauma' while the mind – our consciousness – may be registering 'happiness'. We can 'lie' to ourselves and can believe we are happy while Pain rages quietly within.[21]

This important aspect of 'normalized' trauma is explored in relevant sections later; but it must be emphasized that there is no suggestion that all 'abductees' are mentally ill in any way. Instead, as Janov's work discovered, we all take on board and accumulate developmental trauma and learn to cope with it as part of growing up; it is just that some traumas are more difficult to contain in this way than others, and it is against this background of 'normal' developmental stress that the unconscious utilizes such life situations to propagate the abduction drama – in addition to other expressive outlets, such as dreams, that are also an expression of the unconscious. In fact, vivid 'abduction' dreams are often interspersed with 'abduction' experiences 'proper'. Also, a significant correlation here is the fact that poltergeist activity can occur as a result of externalized stress: this is Jung's exteriorization theory.

This theory certainly supports the ESH and it serves to link the poltergeist phenomenon to the CE experience. Developmental, or normalized, trauma, repressed anger and situational stress can all undermine rational consciousness and result in a dramatized externalization of some type; such factors are common to all of us.

Returning to the 'abduction' experience of Janov's patient, there is also, in addition to the 'time lapse' aspect, another linking feature. This is the confusion that witnesses display regarding the reality-status of their experience (i.e., 'Was I awake or was I dreaming?'). There are so many psychic special effects at the disposal of the unconscious and, as stated, it is in a powerful position to convince the conscious mind of the reality of its 'productions'. The super-real dream or visions on the waking/sleeping threshold are standard methods for presenting purely internal experiences as external events and take place when the brain is subjected to electromagnetic fields. It completely side-steps the complications involved in maintaining an altered state when the percipient is fully conscious. These complications relate to the control of sensory noise, and this extremely important aspect is explored in later sections. In the case of the super-real dream, the unconscious has upgraded the dream state to make it almost indistinguishable from waking perception.

The out-of-body-experience (OBE)

Another super-real dream experience which sometimes occurs during, or in association with, 'alien abductions', and confirms their internal nature, is the out-of-body experience (OBE).

I investigated a case involving this overlap which involved showbiz sports coach, GM. He 'awoke' one night to find two silver-suited 'spacemen' standing by the bedroom window, one of which was holding a small box-like device over a pile of medical books. They had their backs to him, and startled by their presence, he began to step out of bed to cross the room towards them. He suddenly found that he was floating above them, somewhere near the ceiling. Glancing down at his bed, he could see his own body. He stared at the spacemen for a few bemused seconds until they appeared to catch sight of him, when they too reacted in an equally startled manner. They stared up at him with a shocked and horrified look on their faces and then promptly vanished. GM found himself back in bed 'again'.

This 'false awakening' occurs as part of a CE4 which this case could have developed into had the unconscious wished for such an expressive outlet. Thus, it is evident that the two classifications of experience overlap.

An interesting confirmation of this appeared in an article in *New Scientist* by Susan Blackmore. Consider the relevant extract on the comparison of both the OBE and the CE4 with 'false awakenings' which is also what both of the accounts seem to be similar to:

> In all these experiences, it seems as though the perceptual world has been replaced by another world built from the imagination, a hallucinatory replica. Put this way, it becomes obvious that other experiences fit in the same category. Celia Green, of the Institute of Psychophysical Research in Oxford, has called them 'metachoric experiences'. They include the OBE in which you seem to come out of your body to float up to view things from above. Although traditionally thought to involve the separation of an astral body or soul, this experience is better understood as a replacement of the perceived world by one from memory and imagination. Interestingly there is plenty of evidence, including that from my own surveys, that the same people that report having OBEs also have lucid dreams; many of them say the experiences feel very similar, if not identical. Jayne Gackenbach, a psychologist from the University of Alberta in Canada, relates these experiences to near-death experiences and stories about abductions by UFOs. Although the 'UFO abductions' may be the most bizarre, they too involve the replacement of the perceived world by a hallucinatory replica.[22]

The aspect of a perceptual reality being replaced by one based on memory and imagination can be considered as a stage-management strategy. To explain it further, consider the following extract from an unpublished book that I wrote in 1984:

> Notional Duplicates: This concept was proposed as a method by which the perceptions of the witness could be manipulated. Basically, the process involves replacing genuine perceptions with an internal *image* of them. An analogy will make this clear.
>
> The security system of certain companies and government establishments consists of a number of television cameras situated about the building, mounted high up on the walls. They cover various rooms,

corridors and other access points, and the images they receive are monitored in a central security room. This room contains a number of television monitors which correspond to each security camera. If an intruder enters the building he will be 'seen' by one of the cameras, and will register on one of the screens in the central security room. However, if this intruder is able to take a photograph of the image that a camera 'sees', such as a corridor with a door at the end, and then quickly positions the photograph in front of the camera, it will appear as if it is still 'seeing' the corridor, when in actual fact it is really registering an *image* of it. The intruder can then use the access door to gain entry without being seen. The security man will still believe that he is seeing the actual corridor. 'Notional duplicates' operate in the same way. They replace the reality that an individual would normally perceive with an image that duplicates the appearance of that reality. With the human perceptual apparatus, the images that replace reality are derived from a memory of that reality. The unconscious is able to tap in to that part of the nervous system that controls perceptions and introduce another 'staged' signal instead of the one derived from the environment. A similar effect could be produced with our hypothetical closed circuit television system if a screen is erected and a pre-produced moving film is shown. If this film had been altered to include some special effects, so far as the poor security man was aware, he would see apparitions appearing and disappearing or aliens materializing through the walls! With CEs, it is as if the 'normal' perceptual signal is interrupted and a 'psychic video' plays through the perceptual apparatus, giving a simulated reality, just as alternative unconscious imagery is 'played' during sleep as dreams.

It is evident that the human consciousness is vastly underestimated, and that the UI, in conjunction with the powerful energies from the Earth's strata and artificial sources in one form or another, *is* able to present productions with alien *themes*. This is simply evident by examining the content of what are termed 'high-strangeness' encounters in particular, as it is clear that there is a mixing of alien themes with traditional psychic or supernatural phenomena. We find fairies and goblins piloting 'spaceships'; ghosts of relatives appearing during CEs; and even, in one example, 'black shuck', the dark ghostly dog lounging in the corner of a carpeted flying saucer.[23] There is not always a very selective casting director in these psychically staged performances. Overall, then, it is only too obvious that there could only be one origin for all these realities – the unconscious, or more specifically, the UI.

The UAP/close-encounter interface

The 'spacecraft' images that the 'picture library' contains are derived partly from the mass media. They are adapted by the selectivity that the unconscious displays to be almost unrecognizable from the original. However, if the witness has not been exposed to such images for one reason or another (such as a disinterest in science-fiction), then the unconscious uses almost any form to represent an alien 'craft', as long as it is enigmatic. This is why we get such a range of shapes, forms and sizes reported as UFOs, for example, cylinders, ovals, spheres, cigar-shapes, rugby-balls and, of course, discs. These basic forms are the prototype for a personalized alien spaceship with an assortment of embellishments, such as aerials, vents, windows and even propellers! As a result, this makes any analysis of their possible structure and propulsion both intriguingly mysterious and impossibly absurd.

Unexplained lights have also been produced as 'psychic effects' during seances, where the medium, who would be comparable to the witness in an altered state, induces such effects around him or her. Similarly, the 'focus' in poltergeist activity, also comparable with the CE witness, induces unexplained aerial lights around them. If these phenomena are mixed and matched with the luminosities and energetic effects associated with UAPs, there is scope for quite spectacular combinations which can leave physical traces, such as burns on the ground, scorched vegetation, watch malfunction, radio set disruption, water volatization, stopped car engines, retina burns, 'sunburn,' nausea, 'black-outs', amnesia, *petit mal*-epileptiform periods, and hallucinations; in fact, all of the reported CE effects. These 'medium lights' are described in Chapter Five.

Potentially, then, we have quite a complex picture where the witness's unconsciously derived imagery interacts with, and is influenced by, the natural energetic effects of the UAP. The Rowley Regis event (see Chapter Seven) is a good example of this extreme situation where personalized imagery interacts with UAP energies. An example of a hallucinatory CE experience induced by proximity to a UAP is the event which took place on Plumstead Common, south-east London, on 17 July 1978. A woman who decided to rest on the grass while her husband and children went on ahead was suddenly confronted with a large ball of orange light which came hurtling down out of the sky and settled on the ground about 50 yards (46 m) away from her. Totally bemused, she watched as two entities, who changed size as they walked towards her, confronted her in costumes which were a cross between space-suits and chauffeur's uniforms with peaked caps. Then the figure of her father, who had been dead for six years, appeared in a suit and sat on the grass beside her. At this point she felt all the blood drain downwards in her body and she passed out. She lost her sight for about three months and ended up in hospital.

Encounter analysis

This URE includes a number of aspects already mentioned:

1 A UAP emitting a range of radiation types that irradiated the witness. The energies caused trauma to her eyes and induced an altered state. Effects to her physiology included dermal irritation similar to that caused by extreme exposure to ultra-violet and infra-red light.[24] The loss of consciousness was probably caused by exposure to an electrical field, just as the circulatory symptoms could have been due to muscular spasm induced by neurone over-stimulation, squeezing the blood from its normal course.[25] These effects are by no means unique and have occurred in a number of cases, in particular the Rowley Regis event.

2 Non-UFO-related examples of 'black-outs' caused by electrical fields are contained in an environmental study of power-lines over the Dorset village of Fishpond in the 1970s.[26] This is just one example of many that will be given of the overlap in terms of systemic effects between natural and artificial radiation.

3 The entities themselves embodied a number of ideations:

(a) Chauffeurs – those who drive/pilot vehicles.

(b) Technological-looking beings with associated 'body-gadgetry'.

(c) 'Little people'/fairy folklore embodies this imagery. This is a reoccurring theme in encounters of this type, and indicates that the same parts of the CNS are affected by fields from the UAPs in other cases. It is a way of presenting the human form as 'alien'; that is, by reducing it (as an image) beyond the normal range of variation in size. This adaptation of the basic human form is characteristically archetypal and is a descendant of the 'giants and gnomes' themes of traditional fairy tales. In UFO encounters, however, it has basically remained the same but with a technological overlay. The term humanoid is used to describe a basically human-like being.

4 The post-encounter effects include psychic phenomena, (i.e., a sense of presence and associated disembodied voice). Both of these have been reproduced under controlled conditions during Persinger's experiments on the effects of fields on the temporal lobe of the brain. Similarly, research by ophthalmologist Anne Silk into the effects of acute exposure to ELF fields revealed the following disturbances to the eye:[27]

(a) magnetophosphenes

(b) eyelid oedema

(c) crescentric corneal staining

(d) sudden blurred vision

(e) momentary black-out

(f) pain of cornea

Of course, all of these symptoms would be relevant when considering the witness's post-encounter condition, and also:

(g) feelings of terror and dread, intense fear.[28] These too can be induced by field exposure. Also noted by Anne Silk as a result of the same field stimulus are the hearing of voices or instructions, which result from the stimulation of Broca's area of the brain.[29]

5 I have found that much of the imagery and content of such experiences can be related directly to the witness's background. This encounter 'content tracing' can be applied to all experiences involving imagery. The following case demonstrates this well and it is an example of the unconscious utilizing imagery derived from a typically absurd source: the Superman myth.

DC's experience

In the Lake District, England, on the night of 21 November 1980, the solitary witness, DC, a local despite his Italian-sounding name, was out walking by a river. It was wet and windy. Vaguely at first, he caught sight of an object a few yards in front of him. He thought it was a cow from a nearby field and when he got nearer, a sheep-shelter. Shining a torch on to it, he saw an unidentifiable craft hovering two to three feet (1 m) above the ground. Then he heard footsteps behind him and, as he turned round, still shining his torch in front of him, a thin beam of light struck it, shattering the lens and melting part of the rim around it. The source of the beam was a small pen-like object in the hand of a female entity. She was accompanied by a male and they both looked similar in appearance: very good-looking, about 5 feet 6 inches (1.7 m) tall and perfectly proportioned. They both wore dark, one-piece, skin-tight 'wet-suits' with an insignia on the front which consisted of lettering in dark and light shades. The female had a short cape which came down to the middle of her arms. Both had fair hair, or so it appeared, but, oddly enough, DC was not sure if this was a helmet or a hair-style. Neither entity appeared to be affected by the inclement weather, not in the least dishevelled or appearing even slightly wet. The first words of the female entity were to reassure DC that they were on a mission of peace and that they would not harm him, which was stated before he was able to voice his concern. He could not, for some reason, bring himself to speak at that moment. DC had the impression that she knew what was in his mind because she answered questions before he could ask them. He noticed that the insignia on their chests was the same as the one on the end of the craft; a different one was on another section of it. She asked DC to promise never to reveal the nature of the logo to anyone; a promise which he has subsequently kept. Both entities were fair and white and only the woman spoke. She had no accent and just spoke 'good Queen's English'. At one point during the experience, DC wanted to run away but found that his legs were paralysed. After the female entity had told him that their mission was one of peace, a door opened in the craft and both entered, the man first. There was nothing unusual about their gait; both walked normally. When they were aboard, the craft went straight upwards, out of sight.

DC suffered from a nervous stomach for several days afterwards and did not sleep well. He would lie awake, thinking of the encounter over and over again. He also experienced a 'sickly feeling' for a period of a few days. The police were contacted and they took his damaged torch away for examination, returning it a few days later. It was found to have suffered from severe heating effects. Subsequently, investigators stated that the same effect could be obtained with a blow-lamp. DC repeatedly tried to work out why the entities should not want him to reveal the nature of the logos on their chests and craft. He has not seen it before or since.

Encounter content tracing

It is possible to analyse the elements of the encounter and to correlate them with past events in the witness's life, as they shaped and determined the nature of the experience. Following three years in the army, DC became a physical-training instructor and trained in boxing and karate. The latter discipline involves mental as well as physical control. DC took up meditation, although at the time of the encounter, he had not practised for a while. Such pre-encounter influences establish mental patterns which facilitate habitual occurrences of altered state of consciousness (ASC), which basically is what meditative practices aim for. It is a low, sensory noise state, which is also conducive to an ASC. Clearly, DC would recognize and appreciate the perfect physiques that the entities were described as having, as his background as a physical-training instructor, together with his involvement in physical activities generally, would easily provide a stock of imagery of physically perfect super-humans. Not only did the entities have perfect bodies (DC said 'they looked very fit'), they also displayed them, indicating that their appearance was an expression of physical culture-orientated ideals rather than relating to some kind of functional aspect of space-suits. This aspect of display is significant in understanding the link between these background influences and the imagery of the encounter. When considering the modern imagery that would account for the entities' persona and appearance, the Superman or less well-known Marvelman of comic and film fame come to mind. Their physiques are shown dramatically and this apparent vanity appears as an incongruous and out-of-character aspect, but it is, of course, essential to display the embodiment of perfect physique and perfect morals. This aspect was indeed expressed in the encounter, as it was made emphatically clear that the entities' mission was one of peace – vague but virtuous. The logos or insignia on their bodies are also reminiscent of the super-heroes – Superman himself is depicted as an alien from the planet Krypton. Captain Marvel, Superman, Superwoman and Batman always display an identifying logo on their chests; the latter, who had access to super-gadgetry rather than super-powers as such, also rode in the Batmobile and Batplane, both of which also carried identifying logos – as did the entities' craft in DC's encounter. The cape is also a feature of dress for the whole Super-family, including, significantly, Superwoman. All of the Super- and Marvel folk-heroes and the characters derived from them, not only have athletic physiques, but attractive faces with no trace of ruggedness, which DC's entities also displayed. Only one of these Super-heroes is depicted as fair, however, and perhaps the avoidance of this characteristic stemmed from a desire on the part of their creators to eschew any hint that could be interpreted as a depiction of Hitler's Aryan 'master race' ideals. This would fit in historically, as the Super-heroes first appeared soon after World War II. DC reports that both his entities were fair but that they had an ambiguous, almost disguised, hair-style that could have been a helmet. Does the ambiguity of the nature of the hair – fair but possibly only an artificial addition in the form of a helmet – reflect an ambiguity of attitude? That is to say, somebody who would appreciate and be sympathetic to the ideals of physical perfection on the one hand, but reject the racial undertones with which such an ideal may be associated, *would* unconsciously disguise the aspect that embodied such racialism. Alternatively, and much more straightforward, as DC had been in the army, a helmet would be an appropriate addition. There is frequently such 'hybridization' of forms, as there is in dreams, and the entities that DC perceived were a combination of various related themes centred around the Super-heroes of modern post-war America. Of course, this is not to suggest that the witness thought of these elements consciously, rather that they were selected in the same way that dream material emerges, according to the stock of imagery that embodies the expressive needs of the unconscious. All I have done is to trace the cultural roots of these images and show how such figures embodied the unconscious influences of the witness.

However, having said that, the witness did not consciously think of these images. Even *if the encounter was fabricated* (I am not suggesting this), there is a good chance that similar elements would emerge. This conscious construction of an imaginary story also draws upon unconscious influences to some extent. In both cases – in a CE experience or in an imaginary tale – the witness 'makes something up'; it is just the level of presentation that has differing personal and social consequences.

Another aspect not covered is the function of the logos in the reality of the encounter. Such insignia are used to identify members of a particular group. Therefore, by appearing as an identifying group-symbol, they functioned as a device to imply that the two entities belonged to a group or race far away from the encounter situation. Such symbols of reference evoked the existence of an unseen and non-existent population of which the two entities were presented as representative members. How could this device arise? Such notions of the collective nature and origin of the entities can only have been intrinsic to the witness's unconsciously originating imagery and reflects another *modus operandi* as part of the myth-building stage-management. It is not too simplistic to look into DC's military background to find the original idea of such labelling of groups using insignia. It is interesting (and confirming) to realize that a similar need for secrecy as that expressed by the entities *would* also be desirable by a military reconnaissance group. Such a scouting party *would* be depicted as carrying weaponry, like the entities were. Also, such nocturnal surveillance *would* involve disabling any illumination or potentially dangerous device which may be a threat. The entities were depicted as doing precisely this by 'shooting out the light'. This dramatic element functioned to eliminate the visual sensory noise produced by the lamp, as this would threaten the ASC that DC was unconsciously maintaining. This act was woven into the encounter narrative or plot, significantly as the very first act of the encounter experience. The beam 'shot' at the torch depicted a high level of marksmanship, having hit the target on the first attempt. This does not seem to fit in with the ideals of physical culture in DC's background. How could such an incident fit into his stock of imagery derived from past experiences? Could its inclusion in the encounter drama be due to the interesting fact that DC had won awards and had qualifications in gun marksmanship?

Anne Silk, in her research into the systemic effects of electromagnetic and piezo-magnetic fields, *does* list *precisely* the physical symptoms reported by DC that *would* result from such exposure (nausea, 'sickly' feelings). This gives us a clue to the energetic stimulus which, I would argue, DC was undoubtedly exposed to, precipitating an ASC and clinical symptoms. Commenting generally, Silk notes:

Electrical energy of specific frequencies and wavelengths can stimulate anomalous activity, perceptions and behaviour through the kindling of neurones in specific areas of the brain, the temporal and occipital lobes being particularly labile in this respect. The hypothalamus controls metabolism and heat production, the limbic zone controls emotions. The pituitary melatonin secretion is sensitive to magnetic fields and affects circadian rhythms.[30]

From this statement, it can be seen that such fields can create ASCs, perceptual and metabolic disturbances. The closing statement regarding circadian rhythms is especially relevant to DC's report of his disturbed sleep pattern. The melatonin production in the pineal gland is also involved in the further production of two hallucinatory-associated organic chemicals: pinoline and serotonin.[31] These are involved in REM dreaming, lucid dreaming and other naturally occurring ASCs, such as meditative states. Therefore, exposure to magnetic fields does seem to have been a likely candidate for having induced DC's experience.

This aspect of 'content tracing' is central to the ESH, and indicates that many of the encounter perceptions can be traced back to their origin – the mind of the witness.

2 Objections to the Electro-staging Hypothesis

Those who insist that we provide absolute proof of the existence of psychokinetic phenomena before proceeding further have misunderstood the nature of scientific enquiry. Except in the fields of logic and pure mathematics there is no such thing as 'absolute proof', for all factual knowledge is provisional. We have to make the most reasonable assumptions from the data available and go on from there.[1]

This sentiment also applies to the ESH. Theories proposing that the UFO phenomenon is psychic in nature have met with a number of standard objections, which fall broadly into three categories:

1 *Physical aspects*. Psychic explanations do not account for the physical nature of the phenomena reported. The classification 'close-encounter of the second kind' (CE2) refers to physical traces left after a UFO has departed, including: ground traces; broken and burnt vegetation; electrical malfunction; car damage; and remaining material traces. There are also a considerable number of reports listing physiological changes or trauma to witnesses, and animals.

2 *Multiple witnessing*. If the UFO phenomenon is all in the mind, how are *groups* of witnesses able to see UFOs and, more rarely, entities? Or, put another way: If UFOs are hallucinatory, how can they be seen by more than one person?

3 *Consistency*. If the phenomenon is visionary or of the same nature as apparitions or manifested by the mind in some way, how do witnesses all report essentially the same experiences, with the same type of entity reported time and again? This is the global objection, or the 'peasants in Brazil to housewives in Brighton' objection. Restated, it asks: If UFOs and their occupants are basically imaginary or the product of individuals' waking dreams, how are the same entities encountered all over the world, or at least, in different unrelated cases?

From the material presented so far, the reader will have some idea as to how I would answer these objections, although 'conventional' psychic explanations do fall short. As researcher Jacques Valleé notes: 'And while it is probable that a complete theory of ghosts could confine the phenomena to parameters within the human nervous system, the same is not true for UFOs.'[2]

It is evident at this stage that my first comment would be that an overall theory is impossible because the UFO phenomenon is made up of *reports* that describe a *mixture* of unrelated occurrences. It would be like trying to find a common origin for cheese, uranium, time and tennis. No doubt most people in the UFO-study field have a very clear concept as to which events are part of the UFO phenomenon proper and which are not. Such selectivity seems absolutely necessary; but the exclusion of some reports in favour of others, that are not regarded as central to the phenomenon, is a subjective and inherently biased process that is even in flux with each researcher, investigator or interested party. Also, reports that some reject as 'rogue cases' that do not 'really' seem to be 'proper' UFO phenomena are ideal case material and are exactly what the phenomenon is all about to others. There is no fixed definition or standard that is universally acceptable; an example will make this very important point clear.

Long-standing member of BUFORA, Roy Rowlands was walking one summer's evening from his place of work at the London Weekend Television building on the South Bank of the Thames, London. It was the middle of the rush-hour and as he approached a section of the South Bank arts complex, called Lower Ground, he became aware of a strange fluttering and whirring sound just above his head. On looking up, he was dumbfounded to see a very strange sort of Heath Robinson contraption floating a little above him. It looked like a combination of mobiles that consisted of small sails, propeller-like appendages, triangular and rectangular plates, wires, bands and a complex half-box, half-cylinder shape all moving, turning and spinning in different directions. He looked around at the reactions of passers-by, but they seemed to be oblivious to the whirling object. Quite frightened, and with a sense of unreality, he began to walk faster towards the entrance to Waterloo Station, adjacent to the complex. As he paced along, he could see the object out of the corner of his eye. It seemed to be following him. Panicking, he ran the last few yards up on to an elevated walkway that leads into the station concourse. Stopping briefly before entering it, he turned and looked for the strange contraption, but it was nowhere to be seen. However, his attention was caught by what he assumed were birds taking off from the top of an office block nearby. He saw these as three small red lights streaking into the evening sky at an angle.

Whatever we make of this experience, it does not fit easily into 'conventional' UFO-sighting reports. It is revealing to ask ourselves, why not? Such cases as this expose our deeply held assumptions about UFOs and challenge the parameters that we attribute to them. For a start, Roy's UFO does not seem to be any type of advanced technological device; indeed the very opposite: it smacks of low tech. Even if it is assumed that it is not any type of vehicle for transporting occupants and has some other purpose, such as a remote-controlled reconnaissance device, it can hardly be said to have met any 'stealth' specifications. But really, there is no reason for not including it in our catalogue of UFOs: it was certainly unidentified and flying; it *seemed* to be a structured craft of unknown design. It is just that the design does not conform to what has come to be regarded as acceptable in UFO-study terms. It is absurd.

The depiction of the UFO seems to challenge Roy's categorization of UFOs reflecting his sophisticated view of the phenomenon – an experienced investigator. It provided, perhaps, an assumption-testing rogue-case and it was as if his unconscious (for it must have been a hallucination) was saying: 'You're a UFO investigator – include this sort of thing in your ideas on UFOs.' It is not known what Roy's preoccupations were at the time, but, like dreams, CEs reflect the witness's inner reality in some way.

Nevertheless, the points being made regarding overall theories are:

1 An overall theory is impossible because we get reports based on a mixture of unrelated phenomena, which include IFOs that remain UFOs due to insufficient information. Also, those cases that involve the witness with an interaction with entities are no less ambiguous, as it is these cases that, typically, have absurd, incongruous elements in common with psychic and sometimes folklore traditions.

2 This leaves the alternative of having to *choose* which cases to include and exclude.

3 This selectivity is by no means obvious, and it is subjective and biased according to preheld assumptions about the UFO phenomenon.

4 The selectivity involved varies from group to group or from individual to individual: that is, there are no universally accepted parameters, so we are left with the situation where each case has to be judged individually, rather than automatically grouped.

5 We are also left with the situation of 'fragmented consensus', where there is general acceptance (with always a few exceptions) of a genuine enigma, but with particular groups or individuals identifying their own study areas, often passively by not actively collecting certain types of data. For example, those who subscribe to the ETH would not accept Roy's UFO as an example of extraterrestrial activity.

6 In practice, what seems to happen is that specific types of phenomena are studied by specific individuals, who choose a field of study because they feel that by studying the cases of their choice (which they usually select because they already feel that they have a certain level of understanding of them), a wider application of the explanations they compile may be possible.

Psychic explanations

Psychic explanations do not account for the physical nature of close-encounter experiences. Considering the objections which are usually raised in opposition to any psychic explanation of UFO phenomena, it would be appropriate to consider Vallée's earlier statement to the effect that apparitional theory could possibly be contained within the parameters of the human nervous system, but CEs could not. I do, of course, agree with this, and add that without the influence of UAPs on the human system, many of the UREs could not be understood in psychic terms. It is the fact of their physical, natural and consciousness-altering nature that provides many of the effects reported, such as those listed earlier. There is much still to be discovered about the UAP, but what we know makes us realize that they are dynamic centres of radiating electromagnetic energy correlated with specific geophysical features. It is their involvement in the UFO phenomenon that largely (but not entirely) contributes the physical aspects of reports.

It is becoming evident to a few researchers that the changes UAPs induce in people's minds and bodies not only cause these individuals to perceive CE realities, but that they can alter seemingly permanent personality structures – actually increase the range of their perceptual apparatus and introduce realities into their life on a permanent basis – that facilitate a deeply spiritual outlook. They may represent a 'new' form of energy, and science needs to take them seriously.

Consciousness and physical reality in encounter experiences

If the characteristics of apparitions are similar to those of UFO-related entities, it follows that apparitional theory must apply to such entities. What, then, does this theory say about the physical nature of apparitions, and therefore UFO entities? Earlier, there was an allusion to their strange physical aspects or that they 'display selective physical characteristics'. From a commonsense point of view, one would be entitled to argue that either something is physical or it is not, and surely there is no selectivity or strangeness about the issue. However, this 'physicalness' is not just 'out there', but it is apprehended by the witness's perceptual system. The unconscious, by duplicating such subjective perceptions, can convince the witness of their concrete nature. These are the processes at work in the unconscious 'staging' of 'physical beings' and their 'spacecraft'.

This staging, as in the theatre, involves producing near copies of the environment, in perceptual terms, and replacing the witness's real perceptions with these copies. When the encounter experience is an internal vision, a realistic dream is produced which fulfils this replacement. In situations when the witness is actually perceiving the environment, such as a wooded area surrounded by hills for example, the unconscious, activated by electromagnetic radiation, creates a perception of a 'spaceship' and 'aliens' which like apparitions can be perceived by more than one person and *behave in terms of the environment* (for example, by apparently choosing a clearing in the trees to land, circling a hill, etc.). *How* the perceptual apparatus of the witnesses accomplishes this is described in a later section (see Notional duplicates and Reality replacement), but the point at this stage is that it is evident that *it is able to*. This is apparent by comparing such CE perceptions with the versatility and apparently physical characteristics of apparitions (described in Chapter One). After all, apparitions have actually appeared *during* encounters.

To conclude, therefore, it is clear that physical traces in our notional wooded area could be produced by a UAP, and all that remain are the actual perceptions of the witness which take place in an altered state. It is on the basis of these perceptions that CE reports are made. By a close examination of these reports, it soon becomes evident that, usually, there is something 'not quite right' about the authenticity of the realities presented (for one thing, they seem unstable and are liable to vanish instantly). The most perceptive description of this dubious authenticity came from psychical investigator Andrew MacKenzie. He is able to identify the salient aspects of what we call 'real' or 'unreal'. Consider this extract:

> Price had earlier discussed his suggestion that apparitions were some-times 'real objects' . . . in which he said that we were inclined to say that a hallucinatory entity was something 'purely mental', as opposed to a 'real object' which was physical. But . . . the difference between the hallucinatory and the physically real was only a difference of degree. A hallucinatory entity is composed of sense-data or appearances just as a 'real' object is. What is wrong with it, what inclines us to call it 'unreal' is

the fact that there is not enough of it. For example, a hallucinatory rat can be seen from the front but not from the back; it is visible but not tangible; it can be perceived by one percipient but not by more; it endures for only a minute or so. But some hallucinations do better than this. Apparitions, for example, are sometimes public to several percipients, can be seen from different points of view, and endure for considerable periods of time – though not as long as they would if they were real human beings. Now suppose there was an apparition which had unrestricted publicity, i.e. was public to an infinite number of points of view and indefinite number of observers; suppose that there are tangible as well as visible particulars among the appearances which are its constituents; suppose it endures for half an hour and then disappears. We should not know whether to call it an unusually prolonged and complex hallucination, or a very queer 'real object'. (Queer, because we should not know how it got into the room or why it abruptly vanished into thin air.) In point of fact, it would be something indeterminate between the two: a complex system of 'cognita' (appearances) but not quite complex enough to count as a material object.

These points . . . are of the greatest theoretical interest when we try to consider what an apparition might be. In fact . . . I will give two examples in which an apparition *was* on view for half an hour.[3]

These comments are also of the greatest theoretical interest when we try to consider what UFO-related realities might be. MacKenzie makes the point that when we are confronted by something strange, there are a series of subconscious tests that we put it through to determine if it is real or not. These are perceptual tests that the unconscious would be aware of from the 'inside', as it were. If the unconscious could satisfy these criteria internally, within the nervous/perceptual system of the witness, without reference to the external environment, then to all intents and purposes, that 'something strange' would be physically real. This is precisely what it does in the 'stage-management' of the CE experience.

Physical traces and the ESH

This aspect is covered in detail in later sections, and it is sufficient to state here that most of the effects are the product of UAP action as thermal electromagnetic or magnetic vortex phenomena.[4] A viable argument for physical structured objects is also presented, although research into this is in its infancy.

Vanishing water

The UAP phenomenon, being electromagnetic in nature, is attracted to elevated metal protrusions, such as radio and television masts. Marine piers, if constructed of metal, would also be powerful conductors for the energies of the UAP, especially being waterbound. Also, there have been cases where water stored in metal tanks on towers has created the same magnetic attraction effect (the Rosedale case in Australia). There are quite a few cases of vanishing water associated with UFO presence, and it is relevant to note that water volatizes at 500 MHz in the UHF microwave range. At this frequency, the hydrogen bonds break down and water changes to a gaseous state, which may then disperse.[5]

The 'blackout/time-lapse' aspect

Once again, the UAP phenomenon as a centre of electromagnetic energy can cause this effect, 25 Hz or 40 Hz (cycles per second) being the frequencies used in electro-convulsive therapy, which, of course, induces unconsciousness.[6]

The psychic case for the physical

Continuing this theme of the physical aspects of the ESH, it has been argued that most physical aspects are created by the UAP. It has also been mentioned that a witness irradiated by this energy can hallucinate a 'flying saucer' theme drama. It has also been implied that such altered states can produce PK effects, which sometimes continue after the encounter is over. The implication is that the witness, during the encounter, and for some time after, is changed into what would be called a 'medium' who, like 'mediums' in the context of a seance, is able to produce a variety of strange phenomena, including lights, sounds, apparent physical forms and contacts with 'spirits'. Mediums typically enter a trance-like state and they are largely unaware of what is going on around them. This is precisely what occurs in some UFO encounters: a person, who is often already psychic to some extent, is transposed into a medium-like trance by electrical or electromagnetic fields either directly from geological strata, an artificial source (like a microwave repeater) or from a UAP, such as an earthlight. However, instead of spirits of the dead, the appearance of visitors from another, other-worldly realm are evoked: that of aliens from another planet. These 'artificially' induced mediums, like the 'natural' ones in seances, suffer black-outs and periods of time for which they cannot account. In UFO-study terms, these are called 'time-lapses'. Because they are 'artificially' induced these mediums continue to experience psychic effects after the UFO encounter is over, sometimes beginning a career as an 'ordinary' medium. Since these 'UFO mediums' do not always remember everything that they have experienced during their trances, UFO investigators use hypnosis to help them 'remember'. However, because what they have experienced is a mixture of internal images and externally produced 'aliens' similar to spirits or apparitions, what they 'remember' is often a *mixture* of realities based on their religious, or at least spiritual, beliefs, in combination with hallucinated space-alien images.

However, sometimes the radiation that alters their consciousness does not induce a total trance but changes them into what poltergeist investigators call the 'focus person'. This 'focus' is usually a teenager whose body and mind is undergoing a radical change from child to adult.[7] The radiation induces similar physiological changes in an adult, and their unconscious, instead of producing a poltergeist, produces a UFO encounter; or, to be more accurate, often a mixture of both. Therefore, it is common to find a UFO, aliens and apparitions appearing in the same experience. These experiences, like 'pure' poltergeist outbreaks, have physical aspects involved: unexplained footprints; voices that nobody can identify; marks on the body of the 'focus'; strange smells; unexplained fog or mist; extreme changes in temperature and atmosphere; and marks on the ground. In UFO encounters, however, because the theme of the experience is not a haunting spirit but visiting aliens, different physical effects occur that are really permutations of 'standard' poltergeist events. One of these is the appearance of a structured craft or 'space-ship'. In order to understand this aspect, we need to look at what occurs in poltergeist outbreaks and compare them with close-encounters. Consider the following case:

The Middleton case[8]

This case, which involved a complex series of incidents, began in 1962 at the home of the Gould family in South Middleton, Massachusetts, a rural community about 15 miles (24 km) north of Boston. The events included sightings of two distinct entity types (helmeted 'spacemen') and an apparition of a man of ordinary-looking appearance (but not of movement), labelled 'the prowler' by the Goulds. Several different UFO types were also involved, including orange BOL and a *landed* structured 'craft'. The American investigators were Raymond E. Fowler and David

F. Webb. They reported that a single UFO landed on the Goulds' property around 9 January 1978 *and remained for two days* before departing on the morning of 12 January. If true, this event is unprecedented. On 9 and 10 January there were two observations of a helmeted, white-suited 'spaceman' in the vicinity of the grounded UFO. Predictably, there were frequent reports of psychic phenomena interwoven in the UFO-related accounts, which included apparitional and poltergeist effects.

Events of 9 January

On the evening of 9 January, the parents were in their sitting-room. At about 7.30 pm, they saw, from an east-facing window, a very large, yellow-white round light moving downwards at an angle just above some trees. Due to the suddenness and the brevity of the sighting, they were not sure, but the BOL seemed to have a smaller light at one end, or, as Mrs Theresa Gould thought later, three round lights. The BOL seemed to have been approaching from the north-east and was in view for at least 15 seconds. The daughter, Nancy, who saw the BOL from a closer vantage point, described it as a huge orange globe. She ran out of the back door in time to see it disappear behind some trees, where it winked out. Her total observation time was about 20 seconds. Five minutes later, she tried to phone someone, but found the line dead; this malfunction lasted for 20 minutes. It was later found that an incoming call had been equally unsuccessful. The youngest child, Douglas, unaware of the UFO, was staying nearby at a relative's house. There the children had just been put to bed when one of them called out to the father, saying that he saw a pale 'man' at the foot of his bed, who had suddenly vanished. Suddenly, the father heard a knocking sound in an adjoining room, which was unoccupied. On pulling the curtains open, he was startled to see a white 'space-suited' figure with a dome-like helmet, about three feet away (see Fig. 1). It must have been standing on the roof of an adjoining porch. Two eyes stared out from the helmet. The father dropped the curtain and ran downstairs. The figure was not on the roof, but, after turning to go back into the house, he immediately saw it standing just outside the glass-panelled outer door.

The following day was very cold and cloudy, with flurries of snow in the area, although there was no overall snow cover. Thomas Gould spent the day working outside his house. At 2.30 pm he began chopping wood in a spot just north of it. Suddenly, he saw the 'spaceman' standing on the path beside a tree about 90 feet away from him. The figure was quite small, about 4½ feet (1.25 m) tall, wearing a squarish, dome-like helmet in which were set two dark eye-holes. The figure had broad shoulders, with

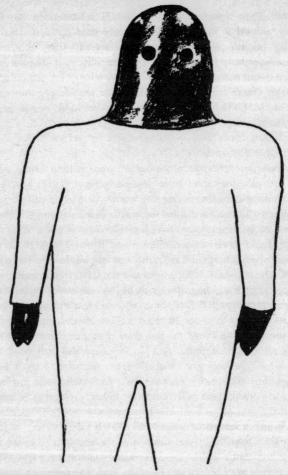

Fig. 1 An 'abbreviated form' of a UFO-associated 'ghost spaceman' in the Middleton case which persisted for 90 minutes. These entities, typically, 'vanished on the spot'. They were 'pale' and 'dark grey', with simplified hands and indistinct feet.

arms that hung down naturally, although its arms ended in simple mitten-like hands with three digits. Only the hands and the helmet were battle-ship grey. This was one of many encounters with this entity that Thomas had experienced and, although it was obviously alone, he often had the strange feeling of another presence near the first figure that he could not perceive for some reason. On this occasion, Thomas and the figure both stared at each other for some time, until Thomas broke the silence by speaking in English. There was no response. He then tried French and for a moment thought he saw the figure move slightly. After that he gave up and, as this was not an uncommon confrontation, he went on with his work *for another 90 minutes*. All the while the 'spaceman' remained, and Thomas noticed when he looked up from time to time that it never moved. In the past he had tried chasing the figures, but *they would vanish* before he could reach them, only to reappear further away. This time, he eventually jumped into his truck and drove a short distance and, on looking back, the 'spaceman' had gone. Then, for the first time, Thomas noticed what seemed to be, at first glance, a 'new' boulder on his land, about 150 feet (46 m) away down a slope in a partially wooded area. He got out of the truck and walked to where he could see the object better. It was sitting on the ground and it was egg-shaped, with one end wider than the other. It had little 'hooded windows' all over it which reminded him of the bulbous eyes of a frog. He drove back to fetch Nancy, his daughter, to look at it too, and she described the windows as protruding from the sides of the object, regularly spaced and side by side. The object was dark grey in colour and rough in texture, like the surface of a brick. No areas of jointing or seams of any kind were evident. The area where the object had rested was measured by the investigators, who estimated that it would have been about 40 feet (12 m) long and 14 feet (4.25 m) wide. The 'spaceman' was seen about 300 feet (91 m) to the west of the object. Thomas had been afraid to approach the object very closely, and he later took his elder child, Allan, and Nancy to look at it. This was at dusk and, due to the failing light, Thomas claims to have seen only seven windows. Allan could only see what looked to him like a huge boulder. However, the next day, from an upper-room window, he saw a disc-like object ascend. It had a smooth, silvery surface and it was shaped-like two shallow dishes pressed together. He also saw 'legs' underneath, which he took to be landing gear. A short while later, he found what he described as 'pod marks' in the ground and the investigators were shown one that still remained.

Encounter context

These UFO-related events (URE) were interspersed with a range of psychic phenomena, including apparitions and poltergeist effects. The area was what investigators would call a 'window area' or 'ufocal' – that is, prone to the type of activity described. It will be shown that, in fact, such areas are electromagnetic hot spots. The earliest event was observed by the grandmother. It was a UFO sighting following a thunderstorm. She saw an orange BOL which grew in size and then divided into a number of smaller lights. These BOLS appeared against a background of multi-coloured beams, and the whole sighting lasted five minutes, which is quite a long period for such events. This and other URE seem to have been electrical phenomena with related UAPs, indicative of an energy potential in the surrounding area associated with sites directly over fault-lines. This is borne out by the continual poltergeist activity which may also be associated with the younger family members. Other cases have shown that UAP/BOL activity is attracted to open stretches of water in 'window areas' and it was no surprise to find that in 1974, when Allan was 17, he saw an orange BOL phenomenon just behind the family pool, which at that time lay 150 feet (46 m) north of the house, not far from the spot where Thomas confronted the 'spaceman' for one and a half hours while chopping wood. Allan's 1974 sighting took place at about 10.45 pm, when he was in bed. The orange light from the UAP was so intense that it shone through the heavy curtains. It was cigar-shaped, with an intensely bright and indistinct hazy edge, and it was much larger than the pool, which was 18 feet (5.5 m) in diameter. It was lost from view when it ascended vertically. Around this time, Allan had another UFO sighting of a huge object which consisted of a dark shape with lights that constantly alternated in colour from white to red and back.

Entities

The entity that became known as 'the prowler' was so life-like that the Middleton police were called on several occasions. This was often at night in the summer months, when the police would drive around the grounds but find nothing. 'The prowler' always appeared dressed in a white shirt and dark trousers. Although it appeared to have short dark hair, no facial features were ever seen – a very common feature of apparitions and it is typical of hauntings generally.

There were other somewhat indistinct and fleeting entities perceived at times and, until the Goulds associated them with their other strange figures, they would sometimes complain to a nearby tennis club that their members were trespassing. 'The prowler' had odd ambulatory charac-teristics which distinguished it from normal human movement. It was nearly always observed in the near distance, just as the 'spaceman' was, and it moved very slowly, with the body held very erect and the arms held rigidly by the sides. The elbows or knees were never observed to bend, like a toy soldier, and when it turned, the whole body rotated in a curious fashion. There were never any footprints seen from either entity type, even when there was snow covering the ground. The grandmother had one encounter with 'the prowler' which was closer than the others. When she was approaching the porch, her grandson was indoors just coming out to greet her, but as she got near the door, she saw 'the prowler' about only 6 feet (2 m) away. It had its back to her and it was motionless. Thinking it was the grandson himself, she called out. When she got a reply from inside the house, she turned her head to the doorway and then quickly back to 'the prowler', but it had vanished.

The Middleton area

The town itself is just 3 miles (5 km) from an area traditionally known for supernatural activity, Danvers, the old Salem of witch-trial fame. Regarding the local geophysical conditions: the area is an earthquake epicentre.[9]

It is usually a combination of natural and artificial fields which produce a hot spot, electromagnetically speaking. It is significant to note that there is an atomic research facility in Middleton, consisting of a linear accelerator (LINAC built by MIT). These sources, in combination, could certainly produce permanent ambient magnetic and electrical fields in the Goulds' house and grounds. Such ambient fields produce altered states of consciousness (ASC) and the type of perceptions the Goulds reported. In fact, it is clear from my own investigations over the past 12 years or more that ghosts, poltergeist effects, UFOs, alien entities, etc., all occur in electromagnetic hot spots, and they are the products of these energies at such locations.

Cazzamalli

It was in the early half of the twentieth century that an Italian professor, named Cazzamalli, conducted experiments in which he exposed human subjects to high-frequency fields in the form of radio waves up to 300 megacyles.[10] He found that these subjects hallucinated at a particular frequency (between 380 to 500 mc) and reported definite 'pulsing' in the brain. (See also the 'Jane Murphy' case-study, in the final chapter, where she described the feeling of field exposure.)

Moreover, electronic pollution expert Anne Silk has listed biological effects of fields, which include 'hum or buzzing apparently exterior to the head'.[11] In this connection, it is relevant to note that a visiting relative of the Goulds heard a sound like a swarm of bees which grew very loud and brought him to the verge of collapse. It is evident that these witnesses were exposed to piezo-magnetic and electronically originating fields. The ESH proposes that the Goulds were affected by the fields and began to act as 'mediums' or poltergeist 'foci' to produce the encounter realities.

Analysis of the psychic/physical aspects

This account represents only a small portion of the strange events the Goulds reported. It indicates that UAPs (the aerial lights), apparitions, 'flying saucers and spacemen', poltergeist effects and, apparently, a physical 'craft' were involved.

However, we are primarily concerned with this latter phenomenon – the physical 'craft' aspect – for this indicates how undeniably physical objects can be part of a UFO scenario that is equally undeniably psychic in nature. This case has been chosen because the 'landed UFO' could not conceivably be the direct consequence of a UAP as a whirlwind or vortex of electrified particles, as some are; nor could it be a simple heating or other direct field effect. How, then, could psychic processes possibly produce a very large, landed, physical craft with bulbous portholes and a textured surface, observed by several witnesses, which, after a few days, vanishes?

The answer is extremely important, because it would reveal how physical, structured objects could be accounted for in CEs generally, using a psychic explanation, which the ESH partially is.

It has already been stated that physical aspects are contained in poltergeist activity. So, what is it exactly about this type of phenomenon that is so relevant to the physical aspects of CEs? It has also been mentioned that poltergeist phenomena constantly occurred throughout the happenings at Middleton, interspersed with the UREs, and we have seen other cases where they are a common post-encounter 'syndrome'. It is evident that whatever causes poltergeists – or more technically, recurrent spontaneous psychokinesis, or RSPK – it is intrinsically involved in many UREs. In order to determine what these processes could contribute to URE generally, and the Middleton case specifically, we need to look closely at the events that occur – that is, what is possible during poltergeist activity, and how does it relate to URE? And in this instance, how could it produce a physical, structured craft?

Examples of poltergeist or RSPK activity

The Reverend Phelps lived in Stratford, Connecticut ... He was interested in clairvoyance, and attempted to treat illnesses by means of mesmerism ... On Sunday, March 10th, the family returned from church to find the front door wide open and the place in disorder. Their first assumption was that they had been burgled; but inspection showed that nothing had been taken ... That afternoon the family went off to church again, but this time the Reverend Phelps stayed behind to keep watch. He may well have dozed; at all events nothing disturbed him. But when the family returned from church, the place again showed signs of an intruder. Furniture was scattered, and in the main bedroom, a nightgown and chemise had been laid out on the bed, with the arms folded across the breast, and a pair of stockings placed to make it look like a corpse laid out for burial. In another room, clothing and cushions had been used to make various dummies, which were arranged in a tableau, 'in attitudes of extreme devotion, some with their foreheads nearly touching the floor', and with open Bibles in front of them. Clearly the poltergeist had a sense of ironic humour.

From then on the Phelps poltergeist practised its skill as a designer of tableaux. The astonishing thing was, that these were done so quickly. One observer, a Doctor Webster, remarked that it would have taken half a dozen women several hours to construct the 'dummies' that the poltergeist made within minutes. One figure was so life-like that when the three-year-old boy went into the room he thought his mother was kneeling in prayer, and whispered 'Be still . . .'

That it *was* a poltergeist became clear the next day, when objects began to fly into the air. A bucket flew downstairs, an umbrella leapt through the air, and spoons, bits of tin and keys were thrown around.[12]

From this case, and numerous others, it is clear that poltergeists have the ability to both *disorganize* and *reorganize* physical objects. How this is accomplished is enigmatic, although there are strong indications that magnetic phenomenon are responsible. However, the point is that this physical manipulation *does* occur. Countless cases have revealed re-arrangements of objects, sometimes to demonstrate specific themes. They also show how materials and objects suddenly and mysteriously appear and disappear. These are known as apports. There seem to be no limits to its material-gathering abilities, although it is usually confined to the local environment. This is the activated unconscious at work again due to the electromagnetically stimulated brain, but instead of influencing the nervous system and perceptions of a witness, it reorganizes the external environment. Therefore, in terms of the 'stage-management' of the Goulds' encounters, it is this organizational ability, utilized in a more specific and directed way, that produced the structured 'spaceship'. It could arrive and depart in the same manner as all apports, and it would be part of the staged reality of an encounter with visitors from another world.

The Middleton events consisted of a *mixture* of non-physical 'spacemen' and 'prowlers' which, nevertheless, could be seen by different family members (as in many cases of haunting), and the addition of a physical element – the 'landed craft'. In other encounters, the mix is different, and phantom 'spacecraft' are combined, for example, with physical 'assembled' entities. If the Phelps poltergeist could produce life-like figures from clothing and houshold items, then, bizarrely, in an encounter with a UFO theme, RSPK activity has the potential to produce 'assembled' entities that pass for aliens from space. It is the ultimate and logical progression from producing apparitions with selective physical features or inducing internal imagery. Therefore, it is evident that *there is no single, simple category into which CE experiences can be placed in terms of whether they are all mental or physical*. There *are* experiences that are purely internal, but others consist of a mixture of levels or 'reality-statuses'. The UI is able to produce these purposely staged realities according to the prevalent conditions. What conditions would these be? What may determine the proportions of, say, hallucination to 'PK-assembly'? Any one encounter depends on:

1 The innate propensity of the witness towards psychic events and environmental sensitivity generally.
2 The type, depth, duration and degree of the ASC that develops or is triggered in a witness or the 'focus' person (which may not be the same).
3 The type and degree of geophysical, electromagnetic and/or electric field exposure.
4 The ambient conditions and circumstances that would allow for the maintenance of the ASC in terms of the control of sensory noise (which interferes with such states).
5 The beliefs of the witness and propensity for fantasy and visualization.
6 The immediate environmental conditions.

To take this assembly and, by implication, animation, concept further, to see how feasible it is as an explanation, we need to look at specific cases in detail. We also need to collate information regarding *what is possible* in terms of effects from a range of poltergeist case-studies. This would give us information as to the repertoire that the unconscious has available, as it were; it would put boundaries around what it can and what it cannot do. We could then examine CE experiences and look for overlapping phenomena.

Men in black

These mysterious perceptions depict visitors dressed in dark clothing – usually suits – and appear to attend to witnesses to a UFO sighting to warn them not to relate their experiences to anyone. Female depictions in this entity category are rare, but the following account provides an example of both sexes. With the 'assembled entity' in mind, consider this extract:

John met the man at the local fast-food restaurant and brought him home with his companion, a woman. Both appeared to be in their mid-thirties; they wore curiously old-fashioned clothes. The woman looked particularly odd: her breasts were set very low, and when she stood up, it seemed that there was something wrong with the way that her legs joined onto her hips. Both strangers walked with very short steps, leaning forward as though frightened of falling. They accepted Coca-Colas, but did not so much as taste them. The strangers sat awkwardly together on a sofa while the man asked a number of detailed personal questions: Did John and Maureen watch television much? What did they read? And what did they talk about? All the while the man was pawing and fondling his female companion, asking John if this was all right and whether he was doing it correctly. John left the room for a moment, and the man tried to persuade Maureen to sit next to him on the couch. He also asked her 'how she was made' – and whether she had any nude photographs of herself. Shortly afterwards, the woman stood up and announced that she wanted to leave. The man also stood, but made no move to go. He was between the woman and the door, and it seemed that the only way she could get to the door was by walking in a straight line, directly through him. Finally, the woman turned to John and asked, 'Please move him; I can't move him myself.' Then, suddenly, the man left, followed by the woman, both walking in straight lines. They did not even say goodbye.[13]

It would certainly appear that when the UI stages UFO encounters, they are more successful, because they are more open-ended in terms of authenticity. The witness has nothing to compare a UFO encounter with to determine its 'correctness', whereas everyone is generally aware of the norms of social intercourse.

It would seem, however, that the unconscious is more devious and creative than it would appear from interpreting the MIB at face value, as it were. Hallucinations are able to present such a reality with more finesse, and this mode of entity production certainly seems to be in severe difficulty. It is significant that in the depiction of the MIBs in this example, there was no real attempt to cover up their obvious ignorance of human society. In fact, it could be said that they were flaunting it. So, instead of seeing them as failed depictions of human beings, they could be regarded as successful depictions of an 'alien humanoid robot', complete with naïve and bizarre enquiries as to how to function in the human world. Only by incorporating their shortcomings as a human depiction could this identity succeed. The principle at work behind such MIB 'constructions' – if that is what this case involved – is: 'If the faults cannot be hidden, make a feature of them.' It has been mentioned that the unconscious uses material from fiction and recycles it, and there is a plethora of sci-fi films that are about human-looking aliens who come to Earth, but who are unaware of what it takes to be truly human.

Therefore, UFO witnesses (and others) are treated to visits by beings who more or less look like us, but who are at pains to 'let it slip' that they are quite weird and not at all human. This is the propagation of another belief or modern folklore myth, and their appearance is propaganda for the existence of 'aliens among us'.

Unfortunately, there is no background information available to make any definitive statement about the electrical/radiation conditions that would support such a 'PK construction'. It is entirely appreciated that such an identification is quite outlandish, but such presentations take place within very narrow and limited conditions. Other MIBs are undoubtedly apparitional, but are more 'finished' in their depiction.

A case which provides another example is the one that involved the Reverend Harrison E. Bailey. It is difficult to classify as either alien or spiritual in theme, as it is both and yet neither. It is precisely these 'hybrid-missing-link' across-category cases that demonstrate their common nature as well as showing how encounters vary according to the witness's background and personal preoccupations, just as dreams express such things. In fact, cases like this, and many encounters, are an external and sometimes physical enactment of the same unconscious material as dreams.

The Reverend Harrison Bailey case

'It isn't that Reverend Harrison E. Bailey minds taking dictation, but when he was stirred at 1.30 am to record the words of two disembodied heads, he started to shake. Bailey's incredible tale is enough to shake just about anyone.' So begins an account by science journalist Alan Vaughn, who brought this strange series of events into the public domain in an article in the science magazine *Omni*, in 1985. The minister awoke in the early hours of 1 November 1978, after a Hallowe'en party at his house. He was confronted with two white, humanoid forms hovering in front of a window in his flat in Pasadena, California. His first bemused reaction was to dash to the bathroom to splash his face with cold water to dispel any feelings of unreality. Returning cautiously to the bedroom, he saw that the entities were still there and, with a presence of mind unusual for a witness in his situation, he snatched his Polaroid camera and took a photograph.

The entities seemed concerned that others should believe his story of alien visitation and posed for full-length photographs (which are too disappointing to reproduce here). However, as they hovered in the room, their feet an inch or two from the floor, they began to lose their humanoid form and became wizened, rather like deflated siren-suits made of muslin. The clergyman took five more photographs, which apparently show them in various stages of deflation. then, suddenly, to his surprise, he looked up to see two Hallowe'en masks from the party positioned over the aliens' amorphous faces (see the plate section between pages 112 and 113). Without warning, they darted towards the bathroom, their humanoid shapes about four feet tall. He took further photographs of them in the hall and, on lowering his camera, he was just in time to glimpse them 'shoot through the ceiling in whirling globes of light'.

Analysis and comment

This 'inflated siren-suit' aspect is especially interesting because it is not confined to this case alone. Witnesses involved in certain UFO entity experiences have independently reported that the 'aliens' wore one-piece 'boiler suits' with no apparent seams or joins, seemingly manufactured as a single continuous cover-all. This is often combined with a helmet which completely covers the head; it has a dark visor so that no facial features can be seen. I am suggesting, therefore, that there is 'nothing' inside such inflated 'suits', and that this is a method by the unconscious of presenting entities with physical characteristics utilizing physical poltergeist-associated magnetic effects. The literature on poltergeist activity is full of just such 'inflatables'.

Another example of the purposeful manipulation of physical material is provided by another 'PK-inflated entity' case, 'The Black Monk of Pontefract':

Jean Pritchard had only just climbed into bed when the disturbances began. The reading lamp rose into the air, sailed across the room, and out through the door. Then they saw something moving around the door – a closer look showed that it was the four small bulbs that produced the glow effect on the electric fire downstairs. Two of them were now dancing around the top of the door, and the other two near the bottom.

Then they saw the hands. For a moment they were petrified. One enormous hand appeared over the top of the door, while the other was near the bottom of the door, about six inches from the floor. A closer look showed that they were Aunt Maude's fur gloves. Whatever – or whoever – was wearing them must have had enormous arms, since there was a stretch of well over six feet between the top glove and the lower one.

Aunt Maude, who was of an evangelical disposition – in fact a member of the Salvation Army – pointed accusingly at the gloves and said sternly: 'Get away. You're evil!' She picked up one of her boots and flung it at the door. The gloves vanished . . . Then the gloves reappeared – floating into the bedroom. One of them seemed to be beckoning to them, as if trying to persuade them to follow it. 'None of us moved,' said Jean Pritchard later, 'we were too scared.' Then the glove clenched into a fist, and shook threateningly in Aunt Maude's direction. Aunt Maude responded by bursting into 'Onward Christian Soldiers'. At this time, the gloves began to conduct her singing, beating in time. Jean Pritchard admits that she had to smile. The gloves vanished again . . . She later found them at the bottom of a cupboard . . . She carried them into the garden with tongs, and burnt them with paraffin on the rubbish heap.[14]

Also recorded in the study is a case where a small, dress-like garment appeared in a household. Made of a papery material, it was, more significantly, all in one piece, with no seams or joins of any kind. Such a poltergeist artefact correlates with the reports of UFO entities wearing one-piece 'space-suits', also with no seams or joins. (The dress was burnt as it was associated with evil by the witnesses.)

Once again, from the poltergeist description, it seems that the unconscious can produce a physical human-like form, and it is this ability that is directed purposefully in close-encounters as part of a staged production.

Notable British cases which seemed to have involved this type of entity presentation were those which occurred in Dyfed, Wales, in 1977 during an intense 'flap' (a concentrated period of UFO activity). BUFORA had one investigator on-the-spot, Lionel Beer, who spoke with many of the main witnesses. Subsequent investigation has made a few events there controversial, but there seems to be a core of witnesses who offer unchanging testimony to something typically British on the UFO-study scene – the tall, silver-suited humanoid.

This entity type was seen repeatedly in the Dyfed area by a variety of witnesses. The authors of a book on the 'flap' also came to the conclusion that these entities were little more than animated 'space-suits'. Consider their comments, which are, of course, completely independent from my own proposals:

A curious aspect of the phenomenon's 'tricks' is the presentation of the humanoids as space-travellers complete with space-suits and breathing apparatus. Earlier literature showed that our grandfathers observed no such equipment and that it is a modern feature. Like the ventriloquist's doll which can be made to behave like a living being by blinking its eyes and performing other functions, the show is very convincing. How convincing it is can be seen by the extent the bait has been swallowed by so many of the UFOlogical literati. This has led the way to the Von Daniken super-cult of men like gods sired by angels. It is a flattering fantasy but totally without scientific foundation.[15]

It is also intriguing that these local investigators came to a conclusion so close to the concept of 'PK constructed' entities. The investigator, Randall Jones-Pugh, is a veterinary surgeon who showed a special interest in another possible 'PK assembled' case involving a dog. The appearance of this entity was very bizarre indeed, and it overlaps with the Dyfed cases in the reported reactions of animals, as well as the 'PK assembly' aspect. It occurred in Dakelia, Cyprus, in September 1968. It is described by leading ufologist Jenny Randles:

A NCO in charge of one wing of an army barracks at Dakelia, Cyprus . . . was alerted at 3 am by his fierce Turkish wolfhound, a large and brave dog. Its fur was standing up very high, and it was obviously terrified. Fearing, perhaps, a terrorist attack which the dog had somehow heard signs of, the soldier tried to soothe the animal, but it would respond to none of his normal commands and became even more upset before crawling under his bed, whimpering.

At this point the officer became aware of a high-pitched whine. Opening the door to confront the origin of this sound, he was horrified to see a weird figure climbing, or rather floating, up the stairs. It wore a light blue tight-fitting suit, and its face glowed orange, with large round eyes and a shock of red hair that stood out in all directions as if charged with electricity (perhaps it was). When the head swivelled through an impossible angle towards him, it is hardly surprising that the panicking man slammed the door and attempted to lock 'it' out.

The normally bold soldier sat on his bed trembling with terror as the humming whine increased. The dog was in an even worse state beneath him. As a sliding sound approached the door, the NCO reached out to grab his underwater speargun and diver's knife from the table beside him . . . He sat there shaking uncontrollably, willing to scythe down the door if the being tried to enter. He managed to restrain himself (something he says is now the most puzzling feature of the whole experience). Presently the sliding and the whine disappeared. At 4.15 am he was found by a guard coming to waken him, still in a state of shock.

The army man survived, with aching joints and muscular pains for a week or so afterward. The dog came out of the encounter less fortunately. To quote his owner: 'My dog was turned overnight into a devout coward.'[16]

Comment

The tell-tale clinical symptoms described are a hallmark of the effects of electromagnetic field exposure. That the witness was in a military base is even further circumstantially supporting, as such establishments utilize ELF waves and microwave beams in a variety of electronic communication systems far more powerful than the average. It appears that the bedroom of this soldier became an electromagnetic hot spot and such field effects on man and dog have also been found in poltergeist outbreaks. Induced fear-states and electrical malfunctions are both found in poltergeist activity and they are produced by the direct effect of electromagnetic fields. These effects are incorporated into the stage-management of encounters to great effect and, interestingly, UFO-study veteran John Keel understood the origin of this effect back in 1975. He relates that when he was driving at night after investigating UFO activity, he passed into an electromagnetic field where 'a wave of unspeakable fear swept over me'. He found that he could walk into and out of a well-defined area that he called 'the zone of fear'. He concluded that 'I was probably walking through a beam of ultrasonic waves' and recognized it as a feature associated with UFO activity and the presence of the bizarre 'mothman'.[17]

It is evident, therefore, that the presence of electromagnetic fields is a common denominator to these experiences, as they transform reality for the witness, and sometimes others, to induce apparitional figures or physical representations of them.

Similarly, in the Cyprus case, the muscular pain which persisted can be directly attributed to an ELF field produced by the difference between two specific frequencies that is termed the 'beat frequency'.[18] It is evident that this radiation causes hallucinations, as well as facilitating personal field emissions which are able to duplicate poltergeist-like effects.[19] Such personal electromagnetic emissions are a symptom of electrical hypersensitivity, and they take the form of coherent beams. They are emitted as a whole body effect, and they can be not only measured on a field-meter or spectrum analyser, but may register as static on a tape-recording made in the subject's presence. They also commonly cause electronic equipment to malfunction, due to their interference with critical microscopic contacts in the construction of such devices. Also, such person-originating magnetic beams are able to move objects, such as those in a domestic environment, and form the basis for poltergeist activity. The individuals so induced to emit in this way are in an altered state of body, as well as consciousness. Not all poltergeist effects have been identified as specific field phenomena yet, but they will; it is just a matter of research and concept development. This transient altered state can be created by subjecting specifically electro-sensitive individuals to field exposure, inducing them to act as a 'focus' in a poltergeist outbreak. In fact, it would seem that this process occurred during the Cyprus event. Such personal field emission is covered later.

Abbreviated forms

Another aspect that links with the idea that psychic phenomena (such as apparitions and 'assembled' entities like the Men in Black, produced by the field-activated unconscious) are also produced in UFO encounters as 'aliens' or 'spacemen' is their abbreviated and limited form. While there are a few reports of brightly coloured entities, the majority reveal the limitations to which the mind, in producing these perceptions, is restricted. Apparitions are consistently reported as pale, grey or dark with indistinct facial features and extremities. Similarly, many alien entities have their faces conveniently hidden by darkened visors or all-covering helmets. When they are depicted, they have simplified features – large black eyes, no nose and a simple line-mouth. There are exceptions, but this is a distinct trend.

These constraints reveal the limited ability of the unconscious to produce colour and fine detail. This monochromatic aspect of entities is a feature shared with apparitions, and it is another indication of their joint nature. Reference has been made by psychical researcher Andrew MacKenzie to the need to understand apparitions as 'dreams while awake'. This would, of course, refer to the fact that the unconscious provides both apparitional and dream imagery. As UFO entities are identified with apparitions, the relevance of dream imagery also applies to them. Therefore, in order to understand why such simple forms are produced, we need to have information on imagery that the unconscious produces in one of these categories (i.e., 'aliens', apparitions or dreams) in more controlled conditions. An area that provides such clues is dream research.

The sleep laboratory

Alan Worsley and Dr Morton Schatzmann carried out research into lucid dreams at the sleep laboratory in St Thomas's Hospital, London, in 1983. From a series of dream experiments, it became apparent that the unconscious abbreviates reality in the production of dream imagery because specific brain functions are incapable of producing a certain level of detail.

Consider an extract from a report on their work:

By concentrating on what he wants to dream about, Worsley has found that he can often dictate the subject of his fantasies. But dictating events is quite another thing. The brain it seems can easily provide a journey through space or time, or a conversation with a dead relative; some very ordinary, everyday things, however, have proved to be impossible.

Worsley has found, for example, that he cannot suddenly light a darkened room. He can turn on a spotlight in his dreams. He can turn on a light in a room already filled with daylight. He can even flick his fingers and produce a flame from them as if they were a pocket cigarette lighter.

But when his imaginary room is in darkness, the light stubbornly refuses to come on. The reason, Worsley believes, is that the brain is unable to create the detailed images necessary to fill a large space instantaneously – so it refuses to co-operate with the fantasy.

But the brain, it seems, does not like to admit such failures, and it can be devious. Recently Worsley was successful in dreaming he had turned on the radio to listen to the shipping forecast and the news. What he heard sounded all right in terms of rhythm and intonation, but as he listened carefully to the forecast he realized that instead of the usual sea areas – Shannon, Rockall, Bailey and so on – his memory was serving up non-existent places such as Wolf and Sofa. When the news followed, it contained the same kind of gobbledegook. That may be because the memory is too erratic to provide the facts, and so the brain hams its way through the performance, like an actor who has forgotten his lines.[20]

This inability of the brain to provide prosaic detail is reflected in the limited form of apparitions and 'aliens'. It does not seem to matter whether a 'PK assembly' or a 'ghost spaceman' is involved, as the same clone-like pattern is reproduced when presenting multiples of 'aliens'. In the language of the report, the brain 'hams' its way through encounters, just providing the bare essentials for 'recognition'. Just as the dream 'broadcast' replaced real names with an impression, facial features are replaced with simplifications or they are avoided by clever stage-management, depicting the entity with a clouded visor or, in the case of apparitions, with the face averted or covered. The famous Cheltenham case depicted a Woman in Black with a handkerchief held up permanently to her face (see Fig. 2).

A SPR case that provides further evidence of the overlap between apparitions and close-encounters occurred in Roxburghshire, Scotland, in 1892. The figure of a tall man with a pale complexion, wearing dark clothing and a top hat, was seen repeatedly on a small country road. His face was indistinct, and 'blue lights were seen after dark near the spot frequented by the ghost; these were not stationary, but moved about in all

Fig. 2 An artist's impression of an apparitional 'abbreviated form' that appeared to the Despard family in Cheltenham, England, in 1884. The face, hands and feet of this dark entity were permanently hidden. Witnesses could hear footsteps and the rustle of clothing as it passed. It appeared on one occasion in bright sunlight in the middle of the lawn, where the family of five encircled it by joining hands. It faded away as it passed between them. At other times it had been seen for over half an hour.

directions.'[21] If this case had occurred recently, it would no doubt have been identified as a 'high-strangeness' case associated with 'nocturnal lights', as the ufological terminology puts it. In fact, a comparable URE also took place on an open road but in a very modern context.

Incident at Junction 36

I am indebted to Joseph Dormer, who investigated this case, for the following details:

> The witness hitch-hiked towards home at 23.30 and was on the A65 junction with the M6 near Crooklands. It had rained heavily, but there was no wind at all. The witness was standing beside a lighted signpost . . . suddenly in the north-north-east he became aware of a white light that began to fade and reappear in pulses . . . then the lights on the road sign went out and he heard a rustling sound and turned to see the bushes shaking violently, as if in a strong wind. Standing only a few feet from him was a figure some 4 foot (1.25 m) tall, looking like a goblin with dangling arms that almost touched the ground. Feeling terrified and a sensation of 'being watched', D. rushed blindly on to the road and was picked up by the police in a state of fear.

Both this and the Roxburghshire ghost were facilitated by witness field exposure from the area and the UAPs. The sudden extreme fear and sense of presence in the 'goblin' case can be induced by specific frequencies. The malfunctioning of the road sign is also an indication of an electrical-field presence.

It has been indicated that the physical aspects of close-encounters can be produced by the effects of environmental electromagnetic fields and UAPs, and that the 'constructed' effects in poltergeist activity overlap with such alien-theme experiences. However, it is clear that very physical-looking flying saucers which appear as structured craft can also be of the same reality-status as apparitions, which can display selective and transient physical characteristics, such effects being due to physical electromagnetic phenomena or the manipulation of the perceptual system. It is equally clear that CEs with seemingly structured UFOs can also be straight hallucinations. Consider the following sighting.

'Spirit Ship'

This case involved a solitary witness to a spectacular 'daylight disc' seen from a taxi in the spring of 1992. Lynn Picknett relaxed in the back of a black London cab as it pulled up at the traffic lights near Haverstock Hill, north London. As she sat there, she became aware that the lights seemed to be taking a very long time to change. Then, to her astonishment, a huge oval object floated slowly into view in the blue sky framed by the taxi window. It seemed quite low and like a 'melon cut in half', with a flat base and a domed top. As it passed over, it banked to reveal an oval-shaped underside that had a single row of white lights all the way round the edge, forming a border. Bemused by this sight, Lynn leant forward and asked the driver if he could 'see anything up there?' 'Nope!' was his curt reply. 'Are you sure you can't see anything?' 'No, can't see anything.' Then the traffic lights changed and the taxi sped away. The UFO was no longer in sight, and Lynn felt that she had been 'given a gift'. Predictably, like so many other CE witnesses, Lynn had a long history of psychic experiences, and described herself as 'very right-brained'.

In summary: it would seem that suitably irràdiated witnesses are able to produce hallucinations that seem totally real to *them*, apparitions that have selective and temporary physical aspects about them, and physical 'constructions' which have a transient existence.

Consistency

Throughout most of the latter part of this chapter, the 'objections to objections' to the ESH have been explored. We began by examining the physical aspects, the implications of which also covered the issue of multiple witnessing. The third main objection to a psychic theory for the CE experience was the issue of consistency. To restate the problem: If UFOs and their purported occupants are basically imaginary or the product of individuals' waking dreams, how are the same entities encountered all over the world, or at least, in different and unrelated cases?

The simplest and most revealing way of answering this question is to ask it again, but replace the words UFO 'entity' or 'close-encounter' with 'dream'. That is to say, there is a direct parallel with dream content that reveals that they are, like dreams, produced ultimately by the unconscious. This applies, to a lesser extent, to UFOs too. Therefore, allowing for syntax, the question would now read: How do dreamers all report essentially the same experiences, with the same type of dream reported time and time again? If dreams are basically imaginary, how are the same dreams encountered all over the world, or at least in different and unrelated cases?

This is a much easier question to answer because we all know about dreams. There is no mystery when we ask how it is that various types of dream are reported all over the world. The answer is simple: every dream is different, but we all have times when we (or others) can recognize our dreams as a type that everyone has. This is, of course, because we all share the same nervous system, biological needs, emotional impulses, etc. Our dreams express the hopes and anxieties that are part of the human condition.[22] The point I am making here is this: the answer regarding the consistency with entity types in UFO encounters is that there are very varied types of entity, with certain kinds repeated over and over, as types. For example, there are the 'greys' as an entity type; the tall silver-suited humanoid; the hirsute dwarf; the small featureless robot; the blond athlete; and the Men in Black – all *types* that repeatedly occur. All dreams are one-offs, but they conform to typical patterns. The same could be said of entities. Similarly, as with dream symbols, there are a number of entity 'specials' that contain typical elements in disguised form, but even these can be traced back to the psychological function they symbolize or embody, or the systemic effect of a field they represent.

This last aspect is the 'cheese makes you dream' effect and it is an indication that, frequently, dreams comply with physical bodily functions to a large extent, which act as cues for the dream content.[23] A parallel process can be detected by comparing the content of encounters with the related field-induced systemic effects, as from this it is clear that the unconscious will react to a field and represent it in encounter perceptions. It has been stated that field exposure is instrumental in the induction of the encounter realities, including physical effects. An obvious and important aspect that contributes to the consistency between unrelated encounter cases is the fact that *the human system reacts to fields in a consistent manner*, resulting in the same small details occurring repeatedly from case to case. To illustrate the degree of consistency involved, it is comparable with the symptoms that reoccur with specific ailments that a doctor would observe to reach a particular diagnosis.

The entities that have been reported – such as the little cloaked entities in the Gateshead case (see *UFO Study* by Jenny Randles); the tall blond 'Venusians'; the silver-suited humanoids; the 'greys'; the robed 'wise men'; the 'watchers'; and the hairy dwarf – will be familiar to those in the UFO-study field. Just as we can make a list of such entity standards, we can do the same with dream types: the flying dream; the falling dream; the paranoid or being pursued dream; the wish-fulfilment dream; the erotic dream (especially applicable to UFO encounters); the dream where you are being pursued but cannot escape due to paralysis; the anxiety dream; the exposed- or nudity-in-public dream and so on. It is clear that entities/encounters and dreams share the same patterns of consistency; both are different but incorporate a range of basic elements in different permutations.

Therefore, alien entities and exotic flying saucers both share the same broad patterns of occurrence, in terms of consistency, with dream types. This is because such perceptions, like dreams, are produced ultimately by the 'picture library' in the unconscious.

Colin Wilson notes: 'Poltergeist phenomena always work their way up from small effects to larger ones . . . The "Bell Witch" poltergeist seemed to take pleasure in developing new ways of upsetting everybody. Strange lights flitted about the yard after dark . . .'[24]

It is clear that the human nervous system, when irradiated by electromagnetic fields, can produce perceptions of aerial lights. This epileptic-like activity is referred to as a visual seizure in neurology. However, such luminous effects can also be anomalous light phenomena produced as a direct physical effect of such fields on the environment. This combination of subjective luminosities and objectively real light phenomena in association with electrical fields is explored in the next chapter, where we find that both are associated with poltergeist outbreaks.

3 Poltergeists, Visions and Close Encounters

There is a vast amount of evidence to suggest that within each of us there is a conscious mind and a separate, subconscious mind · capable of autonomous activity. This evidence is entirely circumstantial; no neurologist's probe has ever established their existence. Nevertheless, Wilder Penfield (one neurologist whose opinion deserves respect) concluded at the close of his career that such a concept was essential to any sensible account of human behaviour.[1]

Psychokinesis (PK) literally means 'movement by the mind' and refers to the spontaneous and anomalous movement of objects during poltergeist activity. It is then called recurrent spontaneous psychokinesis, or RSPK. PK also includes the more controlled parlour tricks, like cutlery bending, and laboratory experiments, such as the effects that psychics have on seed growth. It is clear that much more is involved than the straightforward movement of objects.

Cutlery bending and key distortions have led to thorough research into the processes involved, based on examinations of the affected metal. Metallurgists have used electron microscopes to determine the type of changes that have taken place, and they have found alterations at molecular levels at the critically deformed area in PK-distorted nickel-silver.[2]

Numerous experiments with seeds, where their growth is monitored, have taken place. Those 'exposed' to psychic influence have been found to have developed faster than control seeds without such exposure. Microscopic examination has detected changes in the cell protoplasm associated with the enhanced growth. One researcher, Professor Bernard Grad at McGill University, carried out such tests on barley seeds: 'What he found was that the seeds treated by the healer showed a higher yield than the untreated.'[3]

These are just two small areas of research into PK and they have been chosen here to represent a wider field, the results of which undoubtedly indicate that the human system can manipulate physical reality selectively. The implications of this must be numerous, but the two examples given provide clues as to the possibilities of PK activity in CEs. Stated flatly, if an indiviudal can alter cell processes in plants, then surely he/she could alter processes in brain cells? This has just a little more impact than the length of a barley leaf; it implies that someone with a propensity for producing PK effects can alter the consciousness of another individual. This takes place, it seems, in poltergeist outbreaks, and it is the contagion effect where investigators begin to experience psychic effects themselves, independently from the 'focus'.[4] There are examples of this occurring with UFO investigators also, but the most intriguing ramifications involve encounters where one witness induces another to experience a UFO vision; that is to say, one witness acts as a 'medium' or 'focus' and, by psychokinetic/electromagnetic processes, induces the other to enter an altered state, and that state then precipitates the visionary UFO experience. This scenario *is* actually reflected in CE reports where two witnesses (or more) are involved. One loses consciousness due to the apparent presence of a UFO or entity after sharing the initial stages of the encounter, and the remaining witness then goes on to experience a complex set of perceptions. For those in the UFO-study field, the Pascagoula event seems to be an example of this. This oblivious/trance state is the type of condition that 'mediums' fall into during the early stages of a seance, and then go on to induce 'spirits', etc. 'Physical mediums', as they are known, improve on this and produce objects from remote locations, which are known as apports. Also, as in poltergeist outbreaks, of which the seance situation is a parallel, they reorganize the physical materials around them. These materials may include apports, and perhaps also what could be termed 'ambient materials', such as dust particles, fibres and other waste materials in the vicinity or brought in as apports. In some cases, their own body tissue appears to be utilized. But whatever the materials, they seem to be able to organize them into specific realities, such as 'spirits', 'elements', apparitions, or whatever is relevant to the 'sitting'. The term 'ectoplasm' has been adopted to refer to what appears to be a substance produced from the 'medium's' own bodily tissue.[5] It is evident that the unconscious individual is able to do this, fantastic as it may seem, with varying degrees of success. It is suggested, therefore, that this type of person occurs repeatedly in CE events and in extraordinary altered states. Sometimes the person produces UFO realities which, for a transient period, appear to have superficial physical characteristics.

The implications of this are very strange indeed, but it *has* been found in laboratory tests that molecular reorganization *is* produced. On a macro level, it has also been found that the 'focus' or 'poltergeist medium' can organize household materials into complex structures, more or less instantly.[6] Where is this ability expressed in UREs? How far can this organizational ability by PK be taken? Some researchers use the term 'paraphysical', so perhaps we should speak of 'psycho-engineering', although this is a little misleading, because complexity is not required; that is to say, at the onset of the CE, could metal (or any material for that matter) be shaped and moulded; lights added (these energies occur in poltergeist activity); beams emitted; apparitional 'spacemen' included, etc.? In effect, could a convincing, physically 'staged' flying saucer be temporarily produced, that could travel through the atmosphere in the instantaneous way that apports appear and vanish? Could such a 'psycho-construction' be an encounter reality?

This scenario is a possibility; it is one explanation why structured craft have been observed to have resolved out of an amorphous atmospheric light. If the unconscious can produce images of spaceships as hallucination, it follows, surely, that it could, given the right conditions, use these mental models as the basis for a three-dimensional reality, consisting of organized matter. Could such a 'psycho-construction' be the physical craft that purportedly crashed in Roswell, New Mexico, in the late 1940s?[7] Such a staged event in the early years of the modern UFO era, in a fantasy-prone climate, would certainly kick-start the belief in physical extraterrestrials.

We have noted that PK organization can be rooted at molecular, and presumably atomic, levels, and this could produce a physical object around which the encounter drama could be superimposed. Such an object would not, of course, have to be functional in any mechanical sense – it would be comparable to backdrop scenery in a stage production. It would be put together with entirely different priorities from any conventional engineering viewpoint, and it would be produced to engineer belief. This is entirely consistent with other patterns in CEs and it reflects the *modus operandi* of the electromagnetically activated unconscious in producing such realities.

Close encounters and poltergeist outbreaks – a shared context

There is a background context that is important in understanding both CEs and poltergeist activity. It has already been stated that the unconscious, or more descriptively, the UI, is activated or 'energized' by seismic or artificial fields to create its presentations in the CE mode. It is evident that similar energies are involved in poltergeist activity. As a general statement, where RSPK activity is taking place, and where UFO 'flaps' occur, *there are always ambient electromagnetic or electrical fields, or both*. The aim of this chapter is to show that the two groups of phenomena are two versions of essentially the same basic processes; it is to reveal that, although they are distinct in many ways, they share many subsidiary aspects and, more importantly, the ambient field *context*. Descriptions of isolated UREs often fail to reveal the source of this generalized energy (or even to identify it) and to place the events in this wider EM field context. Once this is done, however, events that at first seem totally inexplicable become more understandable.

We have already mentioned an important overlap with the Bell Witch poltergeist (mysterious aerial lights), and as a general statement, it is the energetic effects in terms of light, heat and electrical phenomena that show the most striking similarities, although the different levels of energetic involvement may give the impression of greater differences than really exist.

By comparing cases, it becomes clear that essentially the same effects are occurring in close-encounters and hauntings or poltergeists, the only difference being that of interpretation; one set of witnesses feel that they are encountering spirits of the dead and the other set, alien intelligences. It would seem, then, that when *houses* or *buildings* are saturated with ambient electrical fields, poltergeists occur; and when wider areas in the landscape are electromagnetically affected, *UFO encounters occur*.

This is a general rule only, for there are cases where houses which are obvious electromagnetic hot spots give rise to UFOs and aliens, but they are scaled down to fit into a domestic environment. This may seem like a joke, so bizarre is the effect. I can only refer the reader to the 'Terror in the House of Dolls' case in the final chapter to see that the family of that house were far from amused to observe a tiny, domed flying saucer trailing sparkling 'oofle dust' around the lampshade while gripped by paralysing electrical forces that sent tingles through their bodies.

Small pockets of incidents often occur in a large area affected electromagnetically. I have mentioned that potent hot spots are those that combine natural and artificial fields. A specific small area, like a road or a house and the land around it (or the house next door), that is already affected by local fault-line(s) has these features 're-energized' when a modern electronic zap is superimposed over the natural background hum. The Middleton case in Chapter Two is a good example of this.

Similarly, individuals who are electrically hypersensitive represent an important set of factors in a 'portrait of a zap-zone'. Broadly, they act as sort of 'switching stations' or 'transformers', where the field energy is 'made' into the high-strangeness phenomena. These events, that are filtered by the human system, often at its expense, are termed *organic* effects. They are distinct from effects caused directly by charged fields, which would occur without a 'focus' or 'medium'. A good example of such *direct* effects which then tail off with an *organic* effect in the form of an apparition/entity comes from the Welsh Triangle:

The house had been unoccupied for six months . . . and the owner was living in a nearby property. On a number of occasions people had informed him that they had seen lights and heard noises coming from the house but after a thorough search of the building he found no traces of anyone . . .

However, a few days later, while looking around his garden last thing at night, he himself heard the noise: a sort of bumping sound, as of something soft and heavy being dragged downstairs. He immediately went to the empty property, let himself in and stood listening for a few minutes before going on. The noise reached him from above, so, moving carefully in the dark, as the electricity had been switched off at the start of the building work, he made his way upstairs.

As he crept up the stairway the noise became clearer, a low humming with a slight throb breaking the tone at intervals of about five seconds. When he reached the landing he was unable to determine from which direction the noise was coming, as it seemed to be all around him.

Then suddenly the noise ceased and he was left with a ringing in his ears which continued for a few minutes. Eventually, as he decided on his next move, a scraping sound reached him from the attic above . . . The humming started up again, reaching a much higher pitch than before and setting his teeth on edge.

He decided to investigate on his own, as whatever it was had set up a strong vibration in the building. As soon as he lifted the trapdoor the noise intensified tremendously and a peculiar smell reached his nostrils like that of burning rubber, but more sickening. Then, as he looked about him, still standing on the steps, he made out a faint silvery shape. Without warning a beam of light hit him and he was unable to see anything more. He remembers falling down amongst the rafters and lying there in complete panic as all he could see was flashing lights before the eyes. He found that he was unable to rise from his face-down position, some unknown force holding him there.

After a while he calmed down and was able to get into a sitting position, though when he held his wrist-watch up to his face he was alarmed he could not see its luminous dial. He thinks he must have remained there for about five minutes before he realized that the noise had ceased and all was now quiet again. He sat still, temporarily blinded by the light and confused, not able to make out his surroundings . . .

It wasn't until some six weeks later that he was informed by neighbours that on the night that he had been in the attic there was a UFO near to the empty house.

. . . the ghost had been no ghost at all, but whatever it was it had caused a huge magnetic disturbance which had ruined his wrist-watch and affected other metal in the property . . . What possible interest the UFO could have had in the attic of the empty property and why the silver-suited figure was snooping around in the dead of night has never been explained.[8]

Comment and analysis

The house was the focus for a number of identifiable field effects. A magnetic field can cause household objects to move, causing poltergeist-like noises. It can also set up vibrations in the inner ear and in the structural materials of the walls, roof, etc.[9] An electrical field can energize circuitry intermittently, causing thermal effects due to shorting, and create localized burning of the wiring, etc.[10] It can also create unearthed potentials in the atmosphere, and from Paget's description of our hapless witness, should he have touched a water pipe, he would have offered a route to earth for such an atmospheric charge, hence to disabling light acting as a mini-lightning strike.

The hum and throbbing effects induced by fields which were emitted by the UFO (a BOL) set up resonant frequencies which, by inducing mechanical vibration and friction, would have enhanced the already charged atmosphere within the loft space with static electricity.[11] This (as can easily be demonstrated with a comb and bits of paper) can induce objects to fly across the room, which is another feature of poltergeist activity.

Very localized air ionization can occur in such a field,[12] especially near a body of water, which in turn can create blobs of electrified particles (another UAP type). In fact, nitrogen, which makes up most of the air we breathe, is elevated to what is known as a metastable state in a charged field, and this produces a soft white glow that continues for some time after such a blob discharges itself. The disabling 'light-beam' effect reported was, it would seem, this electrified cloud earthing on the head and face of the witness. A sudden electrical jolt in this way would paralyse the witness for a short time; it could also cause a migraine-like effect – hence the classic flashing lights symptom.[13] This 'strike' upon the body of the witness would also affect the watch to the point of malfunction. Time pieces are a good indicator of ambient fields, because they are affected strongly by them, especially a digital 'electric watch'. In fact, electronic devices generally may be subject to magnetostrictive effects which cause them to malfunction in an electromagnetic field. Such effects, as touched upon earlier, cause critical contacts to be lost, due to the deformation of the microscopic engineering in the circuitry which returns to normal after the field drops.

The smell like burning rubber can be created by, predictably, electrical discharges in the air. Such discharges change the energy states of various atoms, and numerous chemical compounds can be formed. It has been mentioned that nitrogen, making up 70 per cent of the air, changes to a metastable state. This energized, or excited, nitrogen is called 'activated' because it readily combines with other atoms, whereas ordinary nitrogen does not: for example, it can combine with hydrogen to form ammonia, and with oxygen to form nitric oxide. It also reacts with other gases in the air to form nitrobenzene, which is an oily substance with a strong smell like bitter almonds.[14] Ozone is also produced by electrical discharges (i.e., lightning).[15] This can be smelt around electrical machinery to some extent and it is commonly reported in association with CE experiences.

These processes could account for the smell alone, but it could also have been produced as a hallucination by field stimulation of the brain.[16] We can see, therefore, that such previously mysterious phenomena can be identified as multiple field effects that act directly upon the environment, causing strange smells, movements of objects, apparitions, magnetic effects, etc. These are *direct* field effects as opposed to PK, and general poltergeist activity is a *mixture* of both (i.e., person-mediated and direct field phenomena). It does not appear that this distinction has been made before, as anything strange in a poltergeist-affected house is put down to 'spirit activity' or PK. Instead, fields from natural *and* artificial sources can be *directly* responsible.

In the Welsh Triangle case, the fields produced by the nearby earthlight or UAP must, to a large extent, be the same as the geophysical fields below a poltergeist-active house, as both originate from tectonic strain in the strata. This fact alone is an indication that poltergeist effects and UAP effects are very similar; that is to say, poltergeists and hauntings can occur in houses over fault-lines which emit seismic radiation (EM fields).[17] These reoccurring bursts of energy in fault-located houses precipitate ASCs and an altered physiology in the occupants, who then go on to perceive apparitions and experience the environmental effects referred to as poltergeists. As a geologically originating UAP (i.e., an earthlight) embodies this electromagnetic radiation and is an aerial extension of it, logic dictates that anyone who gets close to one may also hallucinate apparitions and apparently anomalous physical effects in the immediate environment (see 'The man who lives on a fault' in Chapter Six).

The long-term effects of living in such a house varies from individual to individual. In most cases, in combination with fields from powerfully transmitting radio antennae or any other source of artificial EM fields, *it produces a hypersensitivity to electrical things generally*.[18] As can be imagined, this is an important aspect, considering that many UFOs are centres of electrical energy.

Electrical sensitivity: an important factor in UFO encounters and poltergeists

Individuals who have been subjected to prolonged exposure to electromagnetic or electrical fields eventually become 'overloaded' and *actually emit fields of some coherent intensity themselves*.[19] It has been mentioned that seismic activity is one of these EM sources; others are VDU screens; radio and television transmission aerials; radio ham transmissions; microwave repeaters; radar installations; CB radio and cab transmissions; hospital technology; domestic appliances of an electronic/electrical nature; and house-wiring. The list is not exhaustive.[20]

More importantly, however, these electrically sensitive (ES) people are chronically allergic to these emissions once the condition has been induced. It is as if they have become saturated with electricity and cannot take any more. They *can* become very ill in the presence of even very low fields – for instance, the ones given off by fluorescent lighting.[21] Headaches, changes of body temperature, change in cardiac rates, paralysis, etc. occur.[22] This range of symptoms is discussed in later sections. These people are ES or hypersensitive, according to their degree of reaction. When they react allergically, it is then that they actually emit fields themselves. The strength of these varies, but in some cases they can affect street-lights at a distance. Others have rendered all their household electrical equipment totally useless. There are clinics to treat them, but because they emit these quite coherent fields (which increases their effect) patients have to be separated in terms of time and place because they will induce allergic states in each other by their mutual electrical emissions.[23] The implications for the CE experience, where two ES witnesses are involved, are far-reaching and are described later also. In this section, it will be emphasized that *this is a key aspect* to the understanding of CEs.

Invariably, ES people have other allergies associated with their 'electrical allergy' – for that is what it amounts to. This may be *a multiple allergy condition*[24] and these unfortunate people react negatively to a whole range of things that most people do not think twice about – foodstuffs, car exhaust, domestic gas, perfume and cleaning products. This is because their exposure to fields has permanently disrupted their body's ability to cope with these environmental aspects. Perhaps this could be called 'the medium's complaint', or the 'high-strangeness complaint' as *there is, in a substantial number of psychics and UFO witnesses (especially in what are known as high-strangeness cases) a high incidence of electrical hypersensitivity coupled with a multiple-allergy syndrome; furthermore, this aspect is also shared by individuals who exhibit PK abilities.* This is an indicator that their bodily system has been electromagnetically and electrically disturbed, and is an important clue to understanding the CE experience and its relationship to poltergeist activity.

Put simply, it would seem that the electrical or EM field emitted by ES people acts as a 'carrier wave' for psychic effects, including psychokinesis. Such emissions from these witnesses, psychics or foci are bound up with the phenomena that occurs around them, such as PK, visions, apparitions, 'aliens' and UFOs.

There comes a point in these people's lives when they are triggered to produce these things. The triggers can be: field effects; radio waves, especially radar; proximity to lightning strikes; pre-thunderstorm conditions; seismic activity; any dramatic change in metabolism, such as puberty, or even physical trauma (falling off a ladder!).[25] Of course, from a UFO investigator's point of view, an important trigger is the UAP, and ES people can be affected even when these aerial globes of energy are some distance away. Whether they are affected or not would depend on the type of *field mixture involved, its strength, and the particular wavelengths to which the witness is hypersensitive.* Of course, distance is another factor; but it does not seem to be as important as the others. Because ES people also invariably have some degree of food and chemical allergy, they are often characterized as being 'unwell' on a more or less permanent basis.[26] Untreated allergies can go unrecognized for years and become progressively worse until the sufferer is put on a specialized diet.[27]

These food allergies include reactions to gluten in *all* wheat products, milk, a variety of vegetables, certain meats, *all additives* (of the 'E' variety) and sugar, which causes hypoglycaemia (a low blood-sugar complaint).[28] The chemical sensitivity can include just about anything, but volatile substances are the worst. Needless to say, this is a twentieth-century disease and is accelerated by 'electropollution'.[29] However, having said this, if an individual has for a prolonged period been exposed to natural earth-fields, a similar condition can occur.[30] These factors will become evident in the case-studies. During an investigation, one witness emitted a field so strongly that the tape-recorder I was using malfunctioned. Investigators find this all the time during their interviews with witness to UFO and psychic events. In the case in question, the recording came out blank on one occasion and a t a speed too fast on another, so I had to continue the interview with the tape-recorder wrapped in kitchen foil to shield it, which was successful. Tape-recorders are actually used in testing for ES.

However, such emissions are only one important aspect involved in the way that these individuals are able to affect others and their environment. It does seem that another factor, such as an energy, is involved, which may be the 'PK factor'. Events such as this indicate that *PK and electrical fields are intimately bound up with one another in some way*.[31]

In order to confirm the electromagnetic connection with poltergeist phenomena, we need to look at studies of this psychic activity. We have already noted that the energies and radiation of UAPs correlate this electrical aspect with the UFO phenomenon; now there is a need to find a similar correlation with poltergeist activity. Consider the following, concerning a poltergeist 'focus person':

> From this time on, Angelique developed the power of giving people violent electric shocks – she was in fact another 'human electric eel' . . . Objects laid on her apron flew off violently, and the power was strong enough to raise a heavy tub with a man sitting on it. Oddly enough, metals were not affected, indicating that this form of 'electricity' was not the usual kind. When Angelique was tired, the current would diminish. It also diminished when she was on a carpet, but was most powerful when she was on bare earth . . . She had to sleep on a stone covered with a cork mat. The phenomena continued for four months, and were widely studied by men of science; then they ceased.
>
> Mrs Crowe makes the reasonable assumption that poltergeist phenomena may be electrical in nature, and cites a number of other cases, including a Mlle Emmerich . . . who became a human electric battery after receiving a severe fright, the nature of which is not specified. We have already noticed how mediums seem to develop their powers after accidents. The interesting thing about Mlle Emmerich was that she could give people shocks even when they were not touching her. She gave her brother a shock when he was several rooms away; 'Ah, you felt it, did you?'
>
> Mrs Crowe adds the interesting remark: Many somnambulistic persons (she actually means persons under hypnosis) are capable of giving an electric shock; and I have met one person, not somnambulistic, who

informs me that he has frequently been able to do it by effort of will. Clearly, if someone was able to produce electric currents at will, he or she might be in a position to cause poltergeist phenomena – perhaps even at a distance, like Mlle Emmerich.[32]

From this, and other aspects to be described, it is evident that there is an overlap between ES people and poltergeist foci in that both can affect the environment and other people electrically. It is also clear from poltergeist reports that there is a strong aspect of electrical activity which creates a number of effects and is behind many of the phenomena, such as apparitions; malfunctions of cameras and electronic equipment; luminous phenomena; mist; cold spots and hallucinatory realities. In fact, it is proposed that many of these events can be demystified as field effects which emanate from the location and the 'focus'. We saw earlier in the Welsh Triangle case how field effects can produce a whole range of apparently mysterious phenomena, to the extent of giving a house a haunted reputation.

Therefore, if an ES individual – a condition associated with being psychic[33] – encounters a UAP, he or she will react allergically and will emit their own field[34] which, surprisingly, can be extremely coherent (i.e., beam-like).[35] A UAP is only one source of an EM/electrical field that can do this (buried cables, geophysical stress from faults, aerials, etc. are others) and this EM 'signal' appears to act as a 'carrier wave' for PK effects which are organic (i.e., human-originating). There is evidence that this 'PK-enhanced' signal induced by the UAP's field *can feed back to the UAP at a distance*, as the witness's personal field 'signal', or frequency. That this is possible over a distance is evident from the Streetlight Interference Project initiated by Hilary Evans, in which individuals turned off street lamps by their presence. This human link with a distant UAP in the sky can give it apparent qualities of intelligence.

In fact, it has been reported on many occasions that UFOs seem to be aware of the witness's presence. This does, of course, fuel the idea that UFOs are under intelligent control or are intelligences of some kind themselves. This personal link has also been reported as the 'OZ' factor or 'bell-jar effect', where the witness and the UFO seem to be enclosed in their own private world, or 'bubble of influence', and are 'melded' together in isolation.[36] There are numerous reports of this effect, of which the following is an example:

Over in the south-west . . . she saw an unusually bright object . . . The light hovered by Halkyn Mountain at an elevation of just ten degrees. Whatever it was it looked most spectacular.

Ranging her binoculars on to it she saw it in its full glory. There was a large white circle of light and inside this a smaller orange one. Across the middle of the orange circle was a red bar about one quarter the circle's width. This was broken in the middle. The whole thing rotated slowly anticlockwise at an unvarying speed.

Dumbstruck she put down the binoculars and looked at it without them. It was still there. She blinked. The image remained. Never in her life before had she seen anything like this.

She estimated that it was only about half a mile away and positioned over some electricity pylons. As she stared she found herself becoming curiously isolated. The world was disappearing round her as she focused her attention on this visitor from the unknown. It was almost as if she was being hypnotized by the light, forcing her eyes to fixate upon it. Time rushed by. Perhaps only five minutes, she could not gauge this accurately . . . the object began to move, slowly and silently at an angle of about twenty degrees sideways across the sky. It stopped. Quickly raising the camera she pointed it at the object. Just as she did so it streaked away westwards in a blur of motion and in just three seconds had vanished over the horizon.[37]

In this enclosed and linked state, the witness is especially subject to the wavelengths and frequencies that the UAP is emitting, and the sense of time being slowed down is another commonly reported effect (desynchronization). This subjective perception can be produced by exposure to a magnetic field – as Persinger has shown in his experiments – and involves specific wavelengths.

In terms of an EM beam-like signal, the distance between the UFO/UAP and the witness of about half a mile (0.75 km) is not very far at all. Radio waves travel for considerable distances through physical obstacles. That such a process occurs (i.e., that the body emits EM waves) has been shown experimentally by 'electropollution' scientists, Dr Cyril W. Smith and Dr Roger Coghill. The latter proposes radio-wave emission from the human central nervous system. He has found that the human brain is actually structured to facilitate radio-wave transmissions from specific structures (Betz cells) which he describes as a 'radio transmitter of formidable complexity: it's as if the brain had a million or so radio stations in operation simultaneously.'[38]

It is not surprising that these emissions from the human system could link with the UAP emissions, for seismic activity, which gives rise to both UAPs and seismic radiation, produces radio waves (in addition to other parts of the EM spectrum). We have a situation, therefore, where there are two sources of the same frequency (i.e., radio waves); one is emitted from the witness and the other from the UAP, although both are combined with other field types. That is to say, electromagnetic field emissions from the witness and the UAP 'link' through the medium of the ambient field between them, as it seems that an electrical potential builds up between the UAP and the witness. This would not happen with a non-ES witness – or only in exceptional conditions. I would suggest this is similar to the potential difference that builds up between cloud and earth to create a lightning strike. It does not necessarily result in a discharge taking place, of course, but it facilitates a 'signal link' between the two – UAP and allergically reacting ES witness.

Another factor that appears to facilitate this link is the hypnoid state in the witness. From the extract earlier about Mlle Emmerich, it appears that subjects in a hypnotic state can also emit an electrical field – as shown by the community of sensation effect, where the hypnotist and the subject are linked to the extent that each can register the other's sensations.[39]

Therefore, there is a tendency for people in this sort of hypnoid state to emit energies, in addition to their personal fields, as a result of their ES condition. This hypnotic state occurs naturally in some people, and it does not seem to take much to induce them into such a disassociated state. It can be induced by all manner of normal or common conditions, such as streetlights viewed from a moving car which flicker as the car passes a row of trees.[40] ES people slip easily into this blank, day-dreaming state (or they have vivid hallucinatory images) and extreme ES can result in complete 'black-outs' or 'blank-outs'. These people are often psychic and are known in investigation circles as 'trippers', for obvious reasons.

In the OZ factor example during the Halkyn Mountain sighting, mentioned above, it shows how the *behaviour* of the UAP created just such a hypnoid state in the witness by its slow, unrelenting, luminous revolutions. This was noted by the witness, as was the lack of awareness of her surroundings, and this isolating effect is precisely what occurs during hypnosis. It is suggested, therefore, that the UAP and the presence of an ambient field induced an electromagnetic connection, or 'signal link', with the witness during a hypnotic state. Conversely, the UAP was induced to revolve and mesmerize the witness by this link to her. This is a cyclic effect, where one stage propagates the other, which, in turn, reacts back, thereby maintaining it (see Fig. 3).

The cyclical effect is a self-regulating process, and it is only one example of the sort of behaviour of a UAP that the unconscious can induce through a signal link. Other cases demonstrate an organizing process, in which the structure or appearance of the UAP is altered; judging by the number of regular aspects of the Halkyn Mountain UAP, some organization of the 'material' of the UAP can also take place.

This extraordinary electromagnetic link between ES witness and UAP

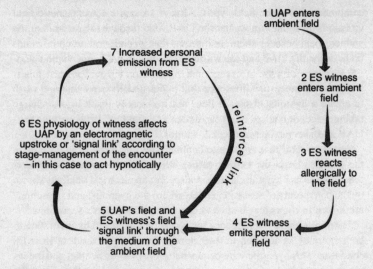

Fig. 3 Cyclic effect of the 'signal link'.

can only take place if both are in a 'connecting' ambient field. The Halkyn Mountain UAP was involved in an extended series of events in Flint, Wales, which are described in the next chapter. This area was the centre for a number of poltergeist-like electrical phenomena, as well as CEs. In terms of electronic pollution, it is surrounded by many powerful transmission antennae from the nearby Ministry of Defence establishment at Neston. There is little doubt that these antennae flooded a small area with ambient fields over an extended period.

Mind the zap . . .

Another more spectacular case where this electromagnetic signal link involved a build-up of an atmospheric charge or potential difference between UAP and witness, actually resulted in a powerful discharge effect. Consider this description by Bob Boyd of the Plymouth UFO Research Group in England:

Here is Denise's story:

'I was coming into my house at approximately 11.15 pm, and as I approached the corner of the bungalow I thought I saw some lights behind the house. As I got to the back door and could see up the hill behind our house, I saw an enormous UFO hovering above the houses on top of the hill. The object was unlit and a dark metallic grey, but coming from underneath the object and shining down on the rooftops beneath it were six or seven broad shafts of light. These were lovely pastel shades of pink and purple and also white. I saw all this in an instant and I was terrified. I hurriedly reached for the door, but as I put my hand on the handle, from the unlit side of the ship, a lime-green pencil-thin beam of light came down and hit the back of my hand. As soon as it hit my hand I could not move. I was stopped dead in my tracks. The beam stayed on my hand for at least thirty seconds, in which time I could only stand and watch the UFO. I was very frightened although the UFO was a fantastic sight to see. It was huge and silent. In fact the whole area seemed very quiet.

'The green beam, which did not give off any illumination and was rather like a rod of light, then switched off and I continued to open the door. It was as if a film had been stopped and then started again. I had stopped in mid-stride and when the beam went off, continued the same movement. I opened the door and rushed in the house. As I did so the UFO lifted into the sky slightly and moved away and out of sight.

'Rubbing my hand I ran in and told my sister. We went back outside but there was nothing there. I went and sat down, and a few minutes later . . . I noticed spots of blood and after washing it saw it was a burn.'

On Friday the 11th, John visited the houses that had been underneath the UFO, and although none had reported seeing the object or having electrical interference, *three* did report very strange behaviour by their dogs at the time in question . . . On Saturday, 12 September, Des Weeks, Group Secretary, his daughter Patsy, a nurse and myself visited Denise. We took a number of photographs and interviewed Denise again . . . The burn itself seemed much worse than it was on Friday . . . Patsy examined the burn . . . she could not say a lot about it but said that it was important that Denise see a doctor as soon as possible as she was in a state of shock. Indeed, Denise was visibly shaking, though she put it down to a lack of sleep over the two previous nights.

A few weeks after the event the wound was very sore and angry-looking. When she came to the Wednesday meeting the burn had a fully-formed scab . . . When she returned from holiday this had gone, leaving a red mark like a pale birth-mark.[41]

Denise Bishop lives only a mile from the largest nuclear and naval base in England, which would produce electromagnetic hot spots in the area. It would seem, therefore, that an energetic UAP, possibly produced as an accidental product of such electronic pollution, had irradiated the area close to the witness's house, inducing a charged area, and she had walked into it. This is precisely as indicated in Fig. 3. Such UAPs are associated with elevated points, like a hill, and it is no coincidence that transmitting radio masts are so often situated on such high ground. As soon as she put her hand on the metal door-handle, she became earthed and the laser-like discharge took place. Schumann waves, which are produced by thunderstorms, set the earth and ionosphere into resonance like a giant electrical bell – a comparable electrical event to this.[42]

We can see from the Lynn Picknett UFO (described in the previous chapter) that this was a hallucinatory spacecraft, or 'ship' as the witness revealingly puts it, grafted on to an objectively real UAP. From reconstructions of encounters, many investigators know only too well that this is a common process: the witness superimposes and subjectively transforms a mundane object – such as a star, the moon or a plane – into an exotic craft.[43] Obviously, a UAP inducing an altered state in the witness would be an even more potent basis for this grafting, especially as the witness has a definite belief and expectation regarding 'them' (i.e., aliens), and so a 'content tracing' approach need look no further.

The muscular paralysis can be obtained by an ELF frequency of about 90 to 110 Hz and it is again induced by the difference between two higher frequencies, known as the 'beat' frequency.[44] The behaviour of the dogs mentioned in the Plymouth case is a common feature associated with CEs: it is due to their heightened sensitivity to electromagnetic fields.[45] The proximity of such events to a military establishment has always been noted by those who adhere to alien activity as an explanation for UFOs, but this association is really to do with the high level of 'electronic smog' produced by their powerful communication systems.[46] (In America, there is no restriction on which bands of the EM spectrum they can use – including the ionizing levels.[47])

Once again the OZ factor silence is reported; this too is indicative of the irradiation of the witness's central nervous system, producing the hallucination of the illuminated flying saucer (visual seizure).[48] The most relevant aspect of this laser-like zap is that it demonstrates the signal link between witness and UAP. Like advanced air-to-ground missiles that are guided back down a radar beam to its source when a military plane is tracked, the electrical potential that built up invisibly was discharged as soon as Denise became earthed. This *Star Wars* theme corresponds closely with the general idea of the sort of weaponry employed by ETs, and it confirms the 'authorized myth'. Also, like the Halkyn Mountain UAP, a structured-looking object was depicted to correspond with a 'ship'.

The Plymouth encounter demonstrates how the unconscious will harness electromagnetic conditions to present such a 'production', and also how UREs, like poltergeist activity, are a mixture of *direct* field effects and *witness-based* effects (i.e., the altered state facilitating the hallucination of the 'structured and metallic spaceship'), with the physically real electrical field effects of the laser-like electrical discharge incorporated into this internally produced imagery. Therefore, we are beginning to build up a picture of a witness–UAP connection through an electromagnetic signal transmission. This signal link is an important step in understanding the CE experience, because it provides a mechanism by which the unconscious interacts with aerial electrical phenomena. It also provides a mechanism by which the unconscious contents of the human mind, with all its strange imagery and dynamic symbolism, can enter the arena of the ET mythology via the UAP.

Before we return to the earlier extracts concerned with poltergeist activity, here is another spectacular example of the signal link between witness and UAP.

An electrical field day . . .

Type: close encounter of the second kind
Date: 27.7.79
Time: 1.40 am local time
Place: near Warren, Minnesota
Investigator: Allan Hendry (CUFOS) and others

Val Johnson is the only witness to the event which occurred in a rural area of flat land with few houses and buildings. The roads there are laid on a rectangular grid pattern, with an uninterrupted view from one to another. As Johnson was driving west from a small town called Stephen he caught sight of a light near some trees which he knew to be 2½ miles (4 km) away near a road junction towards which he was driving. At that junction he turned left (south) on to Highway 220 and headed for the light which as far as he could tell had been stationary. He accelerated to 65 mph (105 km/hr). As he drew closer he could see that the light did not appear to be illuminating the surrounding area. After he had driven about a mile (1.5 km) along Highway 220 the light seemed to 'greatly accelerate' towards him. It covered the remaining half to one mile in an instant. Deputy Johnson heard no sound from the light, and it appeared as a blinding glare. He lost consciousness at this point but recalls the sound of breaking glass.

When he regained consciousness the patrol car was at right angles across the other side of the road, and facing east. His head was resting against the steering wheel and his eyes hurt . . . He was examined by a doctor at 4.00 am. Apparently by this time the red bump on his forehead was not conspicuous and the doctor was not informed that Johnson had been unconscious; therefore he concentrated on the eye pain. This the doctor concluded was due to 'mild welding burns'; the direct light of the doctor's instruments caused considerable discomfort – hurting so much that he did not make a thorough examination. He treated the irritation to the eyes . . .

During this time the patrol car was being moved back to the base garage. The obvious damage was catalogued: one headlight was smashed, a small circular dent was found in the bonnet, the windscreen was shattered, a red light on top of the car was punctured and dislodged from its housing and two radio antennae were bent backwards . . . Johnson's wrist-watch and the dashboard clock were running slow.[49]

An intriguing sequel to this occurred two days later, near Vermillion, South Dakota. Strangely, it involved another Deputy Johnson:

Russ Johnson (no relation to Val Johnson) was driving alone, again on a lonely highway (Highway 50), two days after the (first) deputy's experience *to the hour* and 400 miles (644 km) to the south. Again the sky was clear and the weather was good. This Johnson also described seeing a light like a headlamp just ahead of him on the highway for two seconds. Then, in the space of another two seconds the light rushed at him and suddenly engulfed the car. 'I thought I was in a light-bulb.' Closing his eyes against the blinding light, he slammed on the brakes and hoped for the best. Just like Deputy V. Johnson his car skidded to a stop and spun sideways across the road, facing east. He then opened his eyes . . . to watch the light source rush slightly west-bound and rise in an angle slightly . . . and vanish abruptly . . .

A third almost identical case was reported on 20 August 1979.[50]

These encounters demonstrate the magnetic link between the witnesses and the UAP, which seemed to have happened due to the movement of the cars into the range of the field they emitted. The human body can provide just as potent a conductive medium as a car body – perhaps more so – being made up of 70 per cent water with an embedded electrical system, the CNS. These seem to be further cases of a field connection between witness and UAP resulting in an earthing effect.

Another example is the well-known case (due to the film *Fire in the Sky*) involving Travis Walton, who went too close to a highly charged UAP which earthed on his body like a lightning strike. The departure of such UAPs from a near-ground position frequently involves a vortex and magnetic effect which could have swept the witness up like an electrified mini-tornado, and deposited him some distance away in a battered and amnesiac state, which, predictably, is exactly what transpired. The subsequent 'alien' vision is also a product of the UAP's consciousness-altering effect, in conjunction with later hypnosis.

In the first event, no magnetic after-effects were detected on the car body, which perhaps does indicate that there *was* a signal link with the witness's body, as it was his watch and the car's interior clock that were affected in this way. However, as timepieces are sensitive to EM fields, it is possible that they were affected, while the car's metal was not (a similar situation is where light can be bright enough to register on the retina but not on a photographic film's emulsion).

Once again, however, there is an EM link between UAP and witness/car which was instrumental in the collision. Earlier, the 'substance' of a UAP was mentioned; interestingly, this UAP did not just pass through the car in an ephemeral way: it caused mechanical damage, so it was 'made of something'. One of the important implications of this signal link is that the witnesses, by their own coherent field emissions, can unconsciously mould this 'substance', which undoubtedly includes electrified particles.

In poltergeist activity, luminous phenomena, clearly electrical in character, are fairly common, and they amount to UAPs in a domestic environment. These lights, which sometimes emit their own 'zone of fear', can resolve into self-luminous apparitions (which may be why ghosts have gained a fear-inducing reputation). Similarly, there are numerous reports of lights in the sky (LITS in ufological jargon) as shapeshifting spheres of light (a UAP type) which resolve into 'structured craft'. Witnesses speak of 'silent explosions of light' that clear to reveal an oval object with lights and portholes standing on supports, or hovering; both situations imply a signal link process in operation.

In the Halkyn Mountain case, mention was made of the OZ factor effect: the UAP displayed a certain amount of structure. Although this could be a natural effect caused by its internal fields, it *is* indicative of minimal organization which would certainly be consistent with many of the staging strategies by the UI; that is to say, the unconscious, having insider knowledge of what it would take to create belief in alien intelligence, as it wishes to use this identity, would know that the conscious mind associates structure with intelligence. This is why crop-circles have been 'identified' as alien. Pre-scientific generations attributed all manner of natural things to the work of the Devil, God, 'the little people', evil-spirits, etc. We laugh at these things now, but the same thing is happening when UFOs are identified as ETs; people who suggest this are in their own pre-scientific era. However, there does seem to be reorganization of UAP 'material' via the 'signal link'.

If we look at the studies of PK, we find that some researchers have come to the conclusion that it affects the most flexible, fragile or subtle materials in the environment:

> Rex Stanford has come up with two interesting theories . . . another idea about PK in which he says that PK happens easiest with things that are most flexible . . . The more sensitive a thing, the more unstable, and the easier to influence.[51]

The UAP, being an unstable globe of electromagnetic energy, would certainly qualify as one of these subtle materials, and Stanford's theory lends support to the organization of UAPs by the unconscious. In fact, the same author also presents this idea:

> The hypothesis is that there is some sort of two-way interaction through psychokinesis between our minds and the energy field of the UFO. In R. G. Stanford's conformance theory it is proposed that the more subtle and sensitive the material, the easier it is for our minds to affect it. It is hypothesized that the energy field that we call UFO is a profoundly sensitive energy form responsive to our subconscious mental cues.[52]

This concept of PK in isolation, without the electrical field correlation, and the idea of 'subtle mental cues', are steps in the right direction. However, the introduction of the identifiable and more tangible medical condition of electrical hypersensitivity radically shifts this former approach from an interesting idea into the arena of mainstream scientific method, involving situations which can be measured, tested, detected, reproduced and predicted utilizing established instrumentation. Returning to the case of Mlle Emmerich, indicating the importance of electrical forces in poltergeist phenomena, Wilson mentions that metal was not affected and concludes that the electricity involved was 'not the usual kind.' This, in fact, indicates a field pattern that only affects dielectric materials (i.e., those that do not conduct electricity). This was mentioned earlier in relation to non-conductive materials moving away from the direction of an intense magnetic field. This principle has an industrial use and it can be used to separate particles carried by a non-conductive liquid: 'Paramagnetic tension operates in opposition to gravity. Since the lighter particles respond more to paramagnetic tensile forces and the heavier particles more to gravity, the lighter particles tend to rise and the heavier sink.'[53] This lends support to the electromagnetic field basis for poltergeist phenomena, as paramagnetic forcing field effects, and static charges are able to move objects in the environment, in many instances causing them to float through the air. In his study of the poltergeist, Wilson's comments are pertinent to this close-encounter comparison:

When Esther wore shoes with glass soles(!) the manifestations stopped but she developed headaches and nose-bleeds. Her sensation of electric currents is also highly suggestive. There have been dozens of well-authenticated cases of 'human electric batteries'. Again, nearly all concern girls or boys at the age of puberty. Caroline Clare of Bondon, Ontario . . . developed such powerful electric currents that people who touched her received severe shocks; pieces of metal stuck to her as if she were a magnet. Jennie Morgan of Sedalia, Missouri, became an electric battery at fourteen; when she touched metal objects, sparks flew. Frank McKinistry . . . would develop an electric charge during the night and slowly lose it during the day . . . The Amherst minister, the Reverend Edwin Clay, was convinced that the secret of Esther's manifestations was electricity, and even delivered a lecture to that effect.[54]

This early identification of poltergeist activity with electrical phenomena has been overlooked by subsequent researchers. There is, therefore, a fourfold set of conditions for both poltergeist and UFO encounters:

1 The emission of coherent electromagnetic beams as a whole body effect from the electrically hypersensitive focus or witness as a symptom of their clinical condition.

2 The presence of electromagnetic fields from fault-lines creating hot-spot conditions.

3 The presence of electromagnetic fields as electronic and electrical pollution.

4 Electromagnetic fields emitted by such UAPs as earthlights, ball-lightning, and anomalous light phenomena, such as those created by electronic and electrical pollution from radio antennae and pylons respectively. These could usefully be termed electroforms which occur not only in landscape environments, but also in the traditional poltergeist context, the domestic setting. These 'domestic' UAPs, as I have termed them, also seem to be centres of EM energy fields, frequently as light sources that flicker about the rooms of poltergeist-afflicted houses. Others seem to be more energetic and create the 'zones of fear' by their EM emissions, as described earlier. In the case of the Enfield poltergeist, a member of the household reported:

'I saw this light,' he said. 'It was the equivalent, I should say, of twelve inches vertical. It looked like a fluorescent light behind frosted glass, which burned fiercely and gradually faded away.'

'How did you react?' Grosse asked.

'I was bloody petrified. I'd never seen anything like it, and the feeling I had was one of fear, like there was somebody standing right by me and watching. I've never known such a feeling in my life.'[55]

It has been mentioned that this extreme fear reaction that occurs so frequently in UFO reports, in association with the sensation of a 'presence', can be induced by ELF fields which will trigger the temporal lobe of the brain, producing such feelings.[56] In fact, there is so much scientific literature on the effects of fields on biological systems that it is odd that it is rarely referred to in the UFO study or paranormal literature.

Light phenomena have been repeatedly reported in domestic contexts, for example, in the Enfield case:

> In addition to the shadows and figures, there were lights, which Mrs Harper saw on a wall one afternoon. There were four of them, two round and two shaped 'like keys'. They disappeared after a couple of minutes, then reappeared again.[57]

This is, of course, another example of 'domestic UAPs' in a poltergeist setting.

Ambient field effects

Consider the following example of a strange incident that involved a car parked outside the Enfield poltergeist house:

> A friend called Alan Williams called one night, and left his car parked outside. When he went back to the car, he was surprised to find that the windscreen wipers were working. This should have been an impossibility, since the car was locked and the ignition turned off. Suspecting that there might be something wrong with the car's electrical system, Alan Williams had it checked by a garage the next day. They could find nothing wrong.[58]

Consulting electropollution expert Anne Silk, I found that this is a typical power surge of ambient electrical energy which can generate power to start motors, put lights on, stop and start electronic apparatus, etc.

This is one group of the little-known effects of fields on an environment. It is a sobering thought that if ambient fields can do this, they will have a dramatic effect upon the brain, which is a delicate electrochemical computer. It should not be surprising that individuals affected by such fields should switch in and out of altered states. Such an environment may not only activate the unconscious directly, it can, as we saw in the extract from Colin Wilson's study of Mlle Emmerich, cause them to emit fields themselves that, in turn, affect the system and consciousness of others.

In fact, in Thalbourne's *Glossary of Terms Used in Parapsychology*, this effect is termed 'telergy', which was coined by psychical research pioneer

F. W. H. Myers. It refers to the psychokinetic influence exerted on the brain and nervous system of another organism. This is a key aspect. There have been numerous experiments showing that electrical stimulation of brain centres causes hallucination. Brain physiologist Wilder Penfield found that if he touched specific areas in the temporal cortex (regarded as being the major memory centre) with an electrical probe, the subject would suddenly relive past experiences in cinematic detail. Thus, it is evident that the brain is a vast memory-bank where the conscious self feels like a visitor with only a limited number of access codes. However, if such electrically stimulated visions are possible, then similar effects could be induced by the emissions from one ES individual to another. Therefore, this, too, identifies PK as electromagnetic in nature and it *is* evident that many seemingly anomalous poltergeist- and UFO-related phenomena can be induced by such fields.

It is tempting to hypothesize that the unconscious controls the electromagnetic frequencies in some way, and that the 'focus' emits a selected field level to induce specific 'special effects'. An analogy would be the different programmes on a computer. However, what seems to be happening is that ambient fields are changing and modulating the human physiology, causing the 'focus' to emit coherent electromagnetic beams as a whole body effect.

If an allergic reaction could be induced in an ES witness, he or she would begin to emit their own personal field.[59] Harnessed by the unconscious, this would be an essential step to induce a signal link with a rich source of energy it could use, and there is little doubt that witnesses are induced subliminally to be somewhere or to do something that would lead to this, such as a hallucinated voice or 'instruction'.[60] However, what sort of levels are involved in these personal emissions in terms of voltage or field-strength? And, conversely, which field levels are involved to produce this reacting, and therefore emitting, state? The following extract gives us some idea:

> However, not only are these allergic patients extremely electrically sensitive, they can also, when reacting allergically, emit electrical signals, rather like an electric fish. These signals can be large enough to interfere with electronic apparatus, as clinical case-histories testify. The electrical signals which make it possible to eavesdrop on computers are sufficiently strong to trigger allergic reactions in sensitive patients who are then liable to feed 'garbage' back into the computer or other equipment. The subject area in electronics which deals with such problems is 'Electromagnetic Compatibility'. The problems which allergy patients have described are very wide-ranging. One patient had a robotic system in a factory

completely malfunction each time he stood near it. Another had the electronic ignition system on successive new cars fail as soon as an allergic reaction was triggered by fumes from a diesel truck in front . . . the possibilities for 'zapping' electronics by allergic subjects are many.[61]

We can see from this extract that an allergic reaction in an ES subject will induce their system to emit electrical fields, and this can be prompted by an exposure to such fields or to any chemical to which they are allergic, as they are interchangeable. It would appear that the source for such a triggering could be quite remote and some distance away. In UFO-study terms, a number of possibilities present themselves: for example, if the person suddenly travelled into an ambient field zone, then such a personal emission could occur. It is in this altered allergic state that they signal-link with a UAP through such coherent emissions over surprisingly large distances.

It was hinted earlier that substance allergy and ES are always found in association and that they are interchangeable in terms of an allergic reaction and subsequent electrical emission. This curious state is explained in a further extract from *Electromagnetic Man*:

Allergy used to be concerned with skins and respiration, but in recent years allergic responses have been found to occur so widely that allergy may now be defined as 'the failure of a regulatory system'. The more severely allergic patients have acquired allergic responses to many chemical, environmental and nutritional substances; these may be counted in tens and even exceed a hundred in extreme cases. It appears that about 15 per cent of a given population function to some extent below their best performance capability due to a degree of allergy, that is one or more of their regulatory systems functions inadequately.

It seems that a new allergic response can be acquired, or transferred, by being exposed for a sufficiently long time to some hitherto innocuous substance while reacting strongly to an existing allergen. In such circumstances it seems that exposure to an electromagnetic frequency can sensitize the patient, so that their specific pattern of allergic responses is triggered on subsequently encountering that particular frequency. In general, the pattern of allergic responses is the same whether the trigger is chemical, environmental, nutritional or electrical. In principle, such an accurate 'memory' for frequency is no different to the 'absolute pitch' facility that many musicians possess.

From this extract we find a mechanism whereby ES people, in UFO sighting situations, can suddenly find themselves involved in a hallucinatory encounter. If they are triggered by electrical emissions from everyday sources, such as the local radio ham, or by substances such as car fumes or something they have eaten, to emit or 'broadcast' fields themselves, a simple UAP sighting can become much more significant. However, this is not the end of the story, because it is clear that some witnesses *repeatedly* encounter UFO phenomena, and UFO investigators have certainly gained the feeling that they actually *attract* UFOs in some way. For obvious reasons they are called 'repeaters', and a typical repeater has a history of psychic phenomena.[62] Could it be that their electrical or EM broadcasts have a field effect not only upon their environment, but on UAPs in the area, inducing them to closer proximity? This is certainly a possibility, as we have already seen how a signal link can influence UAPs from a considerable distance.

If we have field emissions induced in a witness by an allergic stimulus, coupled with those that occur during a hypnoid state (also induced by very ordinary situations), *plus* the induction effect to slip into an ASC by direct field influence on the brain, *plus* the effect of telergy (where another ES subject in the company of the witness emits a field, as an effect of the witness's emissions on *them*), we have a very complex situation. We also have a very potent mix, in terms of the production of a CE experience, and the UI could certainly engineer such situations for its own expressive needs.

The telergy effect, or just a straightforward electrical emission from one subject to another, is a real phenomenon and it is a problem that allergy clinics must overcome when treating patients. Dr Cyril Smith mentions this in his clinical procedures:

> The consulting room, particularly if within an allergy unit, should be located as far as possible from the other patients in terms of the number of solid walls and floors separating them. This is important if allergic responses are not to be triggered in all the other sensitive allergic subjects throughout the building during the testing session . . . Even with these precautions we have had patients come into the hospital and say, 'When I came into the building this morning I felt just as I did when I was being tested electrically.' This was without being aware that electrical testing was being carried out in the basement at that particular time.[63]

Therefore, it is not difficult to picture a scenario where two ES people are in the enforced proximity of a car. So many UFO encounters involve witnesses in vehicles that there must be something about this situation that is conducive to UREs. If the electric field from the car engine triggers them to both emit their personal fields, then their response and subsequent emissions will increase. From an electrical field point of view, this is a vicious circle and an escalating field-level could eventually induce an ASC or a 'black-out' in one or both occupants by its effect upon the brain. Assuming they both continue, and are travelling through monotonous scenery at night, they may become subject to highway hypnosis. This occurs when the same visual information is fed into the brain again and again until it 'switches off': an effect called habituation. There is, then, another potent and multiple-cause situation for hallucination or misperception, etc.

Anne Silk has investigated numerous, seemingly causeless traffic accidents where favourable conditions on clear, open, dry roads have given rise to inexplicable lapses of straightforward driving skills. Drivers have reported bemusement and dismay at their own actions or inactions as the case may be. Many of these incidents have correlated directly with combinations of geological faulting or disturbance, RF transmitters, aerials, overhead power cables, etc. A 'blank-out' effect *may* be at the heart of these accidents, although it is just as likely, considering the skills of the UI, that in some cases drivers go on automatic during their 'trance out' and the UI ensures their survival responses. That this is entirely possible was brought home to me on reading the following newspaper article:

BOY DROVE 27 MILES – ASLEEP!

A fifteen-year-old boy claimed yesterday that he drove his father's car 27 miles in his sleep. And the police believe his amazing story.

The youngster had gone to bed as usual in his home in Portsmouth. When he woke up at 3.30 am yesterday he was alone in the family car in Southampton wearing pyjamas and a dressing-gown. The boy, who has never driven before, telephoned his father, who, in turn, alerted the police. And they took him to Southampton police station. 'I know it sounds incredible, but we have no reason to disbelieve his story,' said Chief Inspector Colin Lewis yesterday. 'As policemen we tend to be naturally suspicious, but the boy's story checks out. It seems he has a history of sleepwalking. Astounding as it seems we believe that this boy got up from his bed, went to his father's car, started it up and drove all the way from Portsmouth to Southampton. The car showed no signs of any damage. And the boy's claim that he had never driven was substantiated by his father. The police say that they will not identify the boy, who is still at school. And because they believe his story they will not charge him with driving without a licence or insurance. His parents, on our advice, are taking the boy to see a doctor for treatment for sleepwalking.'[64]

Similar stories appeared in *Fortean Times* in early 1993 and demonstrate this automatic ability. Such 'zombie-like' behaviour is listed as an ES symptom by Dr C. W. Smith in *Electromagnetic Man*.

The more we look into the ES/vehicle-on-the-road-at-night situation, the more potent a scenario for CE situations it becomes. Suppose that, in this highly charged, hypnoid state, our travellers pass through an area of ambient fields due to seismic activity or an underground cable running the length of the road, then they would emit constantly at a high level and could act, potentially, as an electromagnetic 'beacon' creating a magnetic attraction for UAPs. The arrival of an energetic UAP on the scene would precipitate a memorable CE experience as it did earlier for Deputy Johnson; or, it may do the reverse and precipitate a completely blank period of time, known in ufology as a 'time lapse'.

It is evident that there is an important contagion effect involved, whereby witnesses become subject to each others' fields and, it would seem, perceptions.[65] It would also seem that a similar effect occurs in poltergeist outbreaks. Consider the following extract concerning comments by poltergeist investigators:

> Professor Hasted made another very interesting observation during our talk. I had mentioned that some very strange things had started happening to Maurice Grosse, such as the episodes of his car engine and the lost diamond ring. Could this syndrome be contagious I asked him.
>
> 'Exactly the same thing happened to me,' he replied, 'or at least with my wife.' He told me that after his first meeting with Uri Geller in 1974, a number of inexplicable events took place in his own home. This led him to suggest that there might be an 'induction effect' in psychic phenomena whereby they 'rub off' from one medium to another.[66]

We saw this effect in the Subud case (mentioned in Chapter One) which induced electrical sensitivity as a result of being in the presence of those who emit this electrical/PK field effect, which certainly was telergy with a vengeance. They were able to affect the Subud initiate by a deliberate contagion effect which had been passed on to them originally from a UAP! Subsequently, she underwent a year-long period during which her health and mental well-being collapsed, and she developed a multiple allergy syndrome and electrical sensitivity.

The initiate also began to experience a number of startling apparitional phenomena: for example, one night shortly after the Latihan induction ceremony, she awoke to find a beautiful, androgynous 'guardian angel', which glowed with its own light, looming over the bed. She became psychic and generally over-sensitive to all stimuli. The most startling apparitional experience involved the perception of an old woman in a wheelchair, holding a brandy glass aloft, from which sprayed luminous, sparkling particles in all directions. A number of poltergeist effects occurred, including curious malfunctions of electrical equipment. It was clear that her personal field emissions were closely associated with all these events.

Another case of field exposure that was associated with an accelerated deterioration in health, accompanied by allergies and psychic phenomena, involved 'Kathie Davies'.[67] She experienced severe seismic radiation and tremor with associated UAPs. Later she underwent several 'alien abduction' experiences. Her case is so striking that it could be taken as a textbook example for the ES/psychic/CE correlations. Also, similar health problems are associated with OBEs, and it is a further indication that the 'abduction' phenomenon and the OBE are closely related; both involve the human system responding to a disturbed body image due to field exposure.[68]

This is an important research and investigation area that could lead to new understandings of UFO and psychic phenomena, or at least link the two in the minds of researchers in each field. This aspect of electrical sensitivity has implications for new directions of investigation and procedures, involving witness-screening as a result of implementing the ESH.

Broadly speaking, the implication is that the ES factor, like developmental trauma (outlined in connection with Primal Therapy), is a common aspect. Dr C. W. Smith stated that 15 per cent of a given population had been found to be suffering from allergic syndromes and associated ES. This does not make it unusual as this is a sizeable minority, and one aim of further research must be to determine if this percentage corresponds statistically to those of the population who have had CE and/ or psychic experiences in any way, for it certainly does at the individual case-file level of study.

The importance of ES for understanding anomalous phenomena generally cannot be overstated, as it occurs in association with all groups of psychic events, including OBEs. In fact, as percipients and witnesses to these anomalies emit fields as part of their condition, investigators have been affected by these emissions in the same way as people in occupations who are exposed to other field sources have been. Life-long, or at least decade-long, exposure to witnesses and locations during reconstructions and interviews or encounter-site visits, has, in a significant minority of investigators, resulted in a characteristic migraine-like syndrome identified in medical literature as a response to electrical fields.[69] Of course, this is an unwelcome and unexpected contagion effect, as well as a strange occupational hazard – a case of electrical contact rather than alien contact.

Evidently, ES is a common post-encounter effect: that is, some witnesses begin to affect electronic and/or electric equipment after their CE experiences. It would seem, therefore, that although ES is usually induced over a long period of exposure to fields, a CE with a UAP can precipitate the condition instantaneously. This is consistent with the post-encounter effect, where witnesses suddenly begin to have psychic experiences, as these too are associated with ES. It also again ties up with the ESH premise that the witness is changed into a 'psychic' or 'medium' as a result of their UAP exposure. Typical comments by ES subjects in relation to their effect on electrical appliances are given by Dr Smith:

> The patient's comments on 'electrical things around the place' should be sought; do any cause discomfort? What about thunderstorms?
>
> Typical comments are, 'I am no good with electrical things, the children switch them on for me if I need them'; 'The electric iron gives me a pain in the arm'; 'When I switch on the washing machine the programme goes straight to finish without doing any of the washing, the men say there is nothing wrong with it'; 'I cannot wear a quartz watch, it makes me go sleepy'; 'At work there are a lot of VDUs and I just do not like them'; 'The fluorescent lighting makes me bad'; 'Some people coming into the public part of the office make me feel ill as soon as they enter the door.'
>
> These are all typical remarks from patients with electrical hypersensitivity.[70]

These aspects, along with a range of others, should be part of any investigation of CE experiences. The allergic *symptoms*, which can be recognized from CE experiences – if they are reported at all, that is – are:

> bad headaches with disturbances of vision which have persisted for years; *sometimes the legs will not work, the patient gets stuck and cannot move; sometimes the patient becomes completely unable to speak*; then again the patient *may just get all 'zombie'-like* and cannot do the simplest mental tasks; the patient may also get pains in joints, limbs, shoulders, head and sinuses, ears . . . Does . . . standing bare-foot on grass or concrete have any effect?[71]

The last question regarding contact with the ground was also mentioned by Colin Wilson when referring to a poltergeist 'focus' who altered their 'charge' on doing this. The aspect of ES turns up at every turn of the corner in anomaly research.

The following extract from the published diaries of Robert A. Monroe, the well-known 'astral-traveller', must surely represent a final indictment of electrical fields, regarding the fundamental role that they play in anomalous phenomena:

> 7/7/60. Afternoon: This was an experiment I don't want to try again. I was in the charged Faraday cage (copper screen mesh, above ground, D.C.

charge: 50 kv). I got out of the physical (body). OK, then I seemed to be entangled in a large bag made of flexible wire. The bag gave when I pushed against it, but I couldn't go through it. I struggled like a trapped animal in a snare, and finally went back into the physical. In thinking it over, quite evidently it was not the wire itself, but the electric field pattern set up in fundamentally the same shape as the cage, but more flexible. Maybe this could be the basis for a 'ghost-catcher'!

10/30/60. At about three-fifteen I lay down with the intent of going to visit E.W. in his house some five miles distant. After some difficulty, I managed to move into the vibrational state, then out into the room, away from the physical. With mental aim at E.W. I took off and moved slowly (comparatively). I suddenly found myself over a busy street, moving slowly about twenty-five feet above the sidewalk (just above the top edge of the second-storey windows). I recognized the street to be the main street of the town, and recognized the block and corner over which I passed. I drifted along the sidewalk for several minutes, and noticed a filling station on the corner, where a white car had both rear wheels off in front of the two open grease rack doors. I was disappointed in that I had not gone to E.W., my destination. Seeing nothing else of interest, I decided to return to the physical, and did so without incident. Upon return I sat up and tried to analyse why I had not gone where I intended. On an impulse I got up, went down to the garage, and drove the five miles to his town. My thought was at least to make the trip profitable, and check on what I saw. I got to the same corner on Main Street, and there was the white car in front of the two open doors. Little evidential pieces like that help! I looked up at the approximate position I had been over the sidewalk, and got a surprise. At just about the exact height I had floated over the sidewalk were power primaries containing fairly high voltage electrical current. Do electrical fields attract this second body? Is this the medium through which it travels.[72]

What are the implications of these events? Does it imply that the consciousness can actually leave the body and it is contained in an EM centre, like a type of UAP, which can be influenced or guided by electrical fields? There is at least one report in which an 'astral traveller' told observers where he would be in his out-of-body state, and an orange globe of light was seen to flit across a room. Whatever the complexities of OBEs, they are an ASC that occurs in association with UREs, and they too are influenced by electrical fields.

The time-lapse

We can see from the list of symptoms caused by ES that subjects can become zombie-like and slip into a blank, day-dream-like state, where time would pass unnoticed. If such states continue, temporary black-outs occur, during which everything 'just stops' and the subject has a 'blank-out' and 'comes to' repeatedly. It has been mentioned that this is a similar effect to *petit mal*:

> Symptoms of electrical sensitivity include all the allergic symptoms mentioned . . . However, those particularly associated with electric and magnetic fields include . . . muscular aches, noises in the head, pins and needles, especially in hands and feet, dizziness, fits and *black-outs*, disorientation, headaches . . . Electrical sensitivity may also *mimic* neurological diseases such as *paralysis*, *epilepsy* and MS. (my italics)[73]

It is not difficult to see that the cause of 'time-lapses' or 'missing time', where the witness realizes that there is a period of time for which he cannot account, is due to ES. *In fact, all of these symptoms can be plotted within CE experiences, and recognized as such.* The UI will fill this void with material of its own choosing, which appears as dreams or 'flashbacks' in order to link the witness up to the background rumour of ET visitation. A UAP sighting is evocative enough, and the UI will capitalize on this suggestive situation to stage an alien theme drama, or to be more precise, to provide snatches of it as 'previews' or 'trailers'. Another case of a couple driving at night demonstrates these ES symptoms even more clearly:

> About seven minutes later they had climbed higher into the hills, affording the marvellous views . . . Directly ahead Mrs DL saw a brilliant star, similar to Sirius as she puts it, but it looked unusually prominent. She mentioned it to her husband, but he was intent on the winding road and only she concentrated upon the object, which changed into a big oval and moved northwards across the sky. It then dimmed again and was surrounded by a reddish arc of light. It then shot towards the ground and turned deep red, before streaking upwards again . . .
>
> As this is happening Mrs DL is describing the complex manoeuvres of the object to her husband, who seems not too concerned . . . Mrs DL looked behind and directly in a gap between two houses, just above the rooftops, saw a massive object, tilted so that only the underside was visible. In shape it was like two Vulcan bombers stuck together, with a wide central section and protrusions at either side. There was a dim lighting underneath. But the most instantly memorable thing was the complex piping and the 'sticking out bits' underneath. It is imprinted into

her mind like a photograph. For a few moments she tried to tell her husband but the shock prevented her talking. Eventually she blurted it out and said, 'But I only saw it five minutes ago.' However, her husband is insistent she did not tell him until they reached Bakewell, thirty minutes later. The circumstances of this case certainly seem to suggest a time lapse.

Mrs DL says, 'I am sure my husband would have noticed had I been beamed up out of the car and was missing between Buxton and Bakewell.' But she has no answer for the confusion, except she must have been in deep shock for half an hour. MUFORA have endeavoured to persuade her to undergo regression hypnosis, but she has not proven willing to do so.[74]

Once again, there is a 'blank' period in the witness's recollection, and her inability to speak after the sighting could have come straight out of the symptoms of electrical sensitivity that Dr Smith lists in *Electromagnetic Man*: 'sometimes the patient becomes completely unable to speak' or 'becomes "zombie"-like'. Mrs DL may have had 'no answer for the confusion', but I have: electrical sensitivity. She came unwittingly close when she suggests that she may have been in shock, as this term at least has electrical connotations! It would appear that the witnesses were affected by the fields from a UAP. The 'blank-out' would not be noticeable sitting passively in the darkness of a moving car at night. Her husband, from the details given in the report, also seemed oddly detached and mute. This case corresponds closely with the scenario described earlier regarding the outcome of two ES people, where one hallucinated a structured-looking UFO during a nocturnal car journey. As in so many cases where the conditions of low sensory noise and electromagnetic field exposure combine with the sighting of a light in the sky to produce an allergic trance state and hallucination of a structured UFO.

Time distortion

In addition to 'blank-outs', which have the subjective effect of dissolving time, there are findings which show that exposure to high amplitude 60Hz electrical fields results in cardiac change of beat, which has a transient effect on the subject's ability to judge time.[75] Anne Silk comments on the temporal isolation effect:

It could be caused by a field creating an eddy-current in the brain. The effect is called desynchronization. Also, a trance-like effect can be induced by limbic stimulation causing the production of endogenous opiates by peptide receptors in the CNS.

The pineal gland, deep inside the brain, is involved in the regulation of day/night patterns; it is also highly magneto-sensitive, and exposure to fields can upset the subject's biological clock.[76]

CE witnesses frequently report time-dilation effects as well as sudden changes of scene during the experience. These result in time-distortions, where they either feel that they have taken an inappropriately long time to travel a well-known distance, or only remember the beginning and end of a journey. Also the phrase 'it felt like time had stood still' occurs repeatedly in witnesses' reports of UFO sightings – all are indicative of field exposure. This would also indicate that the UFO that they perceived was hallucinatory. As an example from an 'abduction' case, consider the following, taken from an interview transcript:

> that experience I had the other week. I told you I looked at the clock and it were half-past nine and then within minutes, I know that time hadn't changed, only twenty to ten, but when I went out it felt as if, as if the Earth had stood still for about a year. I felt right strange as if I had been missing for a year . . . I felt as if somebody had done something and it [time] had just stood still for ages and ages.[77]

This is desynchronization, and it is clear that all 'abductees' are electically hypersensitive and that their experiences are a symptom of their allergic reactions to an exposure to fields in the environment.

4 Electrical Fields Forever

Cases and places

> Researchers from Kyoto University have developed a model plane powered solely by microwaves beamed from the ground. The microwaves are converted into electricity which powers a motor attached to the propeller. Since all power is provided from the ground, the plane carries neither fuel nor batteries.[1]

Having set out the significance of the background ambient fields regarding UFO and RSPK activity, we can now turn to some examples of phenomena which occur in both areas.

We have already seen how ambient fields can energize electrical systems of a car, causing the deactivated circuits to reactivate in ghostly fashion. We have also seen one example of a 'fear inducing', 'domestic UAP'. Consider another extract from Colin Wilson's poltergeist study:

> Alan Williams made another interesting observation that night. When he looked back at the Pritchards' house, he says it was surrounded by a dim glow of light. This is confirmed by a neighbour who lived opposite; she looked out of her window late at night, and observed the same phenomenon; she told Jean about it the next day. It is tempting to speculate that the effect was either electrical, or was connected in some way with Earth magnetism. Poltergeists . . . appear to be able to control certain electrical forces.[2]

This rooftop glow is a similar effect to mountain-top discharge that has been reported in a number of forms, such as a glowing halo or giant beams of light shining vertically upwards from the peaks of mountain ranges. It is indeed indicative of accumulated piezo-electrical or geomagnetic fields. This rooftop glow also occurred on another house in which a highly strange set of events evolved. They involved the Code family (four children and their parents) in a complex series of UFO and non-UFO visions, UFO encounters (including CE3s), apparitional experiences, precognition, retrocognition (seeing into the past), phantom UAPs, guardian aliens, and a whole gamut of other psychic experiences. The mother and most of the children were psychic, and the UFO experiences were interspersed with 'traditional' psychic events, such as poltergeist activity. The family's experiences were chronicled in a book called *Alien Contact* by Jenny Randles and Paul Whetnall. The Code family lived in Wales, as did another UFO and poltergeist family, the Coombs; the latter far away on the Dyfed peninsula. At the same time as these events in Wales, the Enfield poltergeist was tormenting the Harper family in north London. This area also experienced its own UFO 'flap', of which the Harpers were totally unaware, the details of which were provided for me by a member of BUFORA, Michael Lewis.

Various other cases will be woven into the following comparisons, including a chronicled account by a witness who recalls how he suffered intense EM radiation from a secret Ministry of Defence (MoD) project involving UFO phenomena that he attempted to photograph. From his descriptions, it would seem that both BOLs *and* perceptions of structured aerial craft were involved. The broad aim of these comparisons is to show how URE and poltergeist phenomena are different versions of the same core processes – direct field effects and PK.

These cases have been selected because they show how ambient electrical fields can produce the encounter perceptions described by witnesses. The implication here is that it is not just a comparison of carefully selected cases that just happen to have a common aspect, but that this electromagnetic field context is present in all CE events to greater and lesser extents.

Poltergeist outbreaks and close-encounter experiences

The fear-inducing light connected with the Enfield poltergeist also had another feeling closely associated with it:

> the feeling I had was one of fear, like there was somebody standing right by me and watching. I've never known such a feeling in my life . . . It was as if there was something there, but you couldn't see it; a person . . .

It is apparent that the unpleasantness of this feeling of being watched by an invisible entity can only be appreciated by experience. It would seem at first to be a somewhat intangible phenomenon, but the feeling it evokes is far from abstract. The Code family, who, like the Harpers in the Enfield case, had been told that their house glowed at night, also experienced this feeling of presence:

> It was 24 March, G. was baby-sitting for some relatives who lived nearby. She often did this and it was something she enjoyed . . . she sat downstairs watching television. The time was 9.30. Suddenly she became uneasy. The feeling began to creep over her, icy fingers touching her senses. Something was there within her . . . inside her soul . . . When she [her mother] arrived G. was on edge. She kept glancing round the room in quick jerky movements as if expecting someone to pop up from behind a chair . . . then G. suddenly leapt up . . . 'There's something here – in this room. It's watching me . . .'[3]

This intense feeling of presence was but one experience that intruded upon the Codes, and it is indicative of the presence of ambient electromagnetic fields (probably from an MoD establishment in the area).[4] Experiments with subjects exposed to magnetic fields have been carried out, and the reports from these subjects have matched those of witnesses like the Codes and the Harpers, who both experienced a series of ongoing events. It is worth reproducing the exact text from the *Journal of Bioelectricity*, because it describes a range of effects that witnesses to both psychic and UFO-related events have reported:

> The results of this study strongly indicate that specific types of subjective experiences can be enhanced when extremely low frequency magnetic fields of less than 1 milligauss are generated through the brain at the level of the temporal lobes. Vestibular feelings [vibrations, floating], depersonalization [feeling detached, *sense of a presence* – my italics] and imaginings [vivid images from childhood] were more frequent within the field-exposed groups than the sham-exposed field group . . . Qualitatively, the most unusual experiences were reported by subjects who were exposed to the 4Hz and 9Hz magnetic field conditions. Classes of experiences and specific examples were spinning objects ('I see something mechanical turning round and round . . . and there is something brushing against it'); depersonalization ('this is not real . . . I keep slipping into things [states]'; '*I feel there is something in here with me*'); general vestibular effects ('I am flying in the air'; 'it feels like vibrations are going through my chest'); visual flying imagery ('bats are flying in the air'; 'I see a bird flying'); proprioception and muscle spasms ('tingling over my entire body'; 'my eyes are jerking from side to side'; 'I felt a weird ripple go through my head'); immobilization ('I feel like I can't move'); wave motions ('it sounds like waves'); dissociated thoughts ('I feel like I am in a story') and phosphenes ('I see sparkles in a cave').[5]

From experiments such as this, it is clear that ambient fields can create a sense of presence and a range of other sensations reported in close-encounters. We have also seen that fields can energize electrical circuitry of a car, and it should not be surprising that a similar phenomenon should occur in the Codes' house. Remember, these ambient field effects all preceded their UFO experiences, which included encounters with 'silver-suited aliens'. They are mentioned to build up a picture of *context* in which the more bizarre experiences took place, just as the Enfield poltergeist activity proceeded from similar field effects to full-blown apparitions. The circuitry energized in the case of the Codes took place in the bedroom of one of the children:

> The door was open and a dim light from the landing filtered on to the carpet, casting ominous shadows. D. ignored them but could not shake off the feeling that something was up. It was above him. He noticed the bedroom light flickering. But that was not possible. There was no bulb in the socket. All the same, there were flashes of light. Perhaps sparks from a loose wire, he thought. The radio, too, was crackling a weird faint hiss. Yet he knew it was switched off. Frightened, he moved his hand so that he could see his digital watch. It was going crazy, Numbers were flashing on and off and he could not read the time.[6]

In the Welsh Triangle case we saw how the watch of the witness was severely disrupted, and how he was affected personally by an electric force that disabled him and induced a hallucination of a silver-suited figure. In that case an orange globe of light was hovering just above the roof of the loft. It would be consistent, then, for an orange globe and alien figure to be associated with Master Code's experience also:

> He wondered what to do, but before he could crawl out of bed . . . something appeared – it just materialized on the landing. It was a sphere of orange light, about seven or eight feet high . . . ovoid and spinning quite fast . . . something prevented him from shouting . . . through the doorway he could see a dark patch in the orange and a figure was stepping out. It was one of his aliens, glancing round and then striding boldly across the carpet.[7]

The investigators involved decided that a globe of light of the dimensions described could not have fitted on to the landing of the house, and as deduced earlier, it seems that as D was enveloped in an ambient field (causing the light-wiring to arc), he *sensed* a concentration in the field, 'seeing' it as a globe of light. That he was in some type of altered state was evident from the events that followed:

He felt strange -- a peculiar light-headedness. He got out of bed, but he was not sure why. There seemed no effort in moving. He simply glided across to meet the alien figure. For an instant he wished he were back in bed. Then, an incredible thing happened, he *was* back in bed . . . looking across the room . . . was a figure standing beside the alien. It was D. himself.[8]

Anne Silk comments:

Doppelgänger: Few seconds duration. More common amongst those with brain lesions and epileptics, occasionally associated with migraine. Figure is 'washed out', monochromatic, trunk and head seen, never legs. Often reported as 'like jelly'. It is a mirror image. Technically known as Autoscopy.[9]

It is interesting that the monochromatic aspect occurs in this phenomenon, because we saw earlier how it was part of the 'abbreviated form' of UFO entities and apparitions. Also, in D's case there is an instance of 'false awakening' which has already been identified with OBEs and CE4s, or alien abduction experiences, which incidentally D *then went on to have*.

Turning to the Enfield poltergeist case, it is easy to see that the events were littered with instances of electrical malfunction due to mysterious surges or drainage of power:

Nor was there any reduction in the physical activity. In fact, it increased in range and frequency. One day, no less than ten light bulbs, most of them brand new, blew out in the bedroom, although the wiring was sound.[10]

I played back my tape for comparison, and found that my batteries, bought that day and normally good for at least two hours of recording, had chosen that moment to go flat. I was already getting used to that kind of coincidence.[11]

And a more bizarre electrical event:

On the morning of 23 December, the two little goldfish were found dead in their tank. They had always been well fed and cared for, and Janet was especially fond of them. The Voice claimed responsibility at once.

'I done that.' Grosse asked him why, and how.

'I electrocuted the fish by accident,' he was told. Grosse asked what kind of energy was used.

'Spirits' energy.'

'Is it electrical?' Grosse asked.

'No. Powerful.' We knew that, but it was clear that the Voice would not . . . give us a lecture in interdimensional physics.[12]

One of the first things an investigator learns about poltergeist 'information' is that it is usually false! So far, then, we have had examples of electrical malfunction in a UFO-related case and 'pure' poltergeist activity. In the 1977 'flap' in Dyfed, much of the strange activity centred around the Coombs family at Ripperston Farm. It was no coincidence that the silver-suited, giant entity type haunted this area, and Pauline Coombs – who purportedly had first-hand experience of one at her living-room window, and who had a history of religious visionary phenomena – was also plagued by chronic electrical malfunction:[13]

> When they had been especially worried by the cost of their electricity, they had made a point of switching off every single apparatus in the house as a test and checking against the electricity meter. The dial continued to rotate at high speed and yet the meter had been changed for a new unit and was functioning normally.
>
> Not only had they noticed an incredible number of power overloads, black-outs and voltage variations, but the problem had also caused numerous failures. Electric light bulbs popped and burnt out even when bought the previous day. All kinds of electrical equipment continued to give trouble, including record players and radio sets. The record of television faults was alarming; in one year eight sets had exploded ... sets had just failed and left nothing but burnt-out transformers and circuitry, while others literally exploded ... Though the Coombs seemed to be receiving energy from somewhere ... its effects were most unwelcome.[14]

From these images of electrical mayhem, let us glance back at the ESH, which states that it is the activity of the human unconscious in combination with a variety of natural and artificial energies that produces staged realities identified as the CE experience. From this, it is not difficult to see how the human system would have access to more than enough energy to give a physical reality of sorts to its internally produced imagery. It is one of the central proposals of the ESH that such electrical energy induces mental imagery, giving it a temporal physical status. It is my feeling, when considering this process, that ambient *particles* are caught up in this effect, in the same way that iron filings are organized by a magnet to show the arcs of the magnetic field around it.

We now have three cases for comparison: the Enfield poltergeist; the Codes in Flint, Wales, who had UFO and alien theme encounters, and the Coombs in Dyfed, Wales, who also had parallel close-encounters *and* poltergeist activity. *All three reported dramatic effects that can be produced by ambient electrical fields.*

The Dargle Cottage case

I am indebted to Antony Verney for a fourth case which involved him and his wife, who lived at Dargle Cottage (described in estate agents' hyperbole as a 'Hansel and Gretel cottage'). It is situated about 1½ miles (2.4 km) south-east of Biddenden, Kent, in a mini-nature reserve. Mr Verney had been an inspector for a reputable consumer association. He retired in 1983 and moved to the cottage more or less full-time.

On 1 October of that year, a visitor to the cottage noticed a strange humming that seemed to fill the air. On investigation, it extended from the area at the rear of the cottage into the woods about 20 yards (18 m) away. It sounded as if it were coming up through the ground. This unnerving hum continued over the next four days *and* the next four nights. Sandpit Woods, usually alive with the sound of birds and rabbits running over the fallen leaves, fell silent. It had become empty. (In fact, the birds were not to return to the wood, and no nesting took place there the following spring.)

Mr and Mrs Verney went on holiday at this point. On returning on 25 October, they discovered a great increase in the hum, which sounded as if it were coming from all around the cottage; at times even as if it were actually inside it, especially in the early hours of the morning, when there was throbbing and vibrating. The couple could not sleep due to the level of noise. During the night they also observed the strangest phenomenon from the window facing north-east. The woods were lit up by bright yellow and pink lights which came up through the ground. Mr Verney described it as 'a similar effect to a theatre cyclorama'. Also round about this time, the drains of the house were mysteriously found to be blocked with lumps of broken asphalt.

The Verneys eventually went out one night to look for the source of the vibration, but this proved difficult because, oddly, the sound appeared to move around. Eventually, the police became involved as a result of a complaint made by the Verneys, and they passed the matter on to the Environmental Health Department. Mr Verney comments: 'On the weekend 17–18 December, there was a shortfall in the electricity supply to the cottage . . . an electric fire plugged in scarcely glowed. The house lighting fluctuated at exactly one-minute intervals.' So complaints were made to the local electricity board.

Mr Verney relates the next development: 'It was late-night shopping in London and I found an electrical shop on the Tottenham Court Road with highly sophisticated equipment. I explained to the two men in charge the nature of my problem. They quickly exchanged a look, and quickly said in unison, "It sounds as if you are having trouble with the Ministry of

Defence. You won't get anywhere with them!" ' It had never crossed Mr Verney's mind that the MoD could be involved. It was a stunning realization. The Verneys' curiosity had been aroused by a new 'house' on the other side of the woods from Dargle Cottage. It was described as a farm by the local council's planning department but there were no animals, bar some bee-hives. It had high, double hedges all the way round and it was 'of curious construction'. It had two storeys but no windows above the ground floor or at the back; only at each end. Mr Verney comments: 'The ground-floor windows were obscured by thick, opaque floor-length net curtains, a type of textile manufactured exclusively for the Property Services Agency of the Department of the Environment, and used to protect high security buildings such as the MoD, MI5, MI6 and the telephone-tapping HQ. At the front of the building was some kind of bunker with a large mushroom-shaped air-vent.'

On Boxing Day 1983, the electronic hum and vibrations went on at a high speed and showed no signs of abating during the night. Mr Verney reports: 'The noise peaked at 4.15 am; vibrations and loud humming with a weird metallic note mixed in. At first light there was a new bizarre feature. *Huge, horseshoe-shaped lights moved across the sky from west to east*, one after the other in stately procession, low, against the background of the trees. The objects were lit up like "flying tiaras"; they were three in number. They disappeared losing height over the woods.'

Mr Verney's entry for the day after speaks for itself: 'The "flying tiaras" appeared again, flying from west to east as before. The low-frequency transmissions entering the house were probably attacking the central nervous system, and were also likely to be pumping radiation into the place.'

The following entries over the next week repeatedly reported the 'flying tiaras' and 'pink lights going up and down'. There is a distinctively desperate tone to the brief and evocative entries for the New Year:

3.1.84
Appalling night, worst since Christmas. Wind blowing vibrations. Huge humming and puttering noise like an old-fashioned steam train. Sleep impossible. Peaking after 2.30 am. Loud screaming sound for a short time at 3 am. Then thumping and vibrating speeding up, superimposed by a deep howling noise for an hour.

5.1.84
Something new manifested itself; some kind of electromagnetic beam was directed at the house at about 3 am. No noise, suddenly attacked by excruciating pain in top of head and temples; it was as if head was being bored by an electric drill. Left feeling completely disorientated.

15.1.84

All systems go in early morning. Worst to date. Humming and vibrating worst ever. Zapped at 3.30 am. Lighting going up and down. Got dressed, went out and patrolled the area in car at 4.30 am. Overall loud humming over whole area. Witnessed absolutely spectacular aerial performance; device seen in sky flying under cloud base, its lights flashing on and off. Sound over whole area was one penetrating continuous note, like some kind of signal. Patrolled in car for an hour. No one else about. Whole thing at high level, then increasing with thumping, humming and vibrations at very high speed. Utterly appalling . . .

20.1.84

About 1.30 pm, a succession of loud bangs came from the woods to the north-east of the cottage. These continued at regular intervals of three minutes all the afternoon, to 5.30 pm, when they stopped.

In the middle of these loud bangs Mr Verney telephoned the Environmental Health Authority and demanded that they enforce the 1974 Control of Pollution Act. Allegedly this was not well received. They did, however, mention that members of the public had reported sightings of UFOs over the area.

The inhabitants of the nearest house, over a quarter of a mile (0.5 km) away, in Shorts Wood, complained of hearing the humming noise and continual interference with their television reception. As other people saw the UFOs, it is evident that they were not hallucinations. The Environmental Health Authority even volunteered information of sightings reported by members of the public of what they called UFOs. This case has a very sad 'ending'. Mrs Verney is now a semi-invalid, having contracted a rare and dangerous form of lymphatic leukaemia. Most of Mr Verney's teeth have either fallen out or crumbled and he suffers from a condition described as polythemia, which was discovered in American servicemen exposed to electromagnetism. Mr Verney concludes:

Taking everything into account, the nature of the exercise must have been to do with trials of electronic weapons, which are being developed as the weapons of the future. This development has been in hand in the United States and the Soviet Union since the early seventies. It is known as 'Low Intensity Warfare.'[15]

There are groups who monitor cases like this, and this is not the place to enter into a crusade against this practice by authorities. I have presented this case because it shows that, like the events in the Codes, Coombs and Harper households and surrounding areas, UFOs and associated strange events take place in an electrically charged atmosphere. These ambient fields, whether natural or artificially produced, are the common denominator in the production of such phenomena. These fields can produce altered states, UAPs and a range of apparently anomalous electrical and systemic effects commonly associated with the CE experience.

The Coombs' house, in particular, was clearly saturated in an electromagnetic atmosphere and, to even the most casual investigator, it was equally clear that this was artificially produced by the military establishments in the area. Dyfed in 1977 was a weird mix of strange experimental devices, probably powered by the fields, and hallucinatory realities combined with poltergeist phenomena, all triggered by the ambient fields that flooded the locale. Other phenomena, which also occurred in the Codes case, included apparently landed UFOs of a silvery-metallic appearance which vanished, 'flying saucers' which 'dematerialized', silver-suited 'spacemen' (which in the Dyfed area were sometimes perceived as floating over the rooftops) and a variety of other field-induced hallucinatory realities. Also in Dyfed, the silver humanoids seemed at times to be anomalously light in weight, leaving very shallow footprints in the soft mud of farmland, when such traces should have been substantially deeper.[16] One explanation for this, already mentioned, would be the 'PK assembly' concept, implying that such entities were empty suits, which was the impression of investigators Pugh and Holiday.

The Verney case also shows that the assumption that UFOs, which are apparently secret devices, but are actually rejected as such because it is thought they would not be tested in civilian areas or where they would endanger the civilian population, is erroneous. There are a number of cases that this last statement would apply to: the South American 'chupas' as described by Jacques Vallée in his book *Confrontations* is one; another case involves the huge triangular UFOs sighted in Belgium in the early 1990s.

The ambient field connection, as it could be called, is, of course, central to the ESH, and we saw how they were common to the 'sense of presence' phenomenon specifically, and poltergeist/CE experiences generally. This common context aspect alone is enough to arouse suspicions that the two are different members of the same family of phenomena. In the next chapter, it is shown that artificial fields can produce their own types of UAP and that these 'electroforms', as they have been labelled, were present in all three of the cases under comparison. Also, the field-generated 'sense of presence' has been felt so strongly – and reported so consistently in both psychic and UFO contexts – that it is regarded as distinct a phenomenon as entity sightings and it is clear that it is a forerunner to them.

One of the most convincing aspects of 'structured' UFOs and their 'aliens' that witnesses emphatically put across, is the vivid 'realness' of such confrontations. Witnesses emphasize how they could 'feel' or 'just knew' that the 'aliens' they encountered were solid, three-dimensional beings with nothing ghostly about them. This actually reveals their misinformation as to how 'ghosts' appear, as *exactly* the same heartfelt declarations of 'realness' are reported by witnesses of apparitions. It would seem, therefore, that the unconscious utilizes this 'sense of presence' in conjunction with its visual presentations to consolidate their reality. Put simply, the witness sees *and* feels the presence of entities and apparitions. As an example of this 'realness', consider an example from the Enfield case:

> As before, John kept an eye on their house [that is the home of the poltergeist-afflicted family] while they were away. 'On this day,' he told us, 'I walked into the living-room, paused, looked out of the window at the people walking past, then turned to my right, looking directly towards the kitchen. And there I saw him, sitting at the living-room table, with his back towards me. He had one arm on the table, just sitting there. Dress? He had a white-and-blue striped shirt on, no collar. It was the sort of shirt . . . old, like it was worn in the thirties. Sleeves rolled up, black trousers, leather belt, grey hair, not too thick, sort of sparse . . . he didn't move . . . He had his back towards me, head upright, looking straight ahead. I closed my eyes, like a blink, for a couple of seconds – gone!'
>
> 'Did he look completely solid?' Grosse asked.
>
> 'It looked just like you look now,' Burcombe replied without hesitation. 'Like a perfectly normal person sitting at a table. No haziness, nothing. Clear as a bell. It had been about five o'clock on a summer afternoon. Broad daylight.'[17]

This is a good example, because it demonstrates that if such clear and authentic figures can be produced, then an equally realistic entity figure is within the presentation abilities of the unconscious also. In fact, we saw precisely this mix in the Middleton events described previously. We also noted the overlap between UFO-related 'aliens' and apparitions in terms of their characteristics and behaviour. Randall Jones-Pugh, who investigated the events at Dyfed, commented:

> the phenomena, whatever they are, exist externally in space. We assume, but we cannot by any means be sure, that they also exist in time as we know it. Nor do we know whether they objectively occupy space in any meaningful sense of the term. When the humanoid beings are perceived as occupying space, they appear to react in conformity to the laws governing perspective and optics. They give the appearance of being

three-dimensional objects, although they are manifestly neither physically solid nor organic in any known sense of the words.[18]

These conclusions concern UFO-related entities, but they could just as well apply to the apparition seen by John Burcombe at Enfield, just described.

Pre-event sensations

Another overlapping aspect between poltergeist phenomena and UFO/alien-theme encounters is that of pre-event sensation. Witnesses often report 'feeling strange', 'a certain coldness', 'a tingling', 'a weird headachy feeling', 'a pain like a tight band around my head' and so on, before poltergeist activity begins or before a UFO or 'alien' is encountered. Consider the following example:

> Suddenly G. felt strange and very cold. She could sense that something was about to happen. She looked carefully ahead across the expanse of open field towards the trees cascading fallen leaves. Something was there.
>
> It was many yards off and the sunlight was glinting strongly from its surface. No detail was visible but it looked like some kind of figure wearing a silver suit . . . Then, without warning, the figure began to melt away, blending into the colourful background. It had not run. It had simply vanished.[19]

Another example comes from the Enfield poltergeist case:

> Then Mrs Harper made a very interesting remark, which I took little notice of at the time, in view of the general excitement . . .
>
> 'Before all this happened,' she said, as we picked up cutlery together, 'I came out here and I thought I'd better wipe up. I've got a headache. The front of the head – it's not like a normal headache.'
>
> 'Do you feel it all the time it's here, or just when it comes?' I asked. By 'it' I meant the poltergeist.
>
> 'When it comes, I can feel it,' she answered. 'And when the things go down, the headache sort of goes, I've got it a bit now, but it's sort of eased off.'
>
> Could she have a built-in early warning system in her head? I wondered if it had anything to do with the fact that, as she had already told me, she had a long history of epilepsy in her youth, although it was ten years now since she had suffered an attack.[20]

And another example from the same case:

I asked Matthew (Manning) if he had ever felt headaches like those Mrs Harper felt when something was about to happen.

'I got a prickling sensation down the back of the neck,' he replied. 'That was . . .'

'Excuse me!' Grosse interrupted, excitedly. 'Janet said that half an hour before you came.' He ran back his tape, and we heard her say:

'I keep getting a pain in the back of my head.' She had indicated the back of the neck, just where Matthew had felt his strange sensation.[21]

These symptoms are a response to field exposure, just as D's 'strange light-headed feeling' in the description of the field-activated circuitry and subsequent out-of-body and Doppelgänger experiences were. They can be found in neurological studies, and identified as pre-epileptic and migraine-like symptoms, both of which involve an electrical aspect as a root cause.

Such symptoms are often reported before anomalous experiences and seem to be indicative of an altered consciousness that superimposes or intertwines a UFO-vision with mundane reality, or produces the range of physical phenomena known as a poltergeist outbreak. It is as if in some cases the effect is turned inward and affects the way witnesses 'concoct' their own reality (and to some extent that of others); in other cases, the effect is simply externalized and things are thrown about, fires start, objects are disorganized or reorganized, etc. One results in a CE, the other in a destructive haunting.

Another good example of a pre-event sensation followed by a CE experience is the 1978 Church Stowe, Northamptonshire, case. I am indebted to Jenny Randles for allowing me to use the detailed account from her book *Abduction*:

Mrs Oakensen was head of the teachers' centre in Daventry. At lunchtime on 22 November 1978 she felt a strange tightening sensation around her forehead, like wearing a hat which was far too small. It passed quickly but was unusual enough to remember.

At 5.15 p.m. she left the centre for the six-mile drive home, noticing that a sidelight was not working so she had to travel with dipped headlights all the time. In an account written immediately afterwards, she said: 'When I reached the traffic lights at Weedon, I turned right on to the A5. Ahead of me I could see two very bright lights immediately above the road. The left one was red and the right one was green. My immediate thought was that this was a very low-flying aircraft which would zoom over my head. However, it seemed to be stationary and I drove towards it with my nose practically pressed on the windscreen.' She then drove straight underneath it and observed '. . . an hourglass or egg-timer shape with a light under each circular end. This thing was no more than 150 feet (46 m) up.' There was no sound, and the object was directly over the point where Mrs Oakensen had to turn off into Church Stowe village.

This was about 5.30 p.m. on a very busy main road. Thousands of motorists should have seen this object. Yet, despite a story at the time and the kind assistance of the *Daventry Weekly Express* in this research, not a single traveller has come forward to report seeing anything, even that the lights were an aircraft.

Fascinated, Elsie drove up the road towards Church Stowe, which lies atop a hill. She looked back several times during this half-mile ride and the lights were still sitting there over the A5. It was then that it all happened.

Mrs Oakensen turned right into the village, driving as usual in second and changing up to third gear. 'The next thing I knew, my foot was hard on the accelerator pedal, which was flat on the floor of the car. There was no sound from the engine at all. My lights were still functioning but the engine was dead. The car was slowing down and had almost reached the point of stopping.' She did not switch it back on, but feeling surprisingly calm, changed back to first and depressed the accelerator – the car started normally. She drove another hundred yards and there was a second, more pronounced jerk in reality.

Mrs Oakensen describes what she saw: 'The car was stationary. Everything in complete blackness. My engine had stopped. My lights were out. Suddenly, piercing brilliant white circles of light about a yard (1 m) in diameter came from nowhere, on-off, on-off, starting at the left of my car, round in front of it, to the right, back again and the last one disappeared into the air . . . when the lights hit the ground they lit up the farmyard to my left, the road in front of me and the path and garden of the house to my right . . . [otherwise] it was absolutely black, I could not even see the houses at the side of the road.' Elsie spoke aloud: 'Good gracious!' Then, again without transition, she was moving again. She says: 'I did *not* switch on my ignition. I did *not* put my car into gear. I did *not* depress my accelerator pedal. I did *not* start the car. I just found myself driving along normally.'

She drove into her garage just a few hundred yards away and noticed the sidelights on the car were now working. It never failed again. The village was also as it normally is, quite well lit (there had not been a power cut). Looking at the time, she was surprised to realize it was ten or fifteen minutes later than it ought to have been. Driving the route every day, she had a very good idea how long it takes, but she checked the next night just in case. There was definitely a period of time missing from her memory. That was the whole case, except that same night the tightening sensation occurred one more time . . . Desperate for help to retrieve missing memories, the BUFORA team arranged for researcher Graham Phillips to conduct a hypnosis session. This occurred on 18 August 1979. Elsie relived the sighting only partially, although after the session much flowed into her mind 'as if popping out of my subconscious'.

Elsie felt the tightening as the car slowed down the first time. 'I got hotter and hotter . . . The pressure hurt my head.' Then a brilliant 'pure white light, very bright' hit her full on from the front. It throbbed with circles radiating out from the centre. 'The pain in my head was intense . . . I felt no reaction in my legs . . . I was very frightened.' Then two shapes appeared silhouetted against the glow. Both were grey. They were hazy but from her drawings could be taken as 'people' . . . First many of the symptoms Elsie Oakensen describes (tightening pain, flashing lights, etc.) are suggestive of migraine. But lest you write the case off as a migraine attack, you should remember the UFO in the first place, the effects on the car, and the totally independent second sighting and the fact that Elsie suffered from migraine for several days afterwards and can tell the difference. She believes it was brought on by the bright lights.

The sensations of tightening around the head are associated with an unusual perceptual effect known as microwave hearing, and are caused by an exposure to pulsed microwaves in the environment. These also induce the perception of a bright light, caused by the electrical stimulation of the visual cortex. Doctors who have heard reports of this have dubbed it 'the exploding head syndrome', for want of a better term. It is a symptom of electrical hypersensitivity.

The second case occurred at 7.20 pm on the same night. It involved four young women driving to a meeting in Northampton. They had left Byfield and were travelling near the village of Preston Capes at the time. This is four miles south-west of Church Stowe. They first saw a parallel-sided beam of light shoot out of a cloud across the sky. This was repeated a few seconds later. Then a red and a green light, side by side, appeared and crossed the road directly ahead of the car, which suddenly began to lose power. The driver had to change down from top to third gear to maintain engine revolutions, as the lights paced the car to the south. The women then drove into the village, and the lights merged into one and 'switched off abruptly like a light bulb'.

Case review

It is interesting that the band of pain around the witness's head occurred before *and* after the encounter experience. The significance of pre-event sensations does, of course, vary from witness to witness and event to event. It is the fact that they occur at all, whether they precede a surge of RSPK activity or a URE, that is important. They are a systemic response to EM fields. It was mentioned earlier how long-term exposure to field emission from witnesses and encounter locations can induce migraine-like attacks as an occupational hazard in experienced investigators.

It would appear, then, that Mrs Oakensen may be sensitive to EM fields, and right from the start there are indications that ambient fields were causing electrical disturbances to her and her car. The fact that a sidelight of the car was not working at the start of her journey home, and then resumed its normal functioning spontaneously, as soon as she drove into her garage at the end of her journey, is suspicious enough to alert one to the presence of ambient field effects.

Daventry itself has a fearsome battery of phased array transmitting aerials, which are arranged so that a longer wavelength can be obtained without an increase in power. Military bases always contribute to the 'electronic smog' of an area, and an army HQ, Gibraltar Barracks, is in the vicinity.

Also, Plessey seems to have a centre in the area, which, significantly, is situated over faulted ironstone – a ferrous oxide and iron carbonate, which is unusually close to the surface, although I am not aware of an actual outcrop in the area. Such mineral deposits are indicative of indigenous magnetic activity.

It is also not a matter of chance that the witness's car showed peak disturbance to its electrical system (i.e., not responding to the accelerator) and lost power intermittently and selectively before stalling completely, just before her encounter experience with the circles of light that penetrated an anomalous darkness. It would certainly *seem* that Mrs Oakensen experienced a 'blank-out'; she said: 'While the incident was on, time seemed to stand still. It passed unnoticed, like when one is asleep.'

We have seen from past case-reviews how a subject's sense of time can be disrupted by an EM field (called desynchronization), and it has been shown that in certain conditions magnetic fields can impair the short-term memory. It was young Mark Wilson (winner of the young scientist of the year award in 1992 for a concise experiment in cyclotron resonance) who showed this effect. This is not the place to go into the details of his experiment design (as it duplicated previous experiments that showed this), but it is worth quoting his hypothesis for the more scientifically minded readers:

> My hypothesis was that short-term memory loss may be due to the brain calcium ions (Ca^{++}) being affected by these types of EM fields. Changes in brain calcium motion, caused by magnetic and electric fields that meet ion cyclotron resonance conditions, could affect short-term memory.[22]

The witness *did* report a short amnesiac period or 'time-lapse'. This was investigated by regressive hypnosis and, instead of an alien abduction story emerging, she recalled: 'I got hotter and hotter . . . the pressure hurt my head'. 'Then a brilliant pure white light, very bright' hit her full on from the front. It throbbed with circles radiating out from the centre: 'The pain in my head was intense . . . I felt no reaction in my legs . . . I was very frightened.' In the list of ES-reacting allergy symptoms compiled by Dr Smith, and given earlier, we can immediately pick out: 'bad headaches with disturbances to vision . . . *sometimes the legs will not work* . . . the patient may also get pains in . . . head'.

In a paper based on a study of electrical stimulation to specific brain centres, these effects can also be found. Consider:

Reed Neurological Research, UCLA, USA (1978)
Temporal lobe stimulation: Mesial temporal lobe: 20 categories; including: Somaesthetic: Subjects reported pulsing, tingly and very hot sensations; also sensations of light in combination with headaches. Subjects also said they felt 'odd' or 'funny' – disorientated time and place/amnesia for the duration of several hours, but in one case: for a few minutes.

Stimulation of parts of hippocampus resulted in visual radiation.

Main hippocampus: Subjects reported visual effects, i.e. coloured balls, flashes.[23]

Such results are not surprising, as the brain is, as mentioned, a delicate electrochemical computer. These effects were found in the description of the experiences Mrs Oakensen gave. But, then, if high *ambient* fields were involved, this would be expected. The overwhelming feeling of being hot and the radiating light match well. A common symptom of those exposed to field effects is that of being too hot or too cold, and these extremes can be produced by EM disturbance to the hypothalamus which regulates the temperature of the human body.[24]

Moreover, such controlled studies have been supported by the incidence of chronic electrical and EM pollution in community environments. One of the most detailed analyses of this came from the village of Fishpond, Dorset, from 1978 onwards. This small rural community suffered the effects of electrical fields from power cables mounted on pylons erected on its land. The symptoms described are very relevant, and an extract from an account by one of the unfortunate residents of Fishpond is interesting when considering Mrs Oakensen's experience.

In the spring of 1978, six months before the Inquiry, at least four people in Fishpond had experienced strange and distressing black-outs within the space of one week – one of these people was a visitor who blacked out while riding his bike under the lines, fell off and broke his ribs. Another was my fourteen-year-old son, who had never experienced anything like it before, and indeed did not tell me until we had discovered that we had all suffered in the same way but without telling each other at first, because it seemed so weird. For another villager it was a series of spells of dizziness. For myself, it was an almost indescribable episode *in which the light seemed to go black* (although I could still see) and I was completely disorientated. [my italics][25]

In the light of Mrs Oakensen's darkness, this first-hand report of an apparently anomalous darkness due to electrical and/or EM fields, is illuminating . . . Another extract from the same section provides a relevant perspective:

As soon as an object is placed within an electric field, the field behaves rather like a curtain and drapes itself in close folds over the object, leaving a clear space underneath. The field so folded can reach values up to a hundred times that of the ambient, unperturbed field. In ordinary working or living conditions, such an object might be a car whose top is at head level . . . *The possible biological implications of such field enhancement are considerable.* [my italics]

During the investigation into the Enfield poltergeist, there were *some* measurements taken with a magnetometer – an instrument to measure the presence or fluctuation of ambient fields:

From the landing, we could keep an eye on the dial of the machine, and in the following forty minutes Janet's pillow was twice thrown across the room, just as it had been the previous evening in my presence . . . And each time the needle on the magnetometer did indeed deflect . . . we called off the experiment once we were satisfied that it seemed possible that there was a link between poltergeist activity and anomalous behaviour of the surrounding magnetic field.[26]

This is an important event in the comparison between RSPK and URE, as the field was actually detected by an instrument designed for the purpose, although there seems little doubt that fields are involved in both areas – as we saw in the disturbance to Mrs Oakensen's car. The Enfield activity, as we have seen, was also able to affect cars and Playfair gives another example:

As it was a cold day, he switched on the engine and let it warm up, ticking over slowly and evenly, which it did for a few moments. Then the engine suddenly began to race wildly, as if somebody had put a foot down on the accelerator. It revved up and down as if waiting the starting flag at the Grand Prix.

Grosse might not understand poltergeists, but he did understand engines, and he immediately looked under the bonnet at the carburettor, after checking that both the choke and throttle were closed. None of its mechanical parts was moving. Intrigued by this odd behaviour, he spent some time examining the engine.

This did not take place at Enfield, but happened to one of the main, long-term investigators involved in the case, and it is indicative of the contagion effect. The Coombs in Dyfed also had chronic problems with a string of cars, all of which suffered from electrical 'burn-out'. In their case, however, the fields concerned seem to have been extremely powerful, and like the Dargle Cottage example, do seem to have been associated with a secret military project. The area of Dyfed, during the UFO 'flap', also suffered from unexplained explosions and vibrations of unnatural origin:

> On several occasions a strange glow had been seen in the sky after the boom had occurred, in one case taking the form of a fire-ball that hurtled at high speed across the sky before vanishing . . . Meanwhile the coincidence of UFO activity on dates and in locations not too distant from the area of the noises continued to occur . . . The pattern that emerged out of the numerous reports of both sounds and sightings seemed to indicate that the infamous 'bumps' and 'booms' were definitely manmade . . . There was considerable disagreement as to whether the sounds originated in the air, the upper stratosphere or from underground tremors.[27]

This situation is parallel to the Dargle Cottage events. Mr Verney saw strange LITS (lights in the sky) and in the early stages he too was confused as to the direction and source of the noise. He found the vibration quite overwhelming, and the same conditions prevailed in Dyfed:

> I myself witnessed the phenomena on numerous occasions whilst staying in Wales, and indeed the shockwaves on occasion were very severe . . . There remained the possibility that the actual cause of the vibration was some secret operation, hence the powers-that-be who did know what was causing it did not find themselves in a position to reveal all.[28]

There seems very little doubt, after examining the high-level exchange of correspondence between Mr Verney and government representatives, that the same applied to the Dargle Cottage case. Mrs Coombs also reported unusual vibrations:

125

Pauline Coombs, in one of her statements relating the strange things she had observed in Brides Bay, made the startling comment: 'One day I saw the sea shake.' She went on to explain that she was not referring to ordinary waves on the water but vibration radiating outwards from a point in the bay similar to what one might observe from an underwater explosion or seismic shock wave.[29]

Disturbances such as these, coupled with UFO phenomena, do seem to correlate with restricted official areas and covert military projects. An early conclusion of some ETH-inclined ufologists was that UFOs and their occupants are surveying our technological progress. This was later changed to the myth that the military have crashed saucers and are test-flying or reproducing saucer-technology. I think both are incorrect. In situations where field effects are propagated over civilian areas with associated UFO events, there are indications that there are on-going projects involved with sophisticated communication systems or related matters. It would seem that prototype aerial devices are being tested over such areas, which make use of powerfully projected and/or ambient fields to power them. (Note the quotation at the beginning of this chapter.)

Therefore, field effects also induce poltergeist or poltergeist-like direct field effects in combination, and it is a further indication of their overlap. In fact, the Coombs' household experienced *both*. This was partly due to the psychic background of Pauline Coombs, who experienced Marian phenomena as she was 'activated' by prolonged field exposure to emit personal fields, and partly as a direct consequence of the fields which affected her environment. These, without doubt, emanated from the NATO base in the area:

It came to light that the NATO base of RAF Brawdy, situated directly opposite Ripperston Farm and Stack Rocks on the other side of St Brides Bay, was far from being an ordinary installation.[30]

And:

Although superficially a natural event, information came to light which caused us to question this. Earlier in the winter I had noticed that the Ripperston Farm and its immediate area was unnaturally warm . . . The area around the farm had a strange stillness and calm.[31]

The warmer, micro-climate, strange still atmosphere, UFO sightings, poltergeist activity, entity experiences and numerous electrical mal-functions are all indicative of a zone of high ambient fields. That these emanated from the NATO base, there is little doubt. In conjunction with RAF Brawdy, it was the headquarters of what is known as SOSUS, or

Sound Surveillance System, involved with underwater listening devices.

One strange effect of the fields involved Stack Rocks, which is a small, rocky island a short distance offshore, within the high ambient field zone. Both Pauline Coombs and her daughter, along with a local hotelier, watched silver-suited figures moving about on the rocks:

> There were two of these humanoids . . . they seemed to have moved further over the rock from where I saw them first . . . One of them seemed to be climbing up steps. When you see someone coming up-stairs you see their head, then their shoulders, then the bodies and so on. It was like that. And the other was walking round the edge as if looking for something.[32]

This event is an example of an unusual *direct* field effect called *translocation*. Due to the field, it is possible for objects and people at a considerable distance to appear displaced, due to magnetorefraction. This means that the field acts as a lens which is capable of displacing the normal light reflected in the interior of certain buildings that employ such a field, such as power stations, nuclear plants, *and* SOSUS establishments. It is, therefore, further evidence of the presence of a field. Other examples from field use in the area included the appearance of 'eight-foot (2.4 m) silver-suited figures', which are the workers inside the establishments wearing clothing to protect them from the ambient radiation effects in their place of work. These figures are often complete with helmets and visors. Sometimes, they seem to be holding 'wands', which are rods of the material used in the power-producing process. There are many reports of these 'apparitions'; they are simply images of the workers refracted magnetically through the walls. In Dyfed, in 1977, they were also reported as floating above the rooftops; miniaturized versions even appeared on windowsills. These images are sometimes larger or smaller than the average human, and a study of the laws of refraction will clarify these observations of magnification, or minification, as it is termed.

The fact that images of these figures could appear at remote locations and that they are closely associated with an ambient field also lends support to the concept of imagery being 'imprinted' into a field-medium. The location for such field-bound apparitions would amount to a 'hot spot', electromagnetically speaking. Such points of field-focus could have devastating effects upon the brain and consciousness of those who pass through them. In the case of the Dorset village of Fishpond, which suffered from chronic electrical fields, some of the population 'blacked out'; or, from the *Northern UFO News* case quoted earlier, at least allergic 'blank-outs' can occur.

There was a tragic road accident in the Dyfed area that was reported extensively at the time. There is reason to believe that the location of this fatal accident was a focal point for a field concentration. Consider the sad story:

> On the afternoon of 23 November there was a Welsh Counties rugby cup-match between Carmarthenshire and Brecon which was played at Ystradgynlais. After the match two cars set off back for Carmarthen town. One of these was driven by . . . a former Llanelli Rugby Football Club Chairman . . . At about 8 o'clock that evening a Calor gas tanker . . . left for Swansea. About ten minutes later this tanker . . . was on an incline called Nant-y-Caws Hill. The road was dry, driving conditions were good and few cars were using the highway. Nevertheless . . . the truck apparently jack-knifed and overturned across the three-lane carriageway. The BMW containing the rugby supporters hit the obstacle at speed and was literally torn in two.[33]

What caused the driver of the tanker to lose control is a mystery. However, there may be a clue in the revelation:

> We were particularly shocked at this disaster because we had only recently investigated the case of another truck-driver who had been badly shaken after encountering humanoids by night *at this very spot*.

The report by this truck-driver reveals his and his mate's perceptions:

> I came down into a dip . . . and started to climb up and then the lights just picked up these two things. I saw them and thought: 'It can't be – it must be my eyes', so I never said a word. John, by the side of me, said: 'What the hell's that?' I just said: 'I'm not hanging around to find out.'
>
> Standing on the right-hand side grassy verge were two huge figures about seven feet high and correspondingly wide. They were a reddish-orange in colour and seemed to be wearing single-piece celluloid suits. Their heads were elongated upwards as if carrying a tall helmet. The heads seemed to the witnesses to be about a foot wide and eighteen inches high – rather like those of guardsmen wearing busbies. As the light struck the figures it reflected back.
>
> The two monstrous beings were standing together, slightly turned towards each other. They seemed to be holding some sort of instrument between them, although what this object was the two witnesses couldn't make out. The figures remained still as the truck ground up the slope past them . . . 'I had a weird feeling. I wouldn't call it fright. It was a sort of a cold tingling as we were approaching and passing them . . .
>
> 'I've never seen anything so weird or ever felt so weird.'

Wilder Penfield's homunculus represents the distribution of nerve tissue throughout the human body.

Close-encounter witnesses have consistently reported an entity type that has come to be termed a 'grey'. It represents a sensory model of visual predominance at the expense of other reduced sensory areas.

Top: **Investigator Philip Mantle in the fields behind the back garden of 'Jane Murphy' which appeared in her alien-abduction vision.**

Above: **The Reverend Harrison Bailey case. The entities tried to improve their failing physical structure by donning Hallowe'en masks. (*Courtesy of* OMNI)**

Right: **Artist's impression of the Essington Canal case. (*Michael Buhler*)**

Left: **Jean Hingley with mince-pies and glasses of water 'for the gentlemen' visitors.**

Below: **Investigators' photograph of the mark on Jean Hingley's small lawn where she perceived the 'spaceship'. The bucket (1 ft/ 30 cm high) is for scale.**

Jean Hingley's back-garden fence, over which the UAP must have passed. Note the radio mast in the middle distance, behind and below which is the massive Hailstone Quarry (shown below).

Above: **Jean Hingley's back-garden fence and car-port, over which the UAP was seen hovering.** *Below:* **The very ordinary front of Jean's house in Bluestone Walk.**

An artist's impression of the 'Terror in the House of Dolls' case in Gateshead, England. (*Michael Buhler*)

Opposite: An artist's impression of the Rowley Regis case. (*Michael Buhler*)

Right: **An artist's impression of the Cynthia Appleton case in Birmingham, England. (*Michael Buhler*)**

Below: **UAP seen emerging from the ground at Burscough, Lancashire (*Photo: Sally Wallbank*)**

'Did you notice their legs?'

'No. That's the funny part. I didn't. John didn't either.'

'Could you make out the features?'

'No – and that's another queer part. The faces were there, but we seemed to see through them like. There seemed to be nothing [there]. You couldn't make them out . . .'

Man and boy stared at this spectacle for five or six seconds while the heavy truck rumbled past the monsters and left them behind in the darkness.[34]

Also, after they had passed them, neither of them spoke, which was unusual: '. . . a reaction set in'.

The strange tingling, fear-like feeling, the lack of speech . . . By now the reader will recognize these symptoms as reactions to field exposure and possible electrical sensitivity. Did the other tanker driver involved in the accident 'black-out' at that spot? It would certainly seem so. This does seem to be an example of a translocation-focus creating an electromagnetic hot spot. It is not my intention to blame any party; only to point out that it is an important correlation between field-produced apparitions and 'black-outs' which are interpreted as 'time-lapses' (i.e. periods of 'missing time'). Once again, we find that the combination of sensitive individuals and an ambient field can explain the central features of the CE experience. The identification of such field contexts has important implications, therefore, for both psychical and UFO study.

UFOs over Enfield

It has been argued that poltergeist activity and UFO 'flaps' take place in ambient field conditions. Therefore, we could predict that areas with one will have the other, in conjunction with probative field-exposure effects. This was in fact the case with the Enfield poltergeist in 1977. I am indebted to long-standing BUFORA investigator Michael Lewis for the following reports:

Reports of UFO sightings at the time of the Enfield poltergeist activity

A minor 'flap' was experienced during the early autumn of 1977 over north London and south Hertfordshire. It was centred on High Barnet (which adjoins Enfield). This area had not hitherto been noted for UFO activity. Nearly 20 reports were investigated on behalf of BUFORA.

It can be assumed that, as these reports were compiled by Michael

Lewis, an experienced investigator even in those days, they are not completely 'unfiltered', and obvious IFOs have been eliminated. Probably the most interesting case occurred on 30 August 1977 at 5.30 am in Queens Road, High Barnet, a place that Michael knows well:

> A housewife, woken by the crying of her baby, noticed two glowing circles of green light in her bedroom. They were the size of tennis balls, and made no movement. The witness touched one without suffering any ill-effects. The bedroom window was wide open at the time. During the following two weeks there were five electrical failures in the house, and the alternator on the family car failed.

By now readers will have become familiar with direct field effects, and the glowing circles seem to have been 'domestic UAPs'.

31 August
10.45 pm: Old Fold View, High Barnet, adjacent to Queens Road. A couple noticed a white ball hovering very low near their house as they retired for the night. It was like a car headlight, bright and well defined. After ten minutes, it glided noiselessly away.

2 September
11.40 pm: Hadley Wood. A driver and his passenger saw a fluorescent green ball the size of a cricket ball, directly in front of their car. It dipped across the path of the car and disappeared behind some trees. The driver stopped and gave chase!

4 September
11 pm: Coopers Lane Road, Potters Bar. A young couple in a car witnessed an oval, star-like object move slowly from a nearby copse. It hovered noiselessly for a short while, during which the brilliant light from the object went out and came on again twice. It then moved erratically behind the copse again, pulsating and spitting flame from its left side.

11 September
7.40 pm: Stagg Hill, south of Potters Bar. A family of four, travelling in their car along Stagg Hill, noticed a bright-orange, triangular light hovering in the direction of Enfield. After stopping the car, they viewed the light through binoculars; it had the appearance of a white light on the curved edge of a boomerang. It then rose slowly, and increased speed considerably as it disappeared without a sound. The same light was also seen by two witnesses at Enfield Highway.

13 September
9.20 pm: Dancers Hill, south of Potters Bar. A couple were driving in their

car along a country road on the edge of the Wrotham Park estate, when they observed a circular object hovering fairly low near a road junction. It had two orange-red lights and one green light on the underside. As the witnesses' car reached the junction, the object shot away 'at a terrific rate'.

9 October
4.45 pm: Chanctonbury Way, North Finchley. Two schoolboys watched an object they described as a light-grey disc with a yellow light bulb on top, which emitted light as it sped northwards towards High Barnet, faster than any aircraft.

The fact that this 'flap' occurred in the same area and at the same time as a vigorous poltergeist outbreak is highly significant. Like the other cases which were originally presented as URE, we have an overlap between the two areas, and the common denominators are: the increased presence of ambient fields *in combination with* the presence of physiologically or psychically 'correct' individuals. These two factors, I predict, will be found over and over again in association with URE and 'conventional' psychic phenomena. Where one is found, the other will be close by, and it will 'only' be a matter of detection.

It is the human unconscious reacting to the presence of transient atmospheric conditions that have been enhanced and activated by natural or technology-borne fields. Also typically associated will be electrical sensitivity and allergic conditions in the individuals involved.

Electronic pollution: a key aspect in the triggering of close encounters

Before I looked into artificial radio and television wave propagation, I was not really aware that the huge radio masts seen mounted high on hills and buildings actually transmit electromagnetic waves (i.e., radio frequencies) as well as receive them. When a radio frequency current at the transmitting station flows into a transmitting aerial or antenna, a radio wave at the same frequency is radiated. The direction(s) of this depend on the way that the aerial is set up for its radiation pattern.

This radiated energy will reach receiving aerials by five possible modes of propagation.[35] Those that concern us most are called surface waves and space waves (see Fig. 4). These intersect with ground-level locations and irradiate the houses, cars, people, etc. at those locations.

Surface waves are aptly named, since they are supported by the surface of the earth and they are able to follow its curvature as they travel from

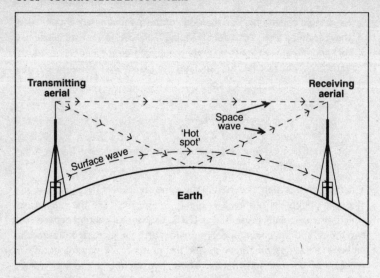

Fig. 4 Surface- and space-wave propagation. Note the reflected component of the space wave.

one aerial to another. Unlike light waves, radio waves do not always travel in straight lines. They are relatively near the surface of the ground and shoot through buildings, etc. and, of course, people. Most of the time, they have a minimal effect, but if people struck by them are electrically hypersensitive, a range of effects, such as altered states, can occur. It is at this point that the correlation of electrical sensitivity and psychic dispositions becomes most relevant to understanding the part such electronic pollution plays in CE experiences.

The space wave has two components. One travels almost in a straight line between the elevated transmitting and receiving aerials. The other component provides possibly the most potent aspect of an electromagnetic hot spot, for it travels by means of *a single reflection from the earth* (see Fig. 5). It literally bounces off the ground, or ground-level locations, which can be houses and roads where people would be in a direct 'firing line'.

An example of a potent hot spot would be a place where several of these reflections converge on to a relatively small or localized area, such as a road junction, forest clearing, or a row of houses. A quarry would be especially potent, since it would either reflect and/or contain the energy transmitted, or actually add to it in the form of geopathic stress. Consider an area that has several surface waves at different frequencies zipping through on their way to a receiving station, that is over a fault-line, that is the location of the ground-reflected space-wave, that happens to be the focus for a magnetorefraction effect . . . High-tension cables mounted on pylons across the area would make such a spot of extremely high potency. An electrically hypersensitive person would certainly react violently with an allergic reaction and add to the electromagnetic and electrical mayhem by introducing their own personal field. This would then be part of a much larger invisible 'cloud' of 'electromagnetic smog'. That is to say, *they* would be 'signal-linked' to a large area of charged atmosphere, measured in volumetric units. Research needs to be done into this important aspect to discern its effect on UAPs, but it may be deduced that such a 'signal-link' situation would connect the witness with any UAPs straying into the area and, as a result, directly influence the movement and form of it, so that it will 'perform' on electromagnetic 'strings' controlled by the unconscious of that person. This is how UAPs *appear* to have an intelligence of their own, and *appear* to react to the thoughts of the witness. As Dr C.W. Smith comments generally: 'It now appears likely that nature is, more than previously suspected, using highly coherent electromagnetic signals within and between living systems.'[36]

Although there is no implication that UAPs are 'living systems', this does indicate the feasibility, in terms of coherence, of the 'signal-link' concept. Another supporting indication of this electromagnetic link

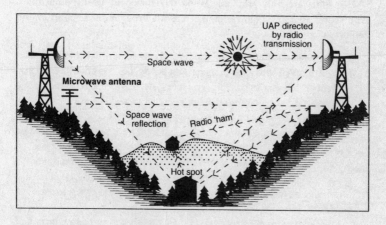

Fig. 5 Possible 'electropollution' scenario: the UAP responds to radio-wave propagation.

between the biological system of electrically hypersensitive persons and lights in the sky can be found in the cases of individuals who have been struck by lightning on numerous occasions. Such unlucky people, it seems, emit a coherent beam of electromagnetic energy as an allergic reaction on encountering the atmospheric charge of a thunderstorm, and offer an easier route to earth than the electromagnetically undifferentiated air of the atmosphere. It is ironic that their first experience of a strike sets their body up for the development of electrical hypersensitivity in later life. These major electrical events can also be triggered by proximity to ball-lightning or UAPs, such as earthlights. In fact, this is why such atmospheric lights seem to pace the cars of such ES individuals (i.e., because they emit a coherent EM beam which the UAP reacts to as a route to earth, rather like the upstroke of a lightning strike).

Anyone whose house becomes a hot spot will experience a range of field effects which, over time, will become progressively more intense. This is due to the development of electrical hypersensitivity or allergy. They will also begin to have strange anomalous perceptions, depending on the type of field (some fields produce physiological effects and little else). These include OBEs, 'alien abductions', 'alien contacts' or even apparent demonic possession. The form of the experiences partly depends on the beliefs and associated 'picture library' of the subjects.

One of the most recent cases published, classified as an 'alien abduction', is the 'Jane Murphy' case in Yorkshire, mentioned in the final chapter. This case could be taken as a textbook model of anomalous experiences due to prolonged field exposure and electrical hypersensitivity.

Hot spots are only gradually being recognized by health authorities. The World Health Organization has recently brought out a report on this important aspect:

> Tell (1990) conducted measurements and calculations directed to applications in the VHF and UHF broadcasting bands, but the concepts are also applicable to assessing RF hot spots near AM radio stations. He summarized the problem of RF hot spots as shown below:
>
> An RF hot spot may be defined as a point or small area in which the local values of electric and/or magnetic field strengths are significantly elevated above the typical ambient field levels and often are confined near the surface of a conductive object. RF hot spots usually complicate the process of evaluating compliance with exposure standards, because it is often only at the small area of the hot spots that the fields exceed the exposure limits.
>
> RF hot spots may be produced by an intersection of narrow beams of RF energy (directional antennas), by the reflection of fields from

RF energy (directional antennas), by the reflection of fields from conducting surfaces (standing waves), or by induced currents flowing in conductive objects exposed to ambient RF fields (re-radiation). RF hot spots are characterized by very rapid spacial variation of the fields and, typically, result in partial body exposures of individuals near the hot spots. Uniform exposure of the body is essentially impossible because of the high spatial gradient of the fields associated with RF hot spots.[37]

It is clear from the author's own investigations that alien abduction and contact experiences take place in such electromagnetic hot spots and they are the product of the interaction of the physiological system of ES individuals with such prolonged irradiation.

5 Unidentified Atmospheric Phenomena (UAPS) and 'Medium Lights'

It is significant that a large portion of UFO sightings are over fault-lines . . . and obviously the state of the earth's crust is causing our space-visitors considerable concern.[1]

The UAP

This generic term refers to a range of aerial phenomena which include ball-lightning, earthquake-lights, earthlights, 'spooklights',[2] plasma vortexes and others. Each of these has been described in the UFO-study literature, and it is not my aim to repeat all of this material, but to expand their parameters to include aspects not previously appreciated. It must be mentioned that much of established science scarcely recognizes the authenticity of UAPs generally.

Ball-lightning, which has been observed countless times for centuries, has been a topic for controversy regarding the possible mechanisms for its production. It is clear that in the past theories have been confounded due to the non-recognition of the fact that such observations are made up of a mixture of light phenomena with differing origins and parameters. Atmospheric physics has not taken into account that there are other forms of spheres of electrical energy which behave in different ways from ball-lightning, and it is proposed here for the first time that electrical and electronic pollution also produces its own ball-lightning-like UAP. These can usefully be called electroforms.

A recent proposal for ball-lightning production has been outlined by David Turner, a chemist at Bristol University in England, and reported in *New Scientist*. Before Turner's conclusions are described, it must also be observed that there is an ultra-conservative attitude towards ball-lightning by the scientific establishment. Some theorists maintain that it does not even exist (which is nonsense) and this may reflect the long-term frustration that they have experienced in accounting for it. This, however, may be due to the reason already mentioned: they are lumping together several different types of light phenomena or UAPs.

So, while some scientists continue with their blinkered approach, ufologists continue to log reliable sighting after sighting of atmospheric BOLs and myriad other shapes and forms, that often (but not always) bring EM and electrical disturbance in their wake. These include a range of extraordinary changes to the consciousness and physiology of the witness, including the production of psychokinetic effects usually thought of as being the exclusive property of poltergeists. Most, however, result in simple UFO sightings.

Examples

I am indebted to Joseph Dormer of the Flyde UFO Investigation group for the following report of an event in 1979:

> I was a Security Officer doing a night duty on Central Pier, Blackpool. I was situated about 50 yards from the front of the pier, in a small toll-booth, on the north side.
>
> At approximately half-past two in the morning, I felt a severe juddering of the pier structure. This juddering only normally happens when the tide is coming in, but on this occasion the tide was out. The vibration of the pier structure continued intermittently for approximately half an hour. At about three a.m. I heard a very loud roaring sound, similar to a low-flying jet aircraft; the sound only lasted about five seconds. As the sound stopped, my reaction was to look through the window facing south, towards the direction from where the sound had come from.
>
> To my amazement, there, between central and south pier, about 50 yards out to sea, and about 300 feet above the sea, was a large orange globe of light. It was about a comparable size to a full moon. The light did not move and there was no sound. I ran out of the toll-booth, and over to the side of the pier in order to get a better look, not taking my eyes off the object. I was shaking with excitement, realizing that I was witnessing something very strange. After about 90 seconds the orange globe just disappeared before my eyes. Just at that moment, the two night-cleaners, who had been working in the Dixieland Disco (which is at the front of the pier) came running over to me and started to ask me what was going on. They had felt the vibrations and heard the roaring sound. I explained to them what I had just witnessed and they were utterly amazed, and asked me to come to the Dixieland Bar to see a magazine – *Weekend* – that they

had just been reading, while on their tea-break. The article in question was on UFO sightings. It mentioned a sighting of an orange ball of light seen over Central Pier, Blackpool, ten years before.

I returned to the deck of the pier and immediately noticed a strong fishy smell which was not there before. Being very excited at what I had seen, I decided to watch the sky for the rest of the night. Over the next four hours I saw four star-like objects rise from the surface of the sea, go vertically upwards a few thousand feet and then accelerate in a horizontal position until they disappeared.[3]

The geophysical origins of earthlights and their associations with aerials, masts, pylons, power-lines, hilltops, etc. have been mentioned, but this object seems to have been originally generated to the surface from strata in a quarry. Consider Joseph Dormer's associated report:

Unfortunately, the witness cannot recall even the approximate date of his sighting. However, the time and location of the sighting, the description of the object, and in particular the juddering of the pier and the very loud roaring sound (geosound) leaves little room for doubt that this was the same object that on 24 February 1979 was first spotted in a quarry in Bacup before travelling some 40 miles or so to the coast. It was sighted by quite a number of people who wrote to Jenny Randles who was able to plot its probable flightpath . . . The juddering of the pier, probably earth tremors, continued intermittently for half an hour, i.e., up until the orange globe was seen, after which it stopped or was too faint to be felt. The structure of the pier and its deep foundations may explain why it registered subterranean tremors when apparently nothing else did. In any case, this 'juddering' may offer a clue to the mechanism involved in the formation of this particular class of UAP.

Review

This fascinating case throws up a number of interesting aspects. Firstly, it is positive proof of the physical, external nature of the BOL or earthlight as opposed to a hallucination, due to the widespread sighting of it by independent witnesses. An object reported by many independent witnesses over a range of 40 miles (113 km) is a sure indicator of its external reality.

Looking at the Blackpool area, there are a number of relevant features. A number of researchers, notably Paul Devereux, have correlated prehistoric stone circles with earthlights. With the presence of this BOL this link is borne out by the presence of an underwater stone circle near the pier. Over the centuries, the sea has encroached upon the land, covering a village called Pennystone. At a particularly low tide in 1588, a stone circle was spotted on the outskirts of the ruined village. More recently an iron stanchion sticking out of a rock was located.

Local geoelectricity and electronic pollution

There is a large fault to the north of Blackpool. The Blackpool Tower has transmitting aerials and dishes which include the local Radio Wave and the BBC meteorological radar. The police station, with its own transmitter, is just opposite the Central Pier. The base station for radio cabs is near the North Pier, although the UFO activity seems to be mostly between the Central and South Piers.

What is the relevance of *this* information in *this* case? If the UAP/ 'earthlight' originated from geophysical activity 40 miles away, and if it was not a hallucination or apparitional, why compile this sort of information? The answer to this is twofold. First, a UAP emits EM radiation and eventually 'burns out'. We saw how the BOL in this case just vanished. It may have been that it just expired in the visible light waveband and it may still have been present as an invisible field concentration. The ambient EM 'smog' acts as a source of energy which can sustain it in the atmosphere. In the Hessdalen investigations, a laser was shot at a pulsing UAP, causing the rate of pulsing to increase. This was done several times. This indicates that UAPs can be boosted by EM beams, of which the laser, being coherent, was a potent source. The same thing happens with coherent RF emissions and the level of electronic pollution in an area provides a gauge of the amount of atmospheric electrical energy that could affect the UAP. An analytical system needs to be compiled here, and it would be of great relevance to investigation if a system of EM levels for any given area could be assessed.

Second, there is the aspect of UAP atmospheric movement. This is indicated in Figure 5 (page 133) of a potential electropollution scenario. The earthlight is made up of a range of field types across the EM spectrum. It is known that seismic stress, at faults, creates radio waves.[4] These have been detected and recorded by seismologists as part of their standard investigation procedures. Therefore, as earthlights are produced by this tectonic stress, they are partially made up of radio waves and would be sensitive to them. Sudden EM pressure, as a projected radio-wave beam, would 'transmit' the UAP in the direction of the transmission and it would be carried along by it in the atmosphere. There would be no question of wind resistance, and as the wave is a stream of fast-moving, charged electrons, it would be carried along by this stream. How fast this is, is the *phase velocity* of the wave. This would explain why witnesses report how UFOs shoot across the sky like 'a tracer bullet' or like 'a stone from a catapult' or 'depart faster than the eye could see'. They are swept along at a velocity comparable with the radio transmission itself (i.e., at the speed of light).

We might wonder if this earthlight was 'patched through' from Bacup by a succession of transmissions, or a single transmission. Previously, it would be at the mercy of ambient fields in a free-floating state. The UAP is a truly mysterious phenomenon at our present stage of understanding. Perhaps if UAPs were produced artificially or one was captured somehow . . . Perhaps UFO sky-watch teams should be stalking the Yorkshire moors and quarries with their miniature radio-transmitters slung like beam-weapons in holsters around their waists, ready to zap a UAP into an electromagnetic net . . .

Paul Devereux has received numerous reports of UAPs hovering round radio or television masts, and predictably, travelling from transmitting to receiving aerial. Consider the following examples:

In September 1983, the Emley TV mast was once more the focus for a light display . . . Again in November, 7.13 p.m., a witness looking through his window saw a ball of brilliant orange light approaching it from a north-north-east direction at a very slow speed. The light passed behind the mast roughly half-way up the 865-foot-tall structure and then headed towards the Holm Moss TV mast further in the distance towards Manchester . . . Another TV mast, this time at Unstone . . . A Cutthorpe farmer . . . reported seeing a strange light darting across the sky . . . 'the pulsating light frequently changed direction and colour . . . it was at one time as intense as lightning and then changed to orange' . . . it seemed to be very close and once stopped as if to inspect the TV mast at Unstone. On 3 January 1986, a family of five saw a strange light hovering around the TV transmitter mast on Moel Parc . . . the light was a hazy-red at the bottom and white on top. After hovering stationary for a time it suddenly flew directly over the witnesses, displaying a rotating ring of coloured lights on the underside.[5]

Broadly stated, it would appear that many UAPs are attracted to the same aspects of the landscape that would induce a lightning strike. Given their electrical nature, this is not surprising. Area of elevation seems to be an important factor for UAP/earthlight activity.

Returning to the Blackpool pier case, another virtually identical orange BOL was encountered in more or less the same area in July 1989. It is intriguing that another was reported, according to the witness's information, exactly ten years prior to that! Consider Blackpool's last reported appointment with a huge orange BOL – certainly a sensational performance on this occasion.

On Tuesday, 5 July 1989, Andrew Billing was driving down Grasmere Road towards the sea-front, when he noticed through the open window of his cab, a large red-orange, brightly glowing sphere in the sky over the sea in the south-west. Its apparent size, he later gauged, could be reproduced by holding a two-pence piece at arm's length. He had barely been watching it for more than a few seconds when it moved 'at fantastic speed, faster than the eye could see' to another part of the sky. Here it hovered for a further few seconds before repeating the manoeuvre, finally disappearing out of sight in the north-west.

Billing, subjected to field exposure from the UAP, then went on to hallucinate an apparitional RAF Tornado firing an air-to-air missile! It may be that this earthlight also originated in the Bacup quarry, and that there is a 'corridor', magnetically speaking, from quarry to coast. A large ferrous structure like a pier could act as a huge magnet, perhaps linking up in linear fashion with the fault to the north.

The presence of the offshore stone circle and the observation by Kevin Cunningham of lights ascending from the sea during the four hours after his sighting (which would have been USOs, unidentified submarine objects) leads me to assume the probability of offshore seismic activity. Indeed, there have been numerous reports of objects emerging from the sea and roaring away into the sky.

The picture we are given in the Billing case of BOL movement across the sky in 'instalments' (i.e., where it hovered, sped away, hovered, sped away and so on) is again indicative of intermittent radio transmissions, which would coincide with the sweep of the BBC meteorological radar: where the transmitting dish is revolving; the beam hits the UAP and is immediately taken off; only to return on the next sweep to push it further across the sky.

Therefore, typical UFO behaviour, in terms of movement and location types, can be identified – that is, 'instalment movement'. The characteristic departure speed is another marker. Devereux has, of course, compiled a typical fault-zone location where earthlights are to be found. From profiles like this, we can then go on to identify purported structured craft as UAPs of some type.

There are consistent reports of 'domed discs', which could be the shape produced by centrifugal forces on a spinning sphere. Alternatively, discoid shapes have been seen to resolve out of a BOL, which may suggest a spinning core that sheds a spherical and luminous 'force-field'. Devereux's collection of reports, many of which are taken from Project

Pennine (an on-going study of UFOs in Yorkshire), are littered with seemingly structured objects with UAP characteristics. Consider an example of the 'disc from sphere' UAP just described:

> About a mile and a half (2.5 km) north of this location, a farmer's wife and her son had been in the fields lambing when they saw a brilliant purple sphere, very fluorescent and moving at a remarkably slow pace. Over Cwm Canol it exploded soundlessly, producing a shower of sparks out of which emerged a white disc. This then descended vertically and was lost to view.[6]

Earthlights: environmental and systemic effects

Let us, then, consider another case, not identified with seismic activity or UAPs by the investigator involved, Budd Hopkins. A series of direct quotations from his book *Intruders* will serve to set out the evidence:

> There was a sudden flash outside in the direction of the Davises' backyard, behind the trees that separate the two houses, *and then a low vibrating sound; Joyce felt her house begin to shake. The chandelier in the dining-room moved slightly*, and the noise increased, the television picture turned completely red and all the lights in the house dimmed and flickered. Then everything returned to normal . . . Thinking immediately that there had been a small earthquake . . . Bernie told me that when he came home that night all the digital clocks in the house were flashing and had to be reset. Something had definitely affected their power supply, at least momentarily.

By now the reader will recognize the clear characteristics of seismic activity and ambient fields from the other cases described. The movement of objects and vibration described can be identified from the Mercalli Seismic Intensity Scale as being between levels II and III. It is worth reproducing the relevant sections of this table:

> Level II: Felt indoors by few, especially on upper floors, or by sensitive or nervous persons . . . sometimes hanging objects may swing, especially when delicately suspended; sometimes trees, structures, liquids, bodies of water may sway; doors may swing very slowly; animals reported uneasy; sometimes dizziness or nausea experienced.
>
> Level III: Felt indoors by several, motion usually rapid vibrations. Sometimes not recognized to be an earthquake at first. Duration able to be recognizable in some cases. Vibration like that due to passing of lightly loaded trucks, or heavy trucks some distance away.

> Hanging objects may swing slightly. Standing vehicles rock slightly.[7]

Readers can draw their own conclusions regarding the matching of characteristics from each source. We have also seen the effect of ambient fields on digital watches from other cases. Returning to *Intruders*:

> Kathie Davis's neighbour that lives across the street ... was awakened by a loud roaring sound that made her house vibrate and so terrified her that she felt sure a jet plane was about to crash into her home.

This distinctive roaring sound occurred in the 1979 Blackpool pier case and it is associated with earthlights. It is, in fact, a phenomenon called geosound, which is produced by subterranean electrical activity during a geomagnetic storm, and it is indicative of seismic stress.[8] I wonder if Budd Hopkins checked the seismological records to eliminate the possibility of this.

It is significant that the roaring sound was not reported in the 1989 events, but instead a hallucination of a silent Tornado. Because of the magnetic field, there was an OZ factor silence and the unconscious, in producing the imagery of the fighter plane, 'lost the sound' from the dramatic presentation. However, the unconscious of the witness would have registered it, and just as external sounds are incorporated into dreams, this geosound roaring served as a cue to access the 'picture library' of the witness for RAF jet imagery, of which Billing had more than an average amount, due to his past exposure to military planes.

Returning to the Budd Hopkins case, we have now identified seismic activity in the area complete with geosound, and electrical disturbance which would also have been due to seismic radiation. To complete the earthlight UAP identification, all that would be needed is a BOL phenomenon near an elevated point, such as an aerial or mast of some kind. Consider the following quotation from *Intruders*:

> Now the pumphouse was dark and the door was closed, but the garage door, which had been shut, was open ... A moment later, however, as Mary stood at the kitchen sink, she noticed a strange round ball of light surrounding the bird-feeder in the backyard. This small feeder, sitting atop a four-foot pole, is located about 12 feet from the kitchen window ... Mary's description: 'It was a pale white light. It wasn't real bright. I could see the bird-feeder through it, and I thought, Gee, where is that light coming from? ... It was round and about as big as a basketball, but I could see the bird-feeder through it. Then it sort of faded out, all at once.

This account provides us with a classical description of a UAP or earthlight or 'earthquake light'. The see-through aspect has been reported repeatedly (for example, the Livingston case). The cryptic comment regarding a door being open when it should have been shut is further evidence of tremor, as we can see this aspect mentioned in the Mercalli table: 'doors may swing . . .'

We now need to look for systemic field effects. Hopkins' description continues: 'I just felt real strange. Something wasn't right . . . The hair on my arms was standing up on end and I felt tingly everywhere.'

It came as no surprise to learn that there was also an open body of water nearby – a swimming pool in the backyard. It is also significant that the swimmers in this pool and the main witness of the case – Kathie Davis (pseudonym) – *felt nauseous and dizzy*. Precisely these symptoms are mentioned in the Mercalli table, although not in the same section. Hopkins states: 'The nausea and dizziness the three swimmers felt suggests the presence of some residual radiation-like effect'. This is, of course, absolutely correct, and it is not surprising that the pool was near to where the globe of light was seen. In fact: 'These peculiar globes of light, somewhat larger than basketballs, seemed to be all over the Davis acreage that night.'

This symptom of nausea was a complaint expressed so definitely that it is surprising that the connection with seismic activity was not made:

Nausea at the Moment of Shock: The curious effect of earthquake shock upon human beings . . . is deserving of more attention than it has yet received. The fact itself, as respects human beings, admits of no doubt. I have direct testimony of the boys of a large boarding-school being suddenly awakened at night by one of the North American shocks, and the greater number suffering from an immediate sense of nausea, amounting to vomiting in many cases. Is the nausea an effect of the sudden disturbance of the nervous system, or due to the movement itself?[9]

Surely the other inhabitants of the area must have been so affected, especially as the area also experienced unusual electrical effects of the kind we have seen in the Enfield poltergeist case, in the Coombs and Codes households. I cannot analyse the full details surrounding the main witness who, Hopkins insists, was abducted by aliens from another planet several times throughout her life. From the details given, it is clear that Kathie Davis is ES, and it is sufficient to indicate relevant background details mentioned in *Intruders* and allow the reader, in the light of the information given so far regarding allergies and ES, in conjunction with the systemic symptoms induced by field exposure, to decide what this case is really about: overweight due to hormonal imbalance (Vasopressin: link with typical metabolic type of 'mediums'); menstruated aged seven years;

stopped growing aged ten years, at 5 feet 3½ inches (1.6 m); high blood pressure; gallstone operation aged 14 years; hepatitis and pneumonia; hospitalized with apparent asthma attack–allergic reaction to medication; ovarian cysts: second child born two months premature. After 'abduction': heart arrhythmia; hypoglycaemia; hyper-adrenalism; allergic reactions to medication; muscular stiffness; eye problems; hair loss; generally felt unwell for days after 'abduction'; low-level pain in ear; food allergies. All of these symptoms are associated with electrical hypersensitivity and hot-spot exposure.

Hopkins describes a typical low-level tremor with associated earthlight UAPs (although he 'identifies' these features as a visit from aliens from another planet, which abducted Kathie Davis in order to gain access to her sex cells). There was also a heated patch of soil with a line extending from it on the ground. This is similar to a trace in the Rowley Regis case, which also involved a landed earthlight which irradiated the lawn, just as this example in *Intruders* describes. The witness involved in this case also hallucinated bizarre entities due to her proximity to the earthlight. There is no doubt that 'Kathie Davis' was subjected to a seismic event and associated geoelectricity, as opposed to being abducted by aliens.

The structure of ball-lightning

A new chemical theory for ball-lightning has recently been proposed by David Turner, which appears to explain two of the phenomenon's characteristics that have puzzled scientists: its stability and its tendency to stay at ground level despite an evident buoyancy.[10]

Unlike earthlights, it is almost always sighted during thundery weather. It seems to be a free-floating globe of luminous gas, typically about the size of a grapefruit. It exhibits a variety of colours and luminosities, but it does not seem to exude a high degree of heat. It has been reported as moving at quite high speeds (up to 33 feet/10 m a second) at about 3 feet (1 m) above the ground. Sometimes it vanishes after a minute or so, or explodes with a loud report.

Turner suggests that during thundery weather, the air is very humid and ions are created by the action of electrical fields on the atmosphere. This causes a localized 'plasma' of ions, at temperatures up to several thousand degrees. When this plasma escapes into a cooler part of the atmosphere irradiated by ambient fields, it is coated by successive spherical layers created by different chemical processes – an onion-like structure. One of these layers is laden with water droplets, which create a cooling effect and a surface tension, thereby giving it shape and a heat-containing layer. This

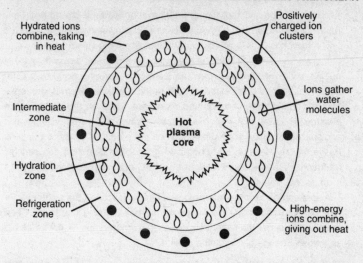

Fig. 6 The structure of ball-lightning. (*After David Turner*, New Scientist, *20 March 1993*)

concentration of water weighs the ball down, counteracting the 'lift' of the hot gases within (see Fig. 6).

The most relevant aspect of this explanation is that the processes involved depend on the presence of electrical fields. We have already seen how UFO-prone areas are correlated with this factor, *and it is likely that processes similar to this also occur in artificially produced fields*; that is to say, intentional, or 'accidental', electronic pollution creates similar conditions and *it is conducive to ball-lightning-like UAP formation, but outside of the pre-thunderstorm conditions described*. These electroforms are just one group of UAP types created out of electromagnetic pollution.

As ambient fields form the atmospheric context that is able to combine in a variety of ways, with correspondingly various weather conditions, there must be a range of electroform types. These can occur, of course, outside seismic conditions, and they are not dependent upon them. All manner of hybrids could (and do) form, in 'flap' areas, with their own properties and consciousness-affecting potentials.

Looking back at some of the UAP reports, there are numerous candidates for these electroforms. Consider the following description from an area that has already been mentioned – the Dyfed peninsula or 'Welsh Triangle':

Another strange and frightening phenomenon alarmed coastguard Tony Dalton at Fishguard in the Pembrokeshire Coast National Park. It occurred on 14 November 1977 at Garn Fawr, near Strumble Head.

. . . a very large, brilliant, yellow-green transparent ball with a fuzzy outline, which descended from the base of a towering cloud over Garn Fawr mountain and appeared to float down a hillside. It emitted intense light for about three seconds and there was static on the radio . . . the coastguard stated that the object slowly rotated around a horizontal axis and seemed to bounce off projections on the ground. Cattle and sea-birds in the vicinity became disturbed and it was this that first aroused his attention. He first thought it might be a UFO but a later explanation wrote it off as 'ball-lightning'.

A spokesman for the Meteorological Office described the sighting as 'a rare case among rare cases'. Apparently ball-lightning has never been seen before larger than about six inches in diameter, but . . . it was 'as big as a bus'. Strange ball-lightning indeed.[11]

While it is impossible to tell the difference between an earthlight and an electroform without a greater knowledge of the area and conditions, this UAP has been chosen as an example because of its comparsion with ball-lightning by someone who, it seems, would recognize it; and also because earthlights are characterized by their earthbound origins – and this phenomenon appeared from a cloud-base. This conclusion is, however, based entirely on second-hand circumstantial evidence. Nevertheless, the point is that in order to begin to understand the UAP as a group of phenomena made up of different types, we have to look beyond earthlights, while realizing their importance. Other possible electroforms are not luminous and appear quite solid and metallic, although they exhibit field effects:

Mrs H called in. She had the experience with her ex-husband (a civil engineer) . . . May 1980 . . . at 14.00 hours on a bright sunny day with patchy high cloud . . . They were on iron-ore tips by Wetherlamb in the Lake District, between Langdale and Coniston . . . They were ferreting through the loose rocks when she had to 'look up' because of an odd feeling. This she likened to the sort of heavy pressure one can get prior to the onset of a thunderstorm; although no storm was around this time. Looking up the slope a strange object appeared. It was like 'a steel kettle in colour and shaped like a ball-bearing, with striations on the surface in no set pattern as if someone had gone over it with steel wool'. A heat haze or shimmer surrounded its surface, even though it was not a particularly hot day. Mrs H insists: 'It was dark bluish-grey . . . very definite and solid looking'. It was 2–3 feet wide.

The object proceeded to move down the slope towards them, noticeably following the contours of the land as it rose and fell. It was no more than 3 feet off the ground and came to an abrupt stop some 50 feet away. Here it hovered for two minutes, then shot skywards and vanished rapidly. During its presence there had been a sound. This was likened to a 'very low almost sub-audible humming'. Mrs H says she 'felt' this more than she heard it, but it was real and disappeared along with the object. She is convinced that this noise precipitated the feeling of apprehension first noted and, 'I couldn't tell whether it was physical or psychological, but the noise was creating such a feeling of "doom" that I was extremely glad when it was gone.' . . . Mrs H says during childhood she remembers how frequently this hill was struck by lightning during storms; possibly because of the attraction of the buried iron ore.[12]

The obvious field effects are the pre-thunderstorm-like atmosphere and the apparent heat-haze effect. An intense magnetic field can interfere with light waves but it can also create visual distortion as an ocular effect. The systemic 'doom' effect in the presence of a magnetic field has been recorded by Persinger, in his co-studies with Rutten (1991), and the witness's description of a struggle to distinguish between a physical and a mental state is typical of a field effect upon the brain. Other UAP parameters are evident, such as its occurrence in a lightning-prone area.

The shiny metallic appearance of this UAP is due to an occasional optical phenomenon called *Heilingenschein* which is caused by the diffraction and refraction of light through a layer of water droplets in a magnetic field. It is significant, therefore, that Turner has proposed that ball-lightning also contains a charged layer of water as part of its structure.

The episode in Poland: a medical emergency and a UAP

Place: Zulawka-Sztum, south-east of Gdansk, Poland
Date: 5 September 1980
Time: 3.15 am
Witnesses: Mrs E. Pluta, Dr B. Piazza, G. Skoczynski, A. Olejuik, J. Kaminska, G. Ludorf

The following description is based on a factual report in *Flying Saucer Review*.[13] In the early hours of the morning, a young mother-to-be began to experience labour pains and an ambulance was called. Travelling along deserted country roads on the way to hospital, she and three others (a doctor, a stretcher-bearer and the driver) encountered a huge crimson globe that came down out of the sky and paced the ambulance for three-quarters of an hour.

The ambulance people were intent on ensuring the safety of the mother and baby and found the UFO's intrusion a distracting threat. It was this single-mindedness that inhibited their emotions, unlike two level-crossing attendants who were found shaking with fear in their hut, when the ambulance halted at the crossing. On this occasion, it was not the passage of a train that blocked its path, but a crimson globe that spanned the road. This road is 19 feet wide and the sphere overlapped its edges by a couple of feet on either side.

Everyone first saw the globe as 'a big red ball in the sky', some distance away. It looked larger than the full moon and dark crimson in colour. It immediately descended to tree-top level and hovered about 500 yards from the ambulance. One second it hung in the sky at cloud level, the next it was seen hovering between two trees either side of the road in the middle distance. All the witnesses then sensed the globe's ominous approach as it cruised towards them at a very low level along the road. The doctor later commented: 'I was always aware that it was never exactly in the sky; it was not very high over the ground at any time.'

The ambulance and the crimson globe approached the level-crossing on a collision course, and when they reached the crossing, each stopped. The globe was a couple of feet above the surface of the road. The doctor left the cab and approached the small hut to speak to the crossing-attendants.

'Can you see what I can?'

'We've been looking at it for some time.'

The doctor returned to the ambulance. 'They cannot help us at all; they're trembling with fear.'

At this point, the labour-contractions grew fiercer and more frequent. There was a feeling of increased urgency, but their path was blocked by the huge sphere. Wondering what to do, the doctor radioed the police.

'There's an obstacle in our way. Please come immediately.'

'What obstacle?'

'A UFO.'

It was 4.10 am and the seconds ticked by as they gazed uncomprehendingly at the unknown visitor. The ambulance crew took in the details of its strange appearance as it hovered there silently. Its surface displayed curved bands and stripes, with a multitude of black lines traversing up and down in irregular patterns. The doctor remarked about how these clear-cut markings reminded her of veins inside the human body. The driver replied by comparing them with a huge net. As they looked on, parts of the surface changed colour. There appeared to be orange-yellow patches on the deep crimson background. Then, the globe dropped to only a few

Fig. 7 An artist's impression of the episode in Poland. (*After Flying Saucer Review*)

inches above the road, constantly changing colour, pulsating, but always with dull muted tones. Strangely, it gave off a strong white light that reflected on the surface of the road.

Out of exasperation the ambulance driver flashed the headlights at it twice. It immediately vanished . . . It was 4.15 am. At 6.10, in hospital, Mrs Pluta gave birth to a daughter. A careful examination of the whole area in daylight revealed . . . nothing.

It would be revealing to carry out an in-depth study of all the witnesses to see if their post-encounter lives are any different. There do not *seem* to have been any consciousness-altering effects, but it would not be surprising if the doctor, who left the ambulance and was therefore more subject to irradiation by the electromagnetic fields emitted by the UAP, developed electrical hypersensitivity in later life, as the unprotected proximity would constitute a major electrical event.

It has been found repeatedly that witnesses experience psychic phenomena after their UFO encounter, and it is clear that such phenomena are due to the development or enhancement of electrical hypersensitivity in conjunction with electromagnetic hot-spot activity;

that is to say, such experiences are intrinsically linked with such environmentally produced illnesses and they are a symptom of it.

Domestic UAPs and 'medium lights'

If the same luminous phenomena as those reported during poltergeist activity were seen in an outdoor setting, they would be called UFOs and incorporated by the ETH into an alien-technology scenario. We have noted that the Enfield poltergeist outbreak included such 'domestic UAPs' and it seemed that the 'focus' can affect ambient electrical fields and may be instrumental in the induction of such domestic luminosities, due to the emission of their personal fields. Investigation of such cases of indoor UFOs, however, has shown that the locations are always within extremely potent electromagnetic hot spots, frequently caused by the intersection of microwave beams from multiple local antennae. The following description will provide an example, taken from the Enfield poltergeist case, of the level of electromagnetic energies that may be involved in hot-spot activity:

> Then followed one of the most remarkable and alarming incidents of the whole case. There was a sudden violent shaking sound, and it was immediately followed by total panic.
>
> 'Oh Lord!' cried Mrs Harper. 'That does it. All that power! I'm getting out.' . . . He [a researcher] was standing in the doorway of the bedroom, wondering if he was seeing things. The entire iron frame of the gas-fire had been wrenched out of the wall and was standing at an angle on the floor, still attached to the half-inch diameter brass-pipe that connected it to the mains. The pipe had been bent through an angle of thirty-two degrees. This was a major demolition job, for the thing was cemented into the brickwork . . . When we finally dismantled the whole apparatus, we found it quite a job to even move. It must have weighed at least fifty pounds.[14]

If there are any doubts about the physical nature of psychic phenomena, then this example would certainly serve to dispel them. When energy levels of this order are involved, in combination with the organizing ability of the electrically activated unconscious, it is easy to see how some CEs could appear as confrontations with physically real machines, for example:

> On 31 October 1963, a UFO, estimated as being 8 m (25 ft) in diameter and shaped like a wash-basin, was observed in broad daylight by several persons at Iguape, south-west of Santos, in Brazil. The slow-moving UFO, which was making a roaring noise, collided with a palm tree before falling

into the nearby Peropava River. The observers watched as the river bubbled and boiled at the point of entry of the object. This was followed by an eruption of muddy water, then one of pure mud. The authorities, using divers, could find nothing in the water, 15 ft deep . . . engineers searched the area with mine detectors, but they too, found nothing.[15]

This is what is meant by a purposely staged event by the UI, utilizing a physical 'PK construction'. The 'crashed' object would not be found, as the UI, being the source of human imagination, is only too aware of how this evocative event would produce imaginative, fantasy-based constructs in all concerned, that would provide a far more complex saucer-interior than its definite but limited physical capabilities could. It would not be found any more than other objects are that vanish mysteriously during RSPK activity, if the strategy of the 'stage-management' directs otherwise. It was apported away, whatever that turns out to be . . .

Apports, when they arrive so mysteriously, are often hot. I have a report where a sheet of metal was so hot that the witnesses had to wait all afternoon for it to cool down before they could handle it. The river water was seen to bubble and boil when the object entered . . . The ESH maintains that geophysical fields – including those that earthlights, by definition, embody – are closely compatible with PK processes. Was this object a combination of geophysical field and 'PK assembly'? After all, the roaring that the object emitted has been encountered in other cases we have met involving earthlights (i.e., geosound).

Returning to the aspect of 'domestic UAPs', we saw that during the UFO 'flap' at Enfield, two luminous rings in a bedroom were reported in association with electrical malfunction. Such effects and phenomena are, once again, indicative of hot-spot activity and are the result of the action of electromagnetic fields on the domestic environment.

During the poltergeist activity at Enfield, the imprint of a human body in a bed was occasionally discovered, the occupants of the house being quite mystified by this. Such physical phenomena as this are due to automatic behaviour on their part; that is to say, prolonged irradiation in hot-spot locations produces epileptiform conditions in the occupants, who episodically undergo automatisms where they have no memory for a period of time, during which they carry out some routine action (this is the cause of 'missing time' of UFO lore).

After regaining awareness they are often startled by alterations in the environment that they have produced. This behaviour, in combination with direct field effects, gives a strong impressionistic feel of an invisible intelligence at work. However, it does seem possible that an intense electromagnetic field can support visual forms which have limited physical qualities (i.e., they can obscure objects and can be obscured by them). Consider the following bizarre account:

> Several years ago in the laboratory of the Rhodes Electrical Company, London, chief engineer Eastman was working on some high-tension wires forming a magnetic field in a dark room. Suddenly he observed a luminous blue sphere form above a nearby revolving dynamo. As the light became more intense, a form resembling a human hand appeared in the centre of the sphere. Eastman and his assistant, Harold Woodew, watched the phenomenon for several minutes before it faded away. The two men spent four days trying to recreate the conditions, and eventually obtained a human head, with indistinct features, white in colour, and revolving slowly. According to Vincent Gaddis, Eastman photographed it.[16]

This account provides an indication that electrical fields *can* act as a medium on to which images of the unconscious can be imprinted, giving them an external form with limited physical properties. Theorists have postulated a 'psi-substance' that the unconscious manipulates in 'staged productions', although the term 'substance' perhaps has implications of 'ectoplasm' and takes the concept further than the evidence warrants. The ESH proposes, instead, a 'psi-medium' of an electromagnetic nature, and it was Jacques Vallée who outlined the need for 'a medium into which the human imagination could be implemented' in *Passport to Magonia*.

In the above account, the categories of direct and organic field effects are blurred, as there seems to have been a *direct* effect upon the *organic* nervous system of one of the electrical engineers, *who seems to have been activated unconsciously into the role of a 'medium'*. This does seem to have been the case, because this engineer went on to induce a *similar* effect in another *similar* situation:

> at the Northern State Power Company in LaCrosse, Wisconsin, a standby boiler had just been put on line at maximum power, when a cloud began to form over the turbine. Fearing over-heating, the men checked and found that the machine was operating normally. They then saw appear in the cloud, 'as clearly as could be', the image of a woman lying on a couch. One of her arms was covered with jewels, and there were rings on her fingers. All of the men witnessed this for about twenty minutes before it faded out.[17]

Regarding these two accounts as pointers only, we should look in the direction of physical mediums who exhibit what have been identified as psychokinetic effects, which, it would seem, are a kind of electrical field emission. It may be that these emissions interact with the consciousness of the observers and in some way 'convince' their senses that what they perceive is physical. Something like this appears to take place in the production of apparitions which display physical aspects. But whatever processes are at work, they represent an important area of study (albeit a rare one) if we are to understand how some UFO witnesses are altered by the UAP emissions to produce CE realities with apparently objective existence.

More precisely, we need to look at those individuals who have not only stood the test of prolonged and close scrutiny, utilizing scientific methods, but have also produced the aspects we are interested in – light phenomena and entities.

We have seen that in many cases, lights – UAPs – have been associated with the appearance of entities. The Stonehenge, Junction 36 and Middleton cases are examples of this, and there are numerous others that demonstrate this UAP/entity link. Most, it would seem, are hallucinatory, but, incredible as it may appear, some may also have a physical basis for a temporary period, if the evidence regarding a very few exceptional physical mediums is to be believed.

Indridi Indridason: a physical medium?

The physical medium I have selected for examination – the Icelandic Indridi Indridason, who lived from 1883 to 1912 – fulfils all of the criteria mentioned. The remarkable phenomena produced in the presence of this man was equalled by the remarkable extent and conditions of investigation which continued for four years from 1905 to 1909. At one point in this medium's career, a completely new and detached building was constructed to house the activity and experiments which involved the élite of the scientific establishment of Iceland at various times.

The monograph describing the case was produced by the Society for Psychical Research and was co-authored by Loftur R. Gissurarson and Erlendur Haraldsson. It was published in January 1989. The introduction states:

> These phenomena, some of which occurred in full light, comprised movements and levitations of various objects, of furniture and of the medium himself, knocks on walls and clicks in the air, odour and light phenomena, materializations of human forms, 'invisible' playing of musical instruments, apports, direct voices often singing forcefully aloud, dematerializations, direct writing as well as automatic writing by the medium, and trance speech.

There is no doubt about the authenticity of the phenomena described, as, apart from the physical restrictions placed on Indridi, the effects that occurred could not have been produced even by a team of special effects technicians today, let alone in the early years of the century. Consider the relevant sections:

The Period of Light Phenomena

Two new phenomena started during the fourth seance in November, 1905. Clicks were heard in the air, as when fingers are snapped aloud, but with a sharper sound. These clicks were heard every evening for some time and they were heard to move all around the room ... Nielsson writes that they had 'obtained' peculiar cracking sounds in the air. These sounds moved around in the room in spite of Indridason's remaining quiet and in the same place.

These auditory effects have been included by the authors because they were associated with the light phenomena. This 'clicking' has been reported in a number of high-strangeness cases and it seems to be a field effect (magnetostrictive acoustics).[18] Magnetostrictive dimensional changes result from a flux in a magnetic field, when materials are either magnetized or demagnetized. If the change in magnetization is rapid, the resulting mechanical transient generates a sound wave. The Page Effect is the 'click' heard when this occurs.[19] The monograph continues:

The other phenomena comprised self-luminous 'lights' or light phenomena. The sitters first saw them manifested as flashing lights or light spots in the air or on the walls ... The lights appeared to be mostly 'tongue shaped'. During the evenings that followed, the flashes grew in strength and had different forms and colours — some were white and some were reddish ... One evening the sitters counted 58 appearances of lights during a single seance ...

They [the self-luminous lights] had somewhat different colours; some were very white; others were more reddish. Once ... 58 lights were counted. These lights were of various shapes; some of the lights were round, while others were oblong. They were different sizes: some were small, about an inch in diameter, but others were stripes of light around two to four feet long.

This report provides a good example of an optical effect shared by multiple witnesses. Once again, this effect, where flitting lights are seen, is produced when the brain is irradiated by magnetic fields (no ES status required). They are known as magnetophosphenes.

Also, such strange lighting effects are produced in a magnetic field, where reflected light becomes polarized, and produces the ellipses described. This is the Kerr magneto optic effect.

During one evening Nielsson counted more than 60 lights while Indridason was sitting in the middle of a circle of sitters. Tongues of light with different colours were seen at different locations in the room. The light spots developed into large flashes with a strong reddish tinge, which spread over one wall of a large room . . . later on the whole wall behind Indridason had become 'a glow of light' [i.e., a continuous mass of light].

There were a few times when a light spread on a whole wall behind the medium, which was twelve feet (3.7 m) wide and ten feet (3 m) high. Sometimes it looked like a sort of net of light, with circular meshes: slightly darker circles around bright flashes. Again the light was sometimes continuous, similar to a glow from a great fire. Those spreads of light were never as white as the small lights were, but were more reddish.

The authors then comment on two associated phenomena:

Often peculiar clicks were heard accompanying the lights. The clicks followed each other very fast (the Page Effect). Nielsson also reports that strong gusts of wind seldom failed to blow through the room before lights appeared. The wind was so strong that the hair waved on the sitters' heads and the pages of notebooks, lying open on their knees, flapped vigorously. Three years later Hannesson also observed a strong wind blowing across the hall . . . Indridason informed them that the gust 'had to accompany the light phenomena'.

Interestingly, inexplicable wind disturbed the bushes before the 'goblin' entity appeared in the Junction 36 case described earlier. This is a significant correlation. This magnetic phenomenon, mentioned earlier, is produced by paramagnetic forcing fields, where a non-ferrous body or material rotates or is otherwise disturbed when suddenly subjected to an intense magnetic field. It is known as a gyromagnetic phenomenon. The authors continue:

From our sources it seems that the purported spirit controls were attempting to produce materializations, the lights being a part of that procedure.

Such 'controls' seem to be separated-off parts of the 'medium's' unconscious, and appear subjectively, to be autonomous intelligences.

The light phenomena continued until eventually, on 6th and 7th December 1905, there appeared for the first time in the light, the full form of a man, whose identity was not recognized by those present. Kvaran describes this:

'On two evenings one could clearly see a man standing in the light. He was slightly above average height, muscular, well built, with broad shoulders. His back was turned towards us.'

Now one would naturally think that it was the medium that we saw in the light. I would assert that it was not. I was certain, at least the other time this vision was seen, that the medium was in the corner, crying out loudly, and screaming, some eight to ten feet from the place where we saw the man standing. The lights, as in all his major phenomena, seemed to cause him much pain. He began to shriek and scream when the lights were coming, and he continued to do so as long as the lights continued. They came in bursts, with small pauses in between, and during the pauses the medium was calm. After the seances he said he felt as if he had been beaten up.

Indridason was undoubtedly an electrical hypersensitive, his condition being induced by prolonged irradiation by geopathic stress from faults after an earlier major electrical event, such as lightning proximity. His pain at such seances is a typical reaction to ambient fields (from natural sources) to which he could 'tune in', re-radiate as a whole body effect and magnify. Such bodily pain is due to the stimulation of the pain receptors in the muscles. However, we are left with the perception of the entity.

We are faced with a number of options, which are by no means exhaustive:

1 The entity was a 'mass-hallucination';
2 The entity was an accomplice;
3 The entity was an objective image;
4 The entity was a physical object or objects assembled by PK;
5 The authors put it in although it did not occur for reasons unknown.

Before we examine these alternatives, there is an aspect that does not seem to be mentioned in the monograph at all – motive. If the phenomenon caused the 'medium' so much pain and discomfort, why did he continually subject himself to situations which induced or accentuated it? Briefly, why was Indridason doing this? This important aspect is not mentioned, but by reading the background material on his daily life, it seems that these phenomena occurred spontaneously wherever he was and they were frequently debilitating and disorientating. 'Things happened to him' as opposed to 'he was doing these things'. The spontaneous occurrences functioned as a disabling illness (like epilepsy might), and it seems evident that the organized seances, with their marginally spiritual overtones, were a way of *managing* what amounted to an illness. In fact, the monograph relates long periods of illness interspersed with seances organized by the Experimental Society in Reykjavik, Iceland. This, of course, correlates with the disabling effects of ES; and generally speaking, systemic dysfunction, somewhat understandably, is associated with acute psychism. To a large extent, this also links with Kathie Davis, who underwent alien abduction experiences. In fact, by examining the events that occurred with this Icelandic 'medium', CE4s are understandable within a psychic context.

Returning to the options presented above, we can only reasonably accept that the entity was an objective image, like many cases of apparitional sighting. There is the feeling that modern instrumentation could have provided essential insights. However, it does certainly appear that such phenomena were perceived. The implications for the UFO CE experience are far-reaching, and become more so as the phenomena in the Icelandic case are examined:

> During sittings in the large room, the smaller seance room started to become filled with very strong whitish light. In this light appeared a human being ... He first appeared between the curtains [curtains between the two adjoining rooms] in the small room and shouted, in a genuine and typical Copenhagen Danish accent, *'Ka' De se mig?'* [Can you see me?]

Very early in the occurrences involving entities, an absurd quality, so typical of high-strangeness encounters, begins to appear:

> Then Jensen became visible in the light. In the New Year he showed himself in the living room, where we sat. He was dressed in a white, very fine robe, which reached down to the floor. The light radiated from him and we saw him in various locations in the room. Sometimes he stood very close to one of us. Once he stood on a sofa and behind his shoulders was something like a tiny sun on the wall. This was a very beautiful sight. Sometimes he stood on the chair-back behind the medium ... He could not stay more than a few moments each time, but he showed himself several times at each seance ... on one occasion Jensen appeared eleven times in one hour ... Jensen appeared and stood upright on a sofa, which was next to Indridason's chair. The light which radiated from this materialized being seemed quite bright but somehow it did not penetrate far into the room, with the result that only people sitting closest to the entity could be seen in the light. On one occasion Jensen stood behind the chair in which Indridason was sitting. In the light from the materialized being sitters could clearly see Indridason in a trance state ... this extraordinary visitor could not be visible for more than a few seconds each time. When he had finished showing himself he tried to touch a few sitters with his hand, arm or foot, and *he always allowed us to touch his materialized body before he dematerialized it again.* [my italics]

Surprising as it may seem, some apparitions can touch and be touched – for example, the 'Grandfather Bull' case.[20] However, the point here is that psychically induced CE experiences could not only involve multiple witnessing, *but a tactile dimension that can also be shared*, making the reality indistinguishable from a physical encounter.

Then follows, from a field-theory point of view, some of the most intriguing details about these entity appearances:

> it always appeared as a luminous, beautiful light-pillar, just above the average height of a human figure and slightly broader. Inside this light we saw a human form but it was not clear enough, for example, for the facial expression to be distinctly seen. This light-pillar was very white but with a little tinge of blue. It was very luminous but did not flicker. However, it did not radiate much light. We saw the medium when the light-pillar stood near where he was sitting in a trance although otherwise there was darkness in the room . . . The appearance of the light-pillar lasted only very briefly each time and was always accompanied by a low buzzing sound . . . Jensen often touched the sitters when he materialized . . . The light-pillar had a colour very similar to moonlight but was translucent at the edges *where folds could be seen as on clothes*. [my italics]

This effect of bright sources radiating very little light is mentioned frequently in the UFO-study literature, as is the acoustic phenomenon of 'buzzing'. It occurs in association with magnetic and electrical fields, and its occurrence with such regularity in association with the 'materializations' and 'light-pillar' is indicative of their presence. It is a phenomenon created by magnetostrictive acoustics. The type of light described is typical of air ionization, which occurs naturally above fault-lines.[21] Such air zones may be columnar, circular or curtain-like (folded as seen in the aurora borealis) according to the form of the field. An observation by Dr C. W. Smith is a further indicator that an electrical field was present:

> As soon as an object is placed within an electric field, the field behaves rather like a curtain and *drapes itself in close folds* [my italics] over the object leaving a clear space underneath. The field so folded can reach values up to a hundred times that of the ambient, unperturbed field.

The monograph continues:

> Jensen seemed to be of average height but 'hardly as thick' as an average man. His figure did not emit much light . . . at one seance forty people simultaneously saw Jensen appear a number of times . . . A little later during this same seance another being appeared, in the doorway, but only the upper part of its body was visible.

This is the 'abbreviated form' aspect that occurs with apparitions and UFO-related entities.

The identity of these figures was the traditional one of spirits of the dead, and the general context of the seances was within a spiritualist framework. How else could the witnesses or, for that matter, the 'medium' make sense of the phenomena? However, if we strip away the cultural overlay, it is evident that under certain unusual conditions, which include the constitution of the 'medium', we are left with the unexpected conclusion that entities can be induced by the UI of this 'medium', with selective physical characteristics, and seem to be able to be induced by the imaging functions of the brain within an electromagnetic field that enables witnesses to interact with them. Such phenomena could usefully be termed emergent consciousness effects. It is this fact, whatever the mechanisms involved, that facilitates the proposal that UFO-related realities are also produced in this way.

Light phenomena/entity correlation

Returning to our initial enquiry, we can see that this link between light phenomena and high-strangeness entity events is confirmed by its occurrence in a non-UFO psychic context. The concept of hallucination caused by field emission has been extended to include PK influences, and the extreme cases of this found in the study of physical 'mediums' provide further evidence that an unknown, but PK-related range of processes are involved. These seem to be able to influence a group of witnesses, causing a convergence of perceptions which result in a 'consensus reality'. It may be that each witness is affected by a sphere of influence, and becomes linked into a central frequency, so that they all share the same or similar perceptions.

It is relevant to note that the 'miniature sun' is a 'domestic UAP' of some type, and it would, in an 'apparitional spaceman' context, be interpreted as an alien technological device or the effect of such a device.

Appendix extract

The monograph about Indridason contains a wealth of related phenomena that cannot be described in detail due to the limited space of this section. Therefore, it is worth reproducing an extract from the appendix to act as a summary of this material:

Light Phenomena
Fire-flashes or fire-balls

Small lights, stars or 'phosphoric balls' in the air
Luminous clouds
Small and large light-flashes on the walls
Light-spreads, as large as 10 to 12 feet
Luminosity of objects, clothes, letters, etc.
Luminosity of medium's head, hands, etc.
Luminosity of materializations

Materializations
Only shadow/shape of apparent materializations seen
Only hand or foot is seen
Complete materialized human being is seen
Sitters touch materialized fingers
Sitters touch materialized limbs/trunks that do not recede
Monster-like 'animal' is seen

It is of the greatest relevance to note that many of the above phenomena have been reported in the literature on URE. While not *all* witnesses produce *all* of these phenomena, it is evident that there is the potential within the human system for phenomena of this order to become manifest. In some UFO-entity descriptions we find the almost obligatory 'one-piece suit', but like the entities described here, there are also descriptions of flowing white robes. The glowing columns of light that contain unearthly beings are also a reoccurring feature, as are the range of field-related luminous effects and the sudden and brief appearances and disappearances. In fact, time and again UFO witnesses speak of the phenomena also 'switching off like a light bulb', just as the seance sitters describe.

The UAP explanation

This chapter is not, of course, meant to be an exhaustive study of UAPs; instead, it has been compiled to extend the parameters of transient aerial phenomena. However, I cannot overstress how important the study of this class of phenomena is, if UFOs are to be understood.

UAPs are the physical objects that register on radar, are seen by airline pilots and that appear to pace planes and cars as 'flying saucers'. They are the physical aspect that creates ground traces, broken branches, witness burns, visions and 'structured craft'. The nature of the radiation emitted by some of them facilitates not only consciousness-altering effects, but it is able to change the physiology of witnesses so that their relationship with physical reality is altered for good (i.e., they act as a major electrical event; an important step towards electrical hypersensitivity/multiple allergy – the medium's complaint). Also, the nature of their energy is such that it is able to interface with the human unconscious (UI) so that its autonomous functions are enhanced to a degree and quality not met with in any other area. When this occurs in specific individuals with specific constitutions (i.e., ES/ESP-conducive) the UAP can take on characteristics of apparent intelligence. If this is coupled with the ability of the unconscious, so activated, to organize not only the energetic material and behaviour of the UAP, but ambient physical materials, a phenomenon is produced that is incorporated into a presentation of an alien spacecraft. It is a key concept that such alien themes are selected by the unconscious intelligence as they reflect how the human system apprehends electro-magnetic fields which impinge upon it from the environment, as externally alien to it.

A phenomenon that represents a link between mind and reality in this way must, surely, be of interest to science.

The potential for the production of this type of phenomena coexists with a wide range of *direct* field effects that can be identified as such and reproduced under controlled conditions. Therefore, a re-evaluation of 'classic' UFO cases is overdue in the light of the UAP phenomenon, which includes ball-lightning, plasma-vortexes, earthlights, electroforms, etc. This latter type is an innovation based on the formation of ball-lightning in ambient fields (i.e., a similar process must take place in artificially produced fields).

Radiation

To conclude: it is evident that UAPs, especially earthlights, can emit a range of radiation types, predominantly, although not exclusively, in the non-ionizing bands. They include: visible light, ultra-violet, infra-red, radio waves (including microwaves). As a general guide, an electrical field refers to a charge which is static and a magnetic field to one which is in motion. Both, however, can induce not only altered states of consciousness in the human organism, but, more to the point, altered bodily states.

6 The Altered State and the Close-Encounter Experience

Energies external to us are given form by one's subconscious. I might be walking home one night and pass through an electromagnetic field of sorts, and this might register to my psyche as a hideosity with green skin and bulbous eyes, or, conversely, as a radiant and beautiful woman with bulbous eyes. We shouldn't underestimate the mind's capacity for image-making. We translate energies into pictures every time we dream. (Graham Fletcher, occult magician, Brighton, England)

Trance states and the close-encounter experience

The light phenomena and entities that appeared during Indridason's allergic trance states in Iceland are an indicator that whatever special conditions were involved, this state is closely associated with them. Could it be that similar states occur during the CE experience, and that the witness is the origin of similar entities, albeit in appropriate guise? This is the proposal that has been suggested, and we now need to look at the behaviour and experience of witnesses to see if we can identify similar states.

Returning to the account of Indridason's case, there is an important clue that indicates which aspect of CEs could be identified with allergic trance states. Among the notables from the Icelandic Establishment who attended the seances was Hallgrimur Sveinsson, the Bishop of Iceland. He asked for seances to be held in his own house, which they then were from time to time. As with most 'mediums', there was the convention of 'controls'. These purported spirit entities were interpreted as 'speaking through' Indridason while he was in a trance. It is astonishing how aspects such as these were (and still are) readily accepted as a way of making sense of 'what is going on'. These 'control personalities' acted as intermediaries, or guardians, while Indridason was in a somnambulistic trance state. They took over his functioning, and were depicted as guiding him generally, at which 'they' were quite efficient (but were parts of his own system in actuality).

This separation of personality and mental functioning, or similar divisions of the self, is called disassociation, and it would appear that CE witnesses become disassociated during a 'time-lapse'. Typically, this is where the witness will be out at night, see a light in the sky, look at it for a while, and then, with no sense of transition, find themselves some distance away, driving or walking. Usually, they later find that there is a period of time for which they cannot account – a void gradually filled by apparent 'flashbacks' of alien abduction, sometimes with a 'medical examination' feature. These 'flashbacks' are a different version of 'breaking the dream', where something trivial happens during the day that suddenly makes one recall the dream.

However, if the witness is experiencing an internal drama involving aliens and a medical examination during the 'time-lapse', and they are in a trance state, how could they walk safely along the road, avoid traffic or even drive their car? Such automatisms have already been touched upon and the account of Indridason taking part in seances at the bishop's house mentions a small detail that indicates that this is possible:

> The sittings were held in the bishop's library, and there the different phenomena occurred with even greater ease. Sometimes the control personalities brought Indridason, *walking in a trance state* directly from the seance room to the bishop's home. [my italics]

This is an indication that an 'abductee' could appear to function normally while in the altered state that facilitates their experiences. We saw earlier how an adolescent could drive a car for a considerable distance in a somnambulistic state and the 'abduction trance' allows a similar degree of functioning. This is due to disassociation, and if we look at the occurrence of this in non-UFO or psychic contexts, it is clear that it is actually closely associated with imaginative conditions:

> 'disassociation', the clinical term, is all too often regarded as something that needs to be cured. Psychiatrists tend not to realize its extraordinary range. Professor Liam Hudson has noted . . . its influence on our memory and our personalities; they do not appreciate its relationship with our dreams, waking fantasies and 'imaginatively conceived actions.'[1]

Trance does not mean inactivity or inaction; that is to say, there is a division in the 'abductee's' consciousness between the visionary state and the functional state, where the subject will be experiencing 'abduction' internally, while in actual fact he or she will 'carry on as normal' with routine low-level activities, such as wandering around a park, driving a car or sitting in a chair. That this is possible is further supported by research into the nature of epilepsy:

> Post-ictal automatism is the phenomenon in which a person can undertake some fairly complex act, such as undressing and putting themselves to bed, of which they have no subsequent memory.[2]

It is clear that subjects can easily lose lengthy periods of time, surprising as it may seem. The ES state, however, can produce a type of pseudo-epilepsy, or 'blank-out', without convulsions, that can be triggered by radio waves or the frequencies emitted from fluorescent light. Consider an incident that happened to an ES 'medium'.

J lived near the campus of Reading University, England, in the early 1970s. One afternoon, before picking her son up from school, she decided to stroll around the campus's spacious park-like grounds. Near the physics block, she walked along the banks of a small river. Passing a stone bridge to her left, she was stopped in her tracks by a strange wall that suddenly appeared in front of her. It was made up of pale strands of a cotton-like material. Totally bemused, J parted the strands like a curtain and passed through. On the other side was an identical 'strand-wall'. Slipping through this, she was immediately confronted by three identical beings dressed in one-piece suits. She was both startled and repulsed by their appearance, as they all had human-sized lizard heads, complete with scaly, folded skin and reptilean eyes.

Rather than continue with this 'abduction' account, it is significant to realize that the witness's conscious memory is quite different from this account, as this narrative was 'recalled' under hypnosis. All J remembers is an intent to 'kill time' in the campus grounds before picking up her son, then calling at the school only to find it closed and quiet apart from the Head who told her that her son was with a friend's mother. School had finished two hours previously and the staff were concerned by J's non-appearance.

The hypnosis was carried out years later, after J had met an investigator who realized the 'significance' of her 'time-lapse'. Such lengthy breaks in consciousness are usually interpreted as a sign of malfunction of some kind, as Inglis points out. However, the UI evidently capitalizes on these 'voids' and uses them as sensory noise-free areas of creativity, and even creates *them*. It may do this by influencing the witness's decisions subliminally, so that the person enters an area of electromagnetic exposure. The witness (or, more accurately, the percipient) involved in this lizard-alien 'abduction', is a 'medium' and, as such, is prone to spontaneous disassociated states. It would seem that, like Indridason, they 'happened to her' rather than being initiated by her. Just such a state occurred while she was asleep, or, at least, in a sleep situation.

Witnesses: CH and partner J
Location: George Street, Reading
Date: 5 August 1985

That night the couple retired to bed as usual and slept soundly until CH, for some reason, suddenly awoke. He found that a small ball of light was hovering in the air at the foot of his bed. It shone 'with a glow as soft and pale as the moon'. He had experienced numerous unusual phenomena at night and was calm and collected. He then turned to wake his partner beside him and shook her gently at first, but she seemed to be totally unconscious rather than simply asleep and did not respond, falling back limply. He felt panicky at first but then, for some reason, angry, grabbing at her hair and shaking her head vigorously. Still getting no response, he glared at the ball of light and shot an angry thought at it. It immediately gave off 'what might have been a cross between the whistle of a kettle with a faint human cry mixed in' and expanded to about three or four feet (1–1.25 m) in diameter. It swiftly shot across the room and out of the door, despite the fact that it was closed. CH could see the glow of it coming through the door, and assumed that it had come to rest in the passage outside. Then, waves of tiredness hit him and he was 'compelled to lay back down'.

In the morning, J was panic-stricken as they found that the right side of her face was red, sore and swollen, and the eye on that side watered uncontrollably. Later in the day, dead skin peeled off, but the soreness was a little more bearable. The next day, 'it was as though it had never happened'.[3]

Analysis

If this event had occurred in an outdoor setting, it would have been classified as a UFO encounter plain and simple, and it is indicative of how context influences our perception of such events. CH's perception, however, seems to have been hallucinatory.

J, being a 'medium' and ES herself, would have reacted strongly to a field exposure in the way that CH described. A 'direct hit' from a transmitting antenna as a reflected ground wave would have put her in the unconscious or 'zombie'-like state that CH found her in. She would have reacted allergically. If this seems like an assumption, remember that she was a 'medium', and the description of her symptoms indicates that she was in an induced 'blank-out' state similar to the one that she had been in during her 'lizard-alien' experience on the riverbank.

The allergic reaction would have produced precisely the facial dermal irritation described, as a response to the field exposure.[4] CH, being in close association with J, would have become 'tuned' to her 'frequency' and would have become ES himself to some degree. (He did suddenly develop mediumistic abilities after becoming involved in a 'spirit manifestation' induced by J.) His inappropriate anger and overwhelming waves of tiredness (already affecting J to an acute level) are both systemic symptoms of field exposure which can be found in the biomagnetics literature.[5] The fact that CH 'saw' the BOL both pass and shine through the closed door is indicative of an electrical or EM field, which *can*, of course, pass through solid materials. We must also be aware that the BOL may have been entirely hallucinatory, rather than a hypersensitive perception of an electromagnetic form, as such hallucinations are reported by epileptics – they are known as visual seizures. However, such neurological phenomena have been due to irradiation by external fields, because the skull is entirely transparent to them.

However, this event cannot be taken as 'merely' being symptomatic of electrical sensitivity, because, as with many experiences like this, there is a meaningful symbolic content from the unconscious: skin-shedding is a growth and rebirth symbol, and lizards emerge anew through this process . . .[6]

From the medical literature on ES, each subject has their own specific EM frequency that will cause them to 'blank-out' – the sort of pseudo-epilepsy mentioned earlier – and the same frequency may have no effect on another ES individual, that is, each person's 'blank-out' frequency is very specific.[7] Of course, not every 'medium' so zapped will produce external light phenomena; in the case of J, her 'lizard aliens' seemed to have been purely internal. Also, not all 'blank-outs' are mediumistic trances: they may be simple oblivion. This is a key factor in making trance states so conducive to unconscious activation; that is to say, they exclude sensory noise completely.

This important aspect will be examined shortly, but before then, take account of the following relevant report in relation to 'pseudo-epilepsy':

> In 1970 we were involved in a case in Forest Hills, New York, in which a 12-year-old girl began to experience hallucinosis followed by mental black-outs and many of the common symptoms of jacksonian seizures. She underwent extensive medical and psychiatric examinations and the

attending doctors discovered she often blacked out when in the presence of fluorescent lighting. Their rather far-out conclusion was that the girl's brain was 'tuned' to the same wavelength as such lights and their radiation directly interfered with her mental processes. The girl frequently saw, and conversed with, beings whom she described as resembling Indians. She saw these apparitions in the family kitchen and in school. Fluorescent lighting was used in both places. Interestingly enough, her mother also saw these apparitions on a number of occasions, but claimed they were diminutive. The girl said they were of normal size and form. The family has now moved, convinced that their old home was 'haunted'. The girl's seizures have diminished since she now avoids rooms with fluorescent illumination.[8]

From this report, we can see that the doctors involved were not so 'far-out' as Keel supposes, and electromagnetic 'tuning' *can* occur with specific frequencies, just as CH became 'tuned' by emissions from J.[9] However, fluorescent lights emit a range of frequencies and not only light. Many ES subjects feel uncomfortable with them. This case, therefore, supports the idea that epileptiform states can be produced by external electromagnetic fields.

Considering this, there is a good chance that on that fateful day in the campus grounds when J was out walking, she 'met her frequency' as it were. This caused her to 'switch off' or 'change channel' from the functional one of receiving direct perceptual information from her immediate surroundings, to receiving internal hallucinatory material and imagery based on a memory of her surroundings. During such periods, the unconscious would be totally dominant; that is to say, it occupies the 'perceptual screen', and it can create as outlandish a scenario as it wishes. This freedom of activity often continues after CE experiences, and it is typical for witnesses to report vivid super-real dreams that they feel are connected with their encounter. This extension of the 'alien vision' into dreams is an indicator that the experience is internally perceived, because once the unconscious is activated, it 'over-runs' into other states that are similarly oblivious to external stimuli and sensory noise, such as sleep; such as the hypnotic state . . .

The hypnotic state (or hypnoid state as it is also known) and the trance state overlap to a large degree. Regression hypnosis, employed in order to retrieve memories during the 'time-lapse', is also characterized as being a low sensory noise condition where the unconscious is induced, it is thought, to give up its memories. In this situation, the unconscious is more inclined to take the initiative and capitalize on the hypnoid condition to produce an internal dramatization of contact with aliens, rather than operate passively as an accessed memory-bank. This is particularly so when such 'regression' takes place in an expectant setting which includes UFO researchers, and especially when the hypnosis is carried out by a UFO investigator-turned-hypnotist. Hypnosis recreates and matches the essential conditions of the 'blank-out', and experiences described during these sessions will either be internal visionary material (like asking someone to recall their dreams), or perceptions of external phenomena they or the electrical field had produced – just as Indridason glimpsed his – or a mixture of the two. Another option is for the 'abductee' to create an experience 'on-the-spot' during the hypnosis session, due to this matching of oblivious sensory-noise-free states.

An example of this was an 'abduction' by seasoned investigator and ex-editor of *UFO Times* (BUFORA), Mike Wooten. His experience demonstrates the possibilities that can be engendered by hypnosis. He was hypnotized and asked to visualize being on a deserted road where a light came down out of the sky and hovered a short distance from him. Nothing else was suggested. He was then asked to 'take it from there'. There emerged a full-blown 'abduction' experience where he vividly 'relived' a confrontation with aliens in which they met him beside a field where their 'craft' had landed. They took him on to the 'ship', where they placed him on a 'table'. It was during this period that he suddenly felt powerful jolts of electricity vibrating through his body, much to the surprise of the investigators and hypnotist, not to mention Mike himself! It is true that this 'abductee' had an extensive knowledge of 'abduction' experiences, and no doubt it was this that precipitated his experience; but the vivid 'reliving' of an imaginary experience, complete with strong physical sensations, demonstrates conclusively how such 'abduction' realities can be produced by the unconscious during hypnosis.

Inevitably, this throws into question the use of hypnosis to retrieve 'time-lapse' memories, especially in the many cases where the investigators carry out the hypnosis sessions themselves, as very little training is required to hypnotize someone. These people have no clinical experience whatsoever, and the first time they conduct hypnosis sessions they try to detect 'memories' of spaceships and aliens. They have not experienced any 'normal' non-UFO control sessions to find out the effects of hypnosis. It is comparable to allowing a novice pilot to fly an experimental prototype.

Sensory noise and the altered state in close encounters

It has been suggested that the CE witness would be able to project his or her unconsciously produced entities in some cases. This brings into play a shift of perception from entirely inner visionary material to a perceptually altered outer environment. We need to consider imagery that is internally generated but superimposed on the environment, such as the 'ghost spacemen' in the Middleton case. However, we need also to consider imagery that is internally generated, but incorporates images of the environment into an entity or UFO encounter: such as the small wooded area that both Dorne and Lee perceived as they approached Stonehenge that later was found not to exist. Why should an encounter require sections of phantom scenery included along with an alien or UFO? The answer seems to be something to do with controlling sensory noise.

In order to understand this, an analogy using TV reception and a video recording needs to be explored. When we go about our daily lives, we are taking in information from our immediate surroundings, and we make sense of the details from our perceptions of our environment: we have built up a catalogue of what we will probably find in our environment, in our memory. This is like the reception of pictures on a television set: we can look at a list of programmes and anticipate seeing what is going to appear. However, if instead of receiving the usual 'transmissions' from the outside (reflected light, sound waves, etc.) through our eyes and ears, a sort of psychic video recording of the sights, sounds and smells of our surroundings is thrust into our consciousness without us realizing it, we will regard this recording as reality. This idea has already been illustrated earlier with the analogy using a security system with TV monitors to explain 'notional duplicates'. In fact, the 'phantom scenery' is an example of a 'notional duplicate'. This concept of the 'psychic video' is based on the same principle and the two ideas and processes overlap.

To extend this analogy, suppose when the 'psychic video' is playing, we keep getting parts of the programmes from the TV station cutting in and interfering with the picture. We would want to control this outside interference, so that the recorded images are untainted by the 'real' programmes. We might notice that the TV transmissions break through into the recording especially when they are showing a bright light or a loud noise in the programme, and the rest of the time the transmitted images and sounds are very faint in the background, just behind the recorded images and sound. These interfering TV station transmissions are the equivalent of sensory noise. I am suggesting that images from the unconscious, of UFO realities, apparitions and 'notional duplicates', are like a video recording that plays though our senses just as dreams do, to give a vivid sensation of reality; but, in order for this to occur successfully, stimuli from the outside, known as sensory noise, have to be controlled. When we are asleep or in a trance state, this is no problem because our sensory apparatus is shut down. This is why we dream while we are asleep.

Our unconscious is dominant and fills our 'perceptual screen'. The same thing happens in sensory-deprivation tanks, where sensory noise is light, tactile sensations and smell, as well as sound. But when we are awake, this sensory noise has to be controlled in some other way, for if it intrudes into the altered state, the witness will 'snap out of it' and revert to normal. This is why seance situations often have to be held in darkness. That is to say, *the altered state is unstable and needs to be maintained by strategies that exclude sensory noise.* When these strategies fail, and sensory noise causes the sudden breakdown of the altered state, witnesses find that apparitions or 'aliens' and their 'craft' suddenly vanish before their eyes as they switch back to their normal state. So often witnesses state that 'the object vanished as if a light had been switched off'. Identical conditions relating to altered states apply to sightings of apparitions:

> Anyone who has studied in depth accounts of apparitional experiences will have noticed that very often the act of looking away from an apparition, even for a moment, causes the figure to disappear. The reason for this is that any such act results in a change of consciousness. It is now generally accepted that apparitions are experienced in what are termed altered states of consciousness.[10]

Returning to the question about how Dorne and Lee's 'phantom scenery' contributed to the control of sensory noise, the following explanation is compiled according to an approach developed over some years and applied to numerous cases in their analysis. It would seem, from their description of events, that the UAP emerged from behind this 'phantom scenery' and was almost obscured by it at first. As the UAP emits light in addition to other field frequencies, this would act as sensory noise at a crucial point when their altered state was in the early stages of becoming established. The field that it emitted would, of course, be invisible, and it would have acted upon the cortex or temporal lobe as they approached. If the BOL was fully visible at that early stage, paradoxically, one wavelength – visible light – would have undermined the establishment of their altered states. There was no cover for this huge light in the open landscape (as was discovered later), so in order to accelerate and ensure the alteration to their consciousness, a 'phantom' copse of trees was induced by their unconscious by creating a hallucination. Their unconscious would be aware of the field presence as they approached the UAP, as it would have been activated by it, but the sensory noise in the form of light needed to be controlled, hence the apparitional trees. In case you doubt if a hallucination could obscure anything at all, remember the catalogue of characteristics of apparitions included the ability to obscure objects and be obscured by them:

They are seen in normal perspective, both when stationary and when moving; they may be reflected in mirrors, may obscure other objects and be obscured by other objects, and in other ways they fit into the physical environment as physical objects do.[11]

The implications of this explanation of sensory noise control mean that some degree of control of, or link with, the UAP by the witnesses' unconscious existed, and the argument for this is contained in the signal-link concept. Another concept devised to explain the function of separate elements within the encounter experience is the 'notional duplicate'. This is really another more specific form of the metachoic experience, which is a term applied to phenomena like the out-of-body experience, where a reality is produced supposedly consisting of hallucinatory images based on memories. From reading the journals of R. A. Monroe, it seems as if the OBE is more a *mixture* of hallucination and straight observation, that is, using the previous analogy, TV transmissions *and* video recordings. The Stonehenge CE experience was also made up of this mixture of internal and external perceptions (see case histories in the final chapter).

Reality replacement in close-encounter experiences

From witnesses' descriptions of the encounter environment, it is clear that the unconscious produces simplified images of their surroundings that merge with their perceptions of the 'real thing'. In a report by investigator/researcher Ahmed Jamaludin on 'abduction' experiences, he describes features of the witnesses' perceived environment at the onset of their encounter:

The situational condition before abduction refers to the normality or abnormality of the environment. An abnormal situation is where the witness reports any of the three following conditions: Strange Total Silence, Presence of Green Mist, an Abnormally Straight Road.[12]

All three of these conditions relate to the control of sensory noise, either visual or auditory, and they are produced either by direct field effects or the effect of fields upon the brain, thereby activating unconscious mechanisms.

Such perceptions as these are frequently reported by witnesses driving at night, and occur at the onset of a strange experience involving apparently real aliens and their 'craft'. They are often accompanied by mechanical and electrical disturbances to their car, which can be identified as typical field effects. They often report that a familiar stretch of road looks different, which adds to the trend towards undermining the rational functions of the brain, as it creates a confused state. It is a hallmark of the onset of an altered state and the introduction of notional duplicates into their consciousness by the unconscious. Again, this is to control sensory noise by replacing direct perception with an internal mental replica.

Perceptual recycling and 'memory loops' in the close encounter

A replacement reality based on memory implies that the unconscious reaches into its stock of 'scenery at night' images and 'plays' them through the perceptual apparatus. Such recordings (for that is precisely what they are) often have the 'sound track' missing or they are made up of the same short bland sequence played again and again like a loop of film. This is the Randles 'OZ factor' effect and the 'abnormally straight road' that Jamaludin reports respectively. However, other 'notional duplicates' are more sophisticated and replace quite lengthy periods of time and surroundings and create an atmosphere imbued with a strange other-worldliness, as we saw with the Stonehenge encounter after the witnesses had driven through the bands of fog.

Another discrepancy in reality that indicates that a lengthy period of time and environment was duplicated at Stonehenge was the fact that the heel-stone that Dorne thinks she touched could not possibly have been reached because of the real height of the fencing around the monument, and the distance of the stone from the fence. This is somewhat specific and it cannot be a duplication based on a 'stock of recordings' as it were. From this, and other examples, it is evident that the unconscious uses information (visual and tactile in this case) based on memories of perceptions that occurred a few seconds previously; that is to say, the unconscious has a long-term stock of recorded material (long-term memories) that it draws upon, and a short-term 'float' of perceptual material built up on the spot and constantly replenished. Memories of the environment need not be long-term ones, but they can be taken from what the eyes, for example, have taken in a second or two before. This is the 'memory loop' concept, and it implies that lengthy encounter experiences are a mixture of direct perceptions that are then recycled immediately in the 'psychic video'. This would make for a more sophisticated 'reality replacement' which would be very difficult to distinguish from the 'real thing', even if the witnesses were aware of it.

Extending this conceptual model, a theory can be presented to explain the 'quasi-conscious' states in which CE witnesses and 'traditional' apparitional confrontations occur. If this recycling of external perceptions takes place instantaneously, a reality can be presented consisting of a high proportion of internal or 'video' material, into which the unconscious could intrude imagery readily; that is to say, because the neuronal signals to the eyes are already engaged by the imaging part of the brain, further signals carrying fantasy or mythic images of spaceships and aliens, or spirits of the dead, could be fed into the perceptual system more easily. This would be how apparitions or aliens of spaceships appear to fit in with their surroundings: for example, they negotiate furniture, fences and trees; that is to say, an entity need not be depicted in isolation, but it can be integrated with the environment. This would, of course, be a particularly convincing portrayal and it represents a sophisticated encounter.

It is relevant to note at this point, that in setting out the parameters for apparitions, Andrew MacKenzie of the Society for Psychical Research notes of apparitions:

> They make adjustments to their physical surroundings and to physically embodied people, in much the same ways in which physically present people would do.[13]

Sensory flooding and the close-encounter experience

The condition of total silence, where all the ambient sounds are absent and a feeling of timeless isolation occurs, can be tracked down to field exposure effects. Persinger's experiments with magnetic fields on the temporal lobe have duplicated an OZ-factor-like condition in the laboratory. However, this eerie silence is also markedly produced by the electrical stimulation of the reticular portion of the mid- and fore-brain. This effect can be induced by exposure to seismic radiation, and at the same time, this field 'turns on' unconscious activity. Occurring at the onset of CE experiences (and other psychic events), it, of course, eliminates sensory noise. This hallucination can easily be shared, due to the fact that different areas of the brain are sensitive to specific field frequencies, and the irradiation of two or more subjects by the same field induces the same perceptual effects.

However, in many cases, instead of an absence of stimuli, the witness, or at that stage, the witness-to-be, is suddenly bombarded with an intense sound or bright light or inescapable pungent smell. These stimuli have the effect of undermining the consciousness and 'knocking out' the rational faculties momentarily; field exposure is taking place simultaneously. These stimuli are an aspect of this exposure; that is to say, by the simultaneous onslaught of a field and an intense sound, for example, the conscious mind is suddenly 'flooded' and rational, function-related thinking is eliminated at a stroke. A comparable situation would be if you were concentrating on counting the number of words on this page and without your knowing, someone switched on the stereo, so that it suddenly blared out. If at that point you were subjected to a burst of seismic electricity, the effect would be complete and you would enter an altered state, and be completely removed, mentally speaking, from the original rational task.

In many cases of 'sensory flooding', the stimulus is geosound which is produced in the earth's strata. It is electrical activity underground – the equivalent of a thunderstorm in the atmosphere. Geosound can be an electronic-sounding squeal, or an intense buzzing like a swarm of bees.[14] Geosound is often accompanied by sulphurous or 'electrical' smells which may be due to an aerosol effect from the strata itself, or internally produced stimulation of the limbic area of the brain.[15] Other geosounds are listed in the Mercalli table, including rustling noises, clicks, raps, roaring sounds like a plane taking off, sounds like horses galloping in the distance. No doubt, these effects are mistaken for experiences of retrocognition (experiencing events from the past, such as battle scenes) where the individual reports sounds of a Roman army marching, etc. If such percipients are also affected by seismic radiation, these external stimuli are incorporated into the altered state to act as suggestions to the unconscious.[16] The percipient may also 'see' the Roman soldiers. This highly suggestible state is very similar to the hypnotic state where anything the hypnotist says – or in some cases, *thinks* – becomes the basis for an internal reality. This has been alluded to as the 'community of sensation' effect. However, Russian experiments have shown that the hypnotized subject can pick up information from the hypnotist unconsciously.[17] Again, this throws the practice of regression hypnosis into doubt.

The incorporation of stimuli into the close-encounter experience

This is an important phenomenon that we have all experienced at some time. Although it need not involve encounter experiences, it has direct implications for them. When we are asleep and dreaming, the perceptual apparatus is inwardly directed and it is oblivious to low-level stimuli, such as sound and light. However, if for example the sound level is raised, it intrudes into the consciousness as sensory noise and we wake up. Sometimes if these external stimuli are at a median level, they are perceived by the sleeper and incorporated into the dream. In dreams a ringing alarm clock can become a fire-alarm; sunlight playing on the face can become a fire; street sounds can become cries of distress and so on.[18] The CE that is an internal visionary experience – or those parts of it that are – can do the same with external lights and sounds, and, even more potently, fields. An ES individual exposed to a variety of fields and frequencies from a transmitting antenna can transpose such fields into perceptions of alien activity, for that is how the brain interprets such fields. Field stimulation to Broca's area of the brain would induce the apparently 'telepathic' perception of words and meaning from an 'alien entity'.[19] In fact, this is an almost obligatory aspect of encounters, where the witness reports that they 'heard words in my head' from an alien 'confronting' them. This would also explain why such 'communications' are almost always in the language of the witness. Other examples may be where the ES witness reacts allergically to the field, which may induce a blotchy rash on the face and neck. This may be perceived as 'a laser beam from the underside of the craft struck me in the face'.

Also, in such an altered state, mundane stimuli, such as aircraft lights, can appear as 'an oval craft surrounded by red, green and white lights flashing in sequence', or something similar. Returning to dreams: we may experience internal stimuli, such as stomach pain, as a blow to the abdomen. Sometimes such images symbolize something that is worrying us and the physical and emotional are fused into a single image sequence, especially as such things are often psychosomatic anyway.[20] Likewise, it is also evident that the systemic symptoms of field exposure can be incorporated into 'abduction' scenarios. A specific example of this relates to a symptom which is caused by frequencies found during seismic activity:

Metallic taste in mouth; usually associated with multiple metal fillings (mercury amalgam) in teeth due to electrical activity in metal/saliva interface.[21]

Budd Hopkins describes a regression hypnosis session where Kathie Davis recalls an alien abduction experience:

Next she twisted in obvious discomfort as she described two thin probes pressing up into her nostrils ... She cleared her throat, swallowing uneasily as she felt something drip at the back of her throat. It tasted bitter and metallic, she told us later, 'like blood'.[22]

In the light of this witness's earlier exposure to seismic tremors, such 'revelations' as this are more likely to be the result of a static charge built up in her saliva and metal fillings, rather than blood from an internal wound caused by aliens inserting a probe in order to monitor her in some way. Such conclusions say more about those who draw them than they do about the state of the witness or alien activity. Earlier, Kathie Davis heard an example of geosound, which was the loud localized 'roaring'. It was accompanied by symptoms and observations straight out of the Mercalli table, which describe the effects of seismic activity. This witness, according to the description given by Hopkins of her medical background, is a typically and chronically ES/allergic individual who has been exposed to a radiating UAP *and* seismic radiation. Like other ES witnesses, her unconscious would symbolize aspects of her physical systemic condition, and the scenario of aliens inserting a probe into her upper nasal cavity happens to reflect exactly that part which contains particles of naturally occurrring magnetic iron. Hopkins, in hypnotizing her, has accessed images from the unconscious symbolizing her system's reactions to environmental fields to which she is allergic.

Shared altered states and the close-encounter experience

Throughout this chapter we have glimpsed the close parallels between 'exotic' UFOs, related entities and apparitions. Earlier it was argued that, although some encounters are internally perceived visions, rarely some may be external images produced by the unconscious imprinted into ambient fields. In a multiple witness case involving two (or more) percipients, both are usually in a similar altered state with nervous systems 'tuned' to a convergent point; that is to say, although one witness may be the 'medium' who produced the imagery due to ES, both are subject to the same field and their central nervous systems are similarly affected. The implication is that someone else outside the field's influence will either not perceive the imprinted imagery or perceive it stripped of detail. However, even mutual field exposure results in inconsistent encounter perceptions. A well-known, but good, example of this is the Winchester 1976 case involving Mrs Joyce Bowles and Edward Pratt. I am indebted to Lionel Beer for the following account:

> They left her house about 8.45 p.m. in her Mini Clubman . . . After three-quarters of a mile, the dual carriage ends and it was about this point that Mrs Bowles said, 'I saw two lights, the first was higher than the second, which in turn disappeared behind the scrub, thus in neither case were they high in the air. I drew Mr Pratt's attention to them.' She also told us that although they were orange they were redder than sodium lights . . . Mr Pratt . . . described them as a bright orange-red object . . . They were seen in the general direction of the lane to Chilcomb . . . At the bottom of

the hill Mrs Bowles took this lane . . . as the Mini was going down the straight piece of lane, it shuddered and rattled (as though perhaps the ignition had stopped firing?) and the steering appeared to lock. Both Mrs Bowles and her passenger struggled with the wheel, but to no avail. On their right was a 280-yard-length of 20–30-feet-wide grass verge . . . Mrs Bowles thought the car was carried sideways, lifting off the ground on to the grass, parallel with the road . . . Mr Pratt reached over and switched off the ignition. When they looked up, they saw an object which she described as 'a fat Winston Churchill cigar' an estimated 5–6 yards slightly to the right in front of their white Mini . . . the object was about 12 feet long and 5 feet high . . . towards the right-hand end of it were what she described as three brightly lit bow-shaped windows . . . She told us that Mr Pratt said *he had only seen one window*. Behind the window(s) they saw three figures positioned as though they were sitting in a bus, one behind the other with only head and shoulders visible. The object was just above the ground with vapour underneath it. Mr Pratt said that the object was 18 inches above the ground and supported by four jets blowing out gasses. He also said the cigar was glowing with a diffused orange-red light . . . she said that during the encounter she had heard a whistling sound (and investigators also heard a definite whistling sound while they were there . . .)

It is possible that a few seconds elapsed before they saw a figure emerge out of the darkness between the cigar's right-hand side and their car, although no opening was seen in the object. The figure . . . took about four or five steps towards the car walking in a normal manner . . . he was about 6 foot 6 inches tall and on reaching the car he must have turned slightly to face the dashboard and the witnesses thought he probably had his left hand on the car roof . . . he looked in the side window at the dashboard and the engine suddenly sprang to life. At the same time, the headlights which were on full beam shone so brightly that they expected them to burn out . . . The figure looked like a tall human being but had no discernible pupils or irises, only piercing pink albino-like eyes . . . She was convinced that they had left some kind of effect on her eyes, like one might expect from looking at the sun . . . he had short hair at the front, which came down to the shoulders at the back and turned up slightly. He had sideboards which met in a roughly pointed beard, but no moustache. His palish face, illuminated apparently by a combination of moonlight and reflected headlights, had a fairly pointed nose, normal mouth, and apart from the eyes, appeared normal . . . Mr Pratt described the man as wearing what resembled a boiler suit, with his hair brushed backwards over his head, reaching down to his shoulders. Mrs Bowles mentioned at one point that he had silvery specks in his hair . . . 'His clothing shimmered as if being shaken by a wind' . . . When he bent down to look into the car window, his overall ballooned out like a cyclist's cape. His outfit did not appear to have buttons, but there was a seam running vertically down the left side of his chest . . . She described the colour of the outfit as being that of baking-foil, a sort of dull silver colour.

As the engine was revving, she probably had her eyes closed, and eventually said, 'Look out, Ted, he is going round your side!' However, Mr Pratt could see no sign of the being behind the car, and by the time they looked back, the cigar and its occupants had completely disappeared . . . When she started the car herself and engaged first gear, 'It was like hitting a barrier.' The car would not move. But at the second attempt, the car started without any trouble, and she was able to drive off the grass.

. . . So far as I am concerned there was no physical evidence whatsoever at the site – not even the narrow tyre marks of a Mini skidding off the road . . . However, there was physical evidence of . . . a subjective nature . . . When we interviewed Mrs Bowles at her home, she told us that the right side of her face had become blotchy the following Monday or Tuesday . . . The rash had cleared by the time we arrived some seven days later . . . but was confirmed by a neighbour who was present . . . she said that her neck and right shoulder had burned for nearly a week. I have already mentioned that she thought her eyes had been affected in some way. She had been feeling slightly sick the whole week, and felt unable to eat proper meals. In passing she emphasized that she was not pregnant! . . . She also said that she felt as if she wanted to sleep for a week.

A further point came to light when Frank Wood asked her if she had been wearing any metal. Astonished, Mrs Bowles said that she had taken her eternity ring off (worn next to her wedding ring) shortly after the event . . . The skin of her finger under the ring had become red and sore . . . As a throwaway line, when we were on the point of departure, she had noticed that a watch that had been with her had gone haywire, and was no longer any use for time-keeping. So far as I know, Mr Pratt has not complained of any adverse physical effects, but if anything, felt mildly exhilarated . . .

Mrs Bowles had come into the public eye in recent years as a result of poltergeist activity in her house . . . She is known locally as a 'psychic healer' and a 'natural medium' . . . The Leyland Mini . . . performed as well, if not better after the incident than before.[23]

Analysis of a multiple-witness encounter

From this detailed Winchester report, it is evident that although the witnesses perceived essentially the same thing, there are a few minor inconsistencies: for example, the number of windows on the 'craft'. It is interesting to note that this experience is classified as a UFO encounter, although at no time was the 'craft' seen in the air, and an assumption was made that the orange aerial lights seen in the early stages were the 'cigar'.

Joyce Bowles produced these apparitions unconsciously in an altered state as a result of field exposure. She appears to be ES, judging from her poltergeist, 'psychic healing' and 'natural medium' history like S in Reading. Like S, too, she reacted to the field exposure by producing an allergic reaction consisting of dermal irritation on the right side of her face. The persisting burning sensation on the right side of her neck and shoulders also indicates the direction of the field. In addition, it indicates that her 'right brain' took the main effects of the field, and this hemisphere is closely linked with imaging and ESP.[24] The unexplained whistling that investigators heard also may have been a field effect.

Joyce Bowles' companion was also caught up in the field exposure, but not being ES, he played a more passive role in the encounter, although some systemic effects were noted relating to an inappropriate calmness during the encounter, alternating with post-encounter elation – both probably due to a sudden intake of a massive dose of negatively charged ions. Alternatively, an exposure to a field of 10 to 15 Hz (cycles per second) has been found during a medical treatment, called Interferential Therapy, to stimulate parasympathetic nerves to dramatically lower levels of excitement.[25]

The fact of their mutual witnessing indicates that either an external image was created that they both perceived, or an internal image was created in the unconscious of Mrs Bowles, and her companion was linked with this through an extra-sensory convergence. Both are viable options, although the second evokes a process that would involve a shared hallucination. This is quite consistent with the other features noted concerning apparitions, and MacKenzie states in his listing of their characteristics: 'They are often seen collectively by two or more persons at the same time.' This may equally apply to the first option regarding an externalized image. There *are* cases where groups of witnesses have perceived an apparition and others, looking from a different viewpoint, have seen nothing. I have suggested that to perceive realities of this order (i.e., apparitional phenomena), *all* parties need to be within, and affected by, the ambient field into which they are 'imprinted' by the unconscious. It has also been pointed out that this is why a group of encounter witnesses may perceive a huge aerial craft, but no confirming witnesses can be found from a wider area.

I myself have been involved in the perception of a shared hallucination and can vouch for their positive existence. During the early 1960s, before the hallucinatory drug LSD 25 was illegal, I followed in the footsteps of Aldous Huxley (or so I imagined) after reading *The Doors of Perception* and *Heaven and Hell*, and took 500 micrograms of the drug with another 'explorer'. After sitting in a room together talking, I noticed two small luminous skulls about six inches in diameter, shining down from a corner of the ceiling. My companion looked up when I pointed and asked him, 'Can you see them?' He replied that what he could see were two luminous 'death's-heads', and he stood on the back of a sofa and reached up and traced their outline, eye positions, etc., with his finger. We were astounded when we realized that we could both see the same hallucination, and later recalled that I made no comments that would suggest the images to him in advance.

Sensory noise in the Winchester encounter

The presentation of the encounter proceeded effectively until the being was depicted as looking in at the dashboard. It was then that an electrical field energized the vehicle's circuitry and the engine produced vigorous sound waves. This coincided with the over-production of light from the headlamps, thereby destabilizing their altered state by the intrusion of sensory noise. The encounter realities were then terminated and vanished from the perceptual field. The field effect activating the car and the being's glance was stage-managed by the unconscious to coincide.

It is typical for electrical equipment (in this case, the car) to be inactivated at the onset of altered states and the encounter dramatization. In other cases this may be a radio or TV set, and in such circumstances, the sensory noise level falls suddenly. The unconscious, however, is activated, and the absence, or low level, of sensory noise then provides a backdrop against which the altered state accelerates and the unconscious speedily constructs a CE or apparitional scenario. The drama that unfolds is dictated by an overall policy of sensory noise *management*.[26] That is to say, apart from the symbolic content which, as in dreams, expresses an individual's psychological state, whatever *appears* to happen in the encounter, *there is always the ulterior motive of preventing, avoiding or distracting from, sensory noise*.

One strategy that the unconscious harnesses to great effect is to make the encounter content so curious or eye-catching that external stimuli are not 'noticed', or, to put it another way, do not 'pull focus'. In the Winchester experience, this was the sparkling appearance of the entity. This effect is produced by the irradiation of the temporal lobes, producing phosphenes as a sparkling effect in the upper left quadrant of the visual field. Other cases have employed bizarre costume depiction, or other-worldly archetypal 'props', such as a 'glowing' sphere hovering above the hand of an entity; or material/imagery taken directly from fairy stories. These images sometimes double-up and express something about the witness's current preoccupations. In these instances, the witness will experience a curious wordless fascination for these realities, as they symbolize something deep within their psyche. This, of course, increases their effectiveness for distracting from potential sensory noise. I have termed these effects 'sensory lures' or 'cognitive lures' according to the levels of the witness's perception they appeal to or engage.

All of these things, however, can be distilled down and attributed to the common motive of *sensory noise control*, for sensory noise acts as a destroyer of these unconsciously produced dramatizations.

In many encounters, the witness reports that they 'heard' or became aware of, a voice 'inside their head' that told them very specifically: 'Do not be afraid.' This is an almost obligatory feature of these experiences. Once again this is a sensory noise-managing strategy on the part of the unconscious. There is 'noise' that emanates from internal sources, such as neural activity in the muscles, which is controlled by paralysis.[27] But there is also mental anxiety that is part of the everyday, survival-orientated consciousness that also has to be eliminated. To do this, so that it does not, like external 'noise', threaten the stability of the altered state, an internal instruction is hallucinated by the unconscious. In a bemused and suggestible state during a CE, the witness is given the comforting and direct command not to be afraid. Figure 8 clarifies and summarizes the sensory noise aspect for altered states during the CE experience.

In the Winchester encounter, the investigators attribute the illumination of the craft and being to the vehicle's headlights, but they seem to have failed to notice that the ignition had been switched off. (A similar field activation of a car's circuitry occurred in the Enfield poltergeist case, when windscreen wipers were seen to be working despite the switched-off ignition.) The entity was perceived as reflecting light primarily from the headlights. It is tempting to suggest that the light level was controlled by the unconscious by adjusting the field level, so that an optimum level of lighting was produced to 'illuminate the stage' as it were, without disturbing the stability of the altered state. This would be a variation of the signal-link concept, where the unconscious is also linked to the energies of a UAP through an ambient field. However, it is also evident

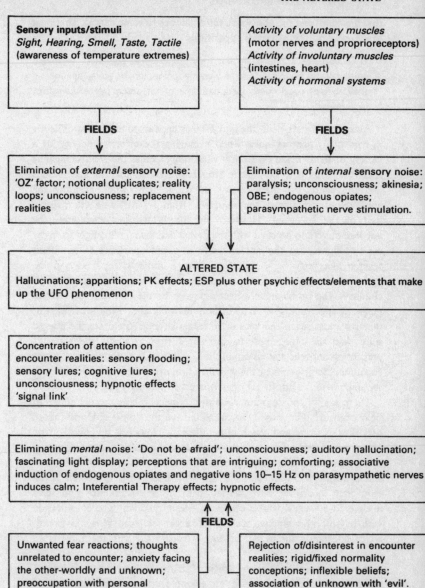

Sensory inputs/stimuli
Sight, Hearing, Smell, Taste, Tactile
(awareness of temperature extremes)

Activity of voluntary muscles
(motor nerves and proprioreceptors)
Activity of involuntary muscles
(intestines, heart)
Activity of hormonal systems

FIELDS

FIELDS

Elimination of *external* sensory noise:
'OZ' factor; notional duplicates; reality
loops; unconsciousness; replacement
realities

Elimination of *internal* sensory noise:
paralysis; unconsciousness; akinesia;
OBE; endogenous opiates;
parasympathetic nerve stimulation.

ALTERED STATE
Hallucinations; apparitions; PK effects; ESP plus other psychic effects/elements that make
up the UFO phenomenon

Concentration of attention on
encounter realities: sensory flooding;
sensory lures; cognitive lures;
unconsciousness; hypnotic effects
'signal link'

Eliminating *mental* noise: 'Do not be afraid'; unconsciousness; auditory hallucination;
fascinating light display; perceptions that are intriguing; comforting; associative
induction of endogenous opiates and negative ions 10–15 Hz on parasympathetic nerves
induces calm; Inteferential Therapy effects; hypnotic effects.

FIELDS

Unwanted fear reactions; thoughts
unrelated to encounter; anxiety facing
the other-worldly and unknown;
preoccupation with personal
problems.

Rejection of/disinterest in encounter
realities; rigid/fixed normality
conceptions; inflexible beliefs;
association of unknown with 'evil'.

Fig. 8 A flowchart to illustrate the formation of the altered state.

that the 'ship' and the entity was self-luminous to some extent. To repeat MacKenzie on this aspect of apparitions:

> Their visibility is erratic, in that they are likely to appear or disappear suddenly and inexplicably, to be invisible to people who would see them if they were physically embodied, to fade in or out, *and to be self luminous*. [my italics][28]

As a general statement, the unconscious appears to have most difficulty in controlling sensory noise when managing the effects produced by a variety of fields made up from a wide range across the electromagnetic spectrum. That is to say, in the Stonehenge encounter, the unconscious had to ensure the management of visible light while ensuring the continuing irradiation of the witnesses (from a UAP) with the invisible part of the spectrum. However, in the Winchester encounter, the unconscious could proceed with the drama and manage the light from the car headlights, but the sudden surge of a field presence (intermittent seismic electricity or a reflection from a radar sweep?) caused the optimum sensory noise level to be exceeded by energizing the car's circuitry. The problematic aspect seems to be the fact that the electromagnetic spectrum is made up of both invisible and visible wavelengths; the first must reach the witness to establish and accelerate the altered state; and the other must be prevented from reaching the witness's perception until the state is established, and then in a subdued way. Close encounters *largely* appear the way they are, in all their variations, due to the unconscious's efforts to juggle these two mutually exclusive criteria.

There are, of course, numerous other aspects relating to the effects of field exposure that caused the car to behave the way it did, and caused Mrs Bowles's ring and watch to be affected. However, by now the type and range of field effects will be evident, and there will be cases described where timepieces and wedding rings have also produced tell-tale signs of EM exposure.[29] Before we leave the Winchester case, it must be noted that once again we have started with a close-encounter and have uncovered a witness who is obviously ES, a 'medium' who is associated with psychic phenomena, such as poltergeist effects. How this trend, which constantly jumps out at one, is reconciled with the ETH is an enigma in its own right.

Returning specifically to the aspect of shared encounter experiences, of which the Winchester case is an example, there is the comparable phenomenon of the *shared dream*. This often occurs between members of a household involved in poltergeist activity.[30] It indicates that the unconscious of the 'focus' or 'medium' can be linked with the unconscious of another individual. This occurs even more readily with members of the same family and suggests a genetic link. The wider implication is that unconsciously produced imagery, such as CE realities, may be perceived by individuals in the presence of the person who is producing them, albeit unconsciously. Equally, it may be that it is not even necessary for the 'medium' to be present.

It would be extremely difficult to determine if an encounter experience was due to the witness's link with a remote 'medium'. The aspect that is far more relevant to multiple-witnessing is whether there is any scientific evidence that will support the viability of the phenomenon; it seems that there is. There is an extremely technical paper by a Yugoslavian scientist, Dejan Rakovic of Belgrade University, who is involved in electrical engineering.[31] *Rakovic outlines a mechanism by which information (i.e., imagery) can be transferred via a 'carrier wave' from one person's nervous system to another's* on a long-range basis. Known as 'remote viewing', this phenomenon has been studied since the mid-1970s at the Mind Science Foundation at San Antonio, USA. The phenomenon has also been developed by Russian scientists to convey information over a long range to personnel in operational submarines. Rakovic shows that because our nervous systems are basically the same in terms of structure and the biological frequencies they radiate, short-range interaction (such as those involved in a CE experience) does not even involve the emission of electromagnetic waves from system to system, because there is an induction process that creates a coupling effect. This produces shared mental imagery.

Consider an extract from Rakovic's paper:

> The model predicts also the short-range transpersonal interactions without any waves emitted, due to electromagnetic induction coupling between two neural networks with embedded ELF waves. This situation is similar to that in primary and secondary coils in electrical transformers, with the only difference being that not only energy but also information are transferred from one neural network to another ... They are even possible in both normal and altered states of consciousness, and could be the biophysical basis for nonverbal hypnosis, suggestion, etc.[32]

In this extract Rakovic is referring to Faradic electricity in relation to the coupling effect between two coils. This is *not* merely an analogy, but a real effect identified as a mechanism in shared experiences between two (or more) individuals. In fact, it seems that by applying the laws of electricity to the human nervous system, and recognizing it as the electrical/EM system that it is, an understanding of what is happening during such phenomena as shared experiences, can be gained. Consider further information on the coupling effect that Rakovic refers to:

Faradic electricity dates only from 1831, when it was discovered by Faraday that if two coils of wire be placed near one another, and if a galvanic current (used to induce muscle stimulation) is suddenly passed through one of them and again stopped, a current is induced in the second coil at the moments of closing and opening of the first circuit. This secondary current differs from the continuous galvanic current in two important particulars: 1) It is only momentary in duration; 2) It has a much higher potential or pressure, and is therefore much more capable of transversing poor conductors like the human body.[33]

From this, we can see why Rakovic has identified this as an underlying mechanism for shared perceptions or the ESP 'scanning' of others by the unconscious to obtain information. That is to say, the field produced seems eminently suitable for a biological/neural context. Such independent confirmation always acts as further evidence for the validity of proposals (i.e., Rakovic's) and I would extend this by placing it in the psychic witness/investigator context as a means by which the ES witness obtains information unconsciously from investigators, which may be subsequently incorporated into further experiences. Perhaps this may usefully be called the 'contamination effect'.

Rakovic also mentions the inter-family-member aspect:

This can provide the biophysical basis for transpersonal interactions; it is only necessary for phases of 90–120-minute ultradian rhythms of two persons to be matched, and exchanged information to be emotionally coloured by the reticular-talmic system of the receiver — which can explain why this phenomenon is mainly recognized between twins, mother and child, or otherwise closely related persons.[34]

Interestingly, Rakovic mentions that during this phenomenon of shared mental imagery, subjects can experience subjective time-dilation, which is frequently reported as part of the OZ factor or 'bell-jar' effect during close-encounter experiences. Witnesses commonly report, for example, that a huge UFO passing over them 'took ages to get from one point to another – it was as if time had stood still.' Consider the relevant section from Rakovic's paper:

The obtained diffusion time matches well with the 90–120-minute ultradian rhythms of both waking conscious experience from normal to altered states, with extremely dilated subjective time base, and mixing of normally conscious and unconscious contents.

Despite the imperfect English, this paper is of great relevance to the multiple-witness CE, as it indicates how purely internal material can be shared by two or more percipients. The UFO-study community has been puzzled by cases in which families have been involved in quite complex interactions during a multiple-abduction experience. Probably the most famous British case is the Aveley abduction, as it is known, which was investigated by Andrew Collins, an investigator of long-standing. This case has been in circulation since it was first discovered in 1977, although it actually took place in 1974, near Aveley, Essex, and it has had widespread publicity. Therefore, it is not my intention to present the case fully, but only the onset of the experience and the post-encounter effects. They relate to altered states, and confirm and extend many of the conclusions I have presented so far. The case provides a good example of a multi-witness 'abduction scenario'.

A UAP-induced vision – the Aveley abduction experience

I am indebted to Andrew Collins for the following account:

> The 'big star' seemed to be travelling in a similar direction as that of the car, and appeared to be 'stopping and starting' as it moved . . . Karen and Stuart were still asleep . . . Kevin (their son) was standing on the floor behind . . . John commented on the lack of traffic for a road that is usually very busy at that time of night. The time was approximately 22.10 hours . . . Elaine (the mother) saw the light . . . which was oval-shaped and was bluish iridescent . . . The miles passed without any incident . . . The car was travelling at around 30 mph which is sufficient to turn the corner in fourth gear. Just then, as they were about to turn the bend they had a terrible feeling that something was wrong. The only sound that could be heard was the radio, neither the car tyres nor the engine were audible. Then, as they turned the bend, they could see no more than thirty yards. In front of them, covering the whole road, was a thick 'mist', 'gas' or 'fog'. It was dense, green, and about 9–10 feet high, and was bordered on the left-hand side by thick bushes. On the right, the 'gas' seemed to curve down to the ground, just behind a thin line of trees along the road's verge. The top was flat and the bottom was touching the ground. Just as the mist was noticed, the car's radio started crackling and smoking. John then pulled out its wires. Then the car lights went dead, and they were engulfed by fog still travelling at around 30 mph. Elaine remembers the car jerking violently as the mist curled around it, greatly different from any thick fog they had ever encountered before.
>
> The windows were up, and Kevin was still standing on the car floor behind them, and the other two children were still asleep. Inside the 'fog'

it was very light and they felt very cold, a tingling sensation was felt and it was dead silent. Everything was hazy and nothing more could be remembered, not even if the car was still moving. They were in the mist for what seemed like a second or two, when suddenly there was a jolt like the car going over a humped-back bridge and the mist was gone. The car now, according to John, was exactly one and a half miles along the same road. Things at this point were very confusing for John, but he swears he was on his own in the front of the car . . . Elaine's first recollections began about half a mile further on . . . Both said that the coldness had now left, and the car was functioning normally, besides the radio that was still unwired. Things were unclear driving home, but they can remember that Kevin was still awake and the other two children were still asleep. Elaine vaguely remembers that the interior light was on in the car, she said, 'Is everybody here?' John and Elaine think that they may have talked about the mist but cannot remember exactly. Both felt very nervous and frightened, although no ill-effects were remembered.

. . . On reaching home . . . both Karen and Stuart were still asleep, and were carried up to bed. Then Elaine looked at the clock, and became very worried as the clock which should have read about 22.20, instead read about 01.00 . . . they realized that three hours were missing from their lives . . . They had no idea what had happened, or even what could have happened . . . The only ill-effects noted the following day were that both John and Elaine felt tired. All three children went to school as usual.[35]

Sensory noise in the Aveley abduction experience

The 'big star' which appeared to pace the car travelled in the characteristic 'starting and stopping' motion that was described in one of the Blackpool cases. This may indicate the presence of a radio-wave transmission applied intermittently, pulling it through the atmosphere. Alternatively, and judging by the relatively slow speed, it may just have been that the car, emitting a field itself, being primarily constructed of ferrous metals, acted as a magnet and the obstructions and varying distances interrupted the magnetic attraction effect. It is also significant that the trajectory of this aerial light coincided exactly with a line of pylons which runs parallel to the road near by. It may have been an electrical corona or St Elmo's fire effect travelling along the high tension cables overhead, running north-east to south-west.

After this event, the two parents and one child recalled a complex 'abduction' into a flying saucer, where they were medically examined, they reported, by a number of different alien entity types.

However, whatever the UAP type, in combination with a powerful ambient field, both sources revealed their presence by a number of recognizable electrical effects upon the car, similar to those in the Winchester case. The violent jerking is indicative of an intermittent loss of ignition, where a 'juddering' effect created by alternate gear-driven and free-wheeling motion would be produced. Throughout the initial pre-'fog' stages, there is a progressive decrease in sensory noise due to the malfunction of the engine, radio and lights. By the time they had encountered the 'fog', all three were silent, and the 'green mist' eventually eliminated virtually everything in the visual field. At this stage, sensory noise had dropped to an optimum level for the establishment of the witnesses' altered states, combining with the irradiation of the witnesses by the field present. The conscious mind, which thrives on sensory input, was starved of external stimuli and the unconscious could then become dominant.

It will be noticed that the 'green fog' eliminated the need for detailed 'notional duplicates' for the witnesses, which throughout the encounter involved John, Elaine and Kevin (that is, father, mother and son). The other two younger children slept throughout the event.

This 'electrical fog' seems to be the effect of an intense electrical field (in this case emanating from the row of pylons which ran beside the road, along its length) on atmospheric water. The charge electrically excites the inert gasses in the atmosphere (neon, argon, krypton and xenon), causing them to become fluorescent, giving an overall luminous green hue. Therefore, strictly speaking, such an 'electrical fog' is a type of UAP, which in this case enclosed the witnesses, irradiating them severely.

The 'fog' had external reality and induced the tingling and cold sensations: both are systemic responses to acute field exposure. However, these effects provided sensory noise, and it is clear that there are internal sensors within the body that need to be 'quietened' before an effective sensory noise-free state is established. These nerve centres are called proprioreceptors and are located throughout the body.[36] They send monitoring neural messages to the brain about the posture of the body, orientation of the limbs, tension and tones of the muscles and so on. This constant internal busy traffic of sensory signals needs to be eliminated also. Some encounter experiences involve a trance-induced inactivity (which involves the habituation effect where the same visual messages are fed into the brain over and over, and is the basis of 'highway hypnosis'). This paralysis creates an internal stillness. In the Aveley case, however, the witnesses 'blanked-out' *and* suffered electrically induced paralysis.

A table compiled by Dr Mark Payne indicates the condition called electrosleep which can be induced by a frequency between 100 and

1500 Hz, which is used medically by a trained practitioner to induce unconsciousness. For the witnesses to have been oblivious for three hours, the phenomenon known as electroanaesthesia, in combination with closely related states, would have to be induced. It takes place in the same frequency range as electrosleep, and it would have quietened the internal sensors mentioned. It would have reduced or removed pain induced by muscular stiffness due to inactivity. In fact, it would explain how all three witnesses were 'frozen' into permanent postures for the period of their unconsciousness, for this is what appears to have happened.

Andrew Collins mentioned that one aspect that puzzled him in particular (apart from the enigma of the CE4 generally!) is that when parents and child *all* regained consciousness, they were *all* in *exactly* the same positions and postures as they were just before they all lost consciousness, even down to Kevin standing up behind the front seats with both his hands on the seat-backs. The perception that John had of being alone must have been a negative hallucination (as his wife could not have joined a moving car) which excludes people and objects that are present, rather than creating the perception of something not there. It is not surprising, therefore, that they slept so soundly after the event, because being frozen in the same position for three hours would have been extremely wearing on the system.

This 'frozen' attitude is motor paralysis or akinesia, and it occurs when motor neurones in the muscles experience electrical interference which causes them to malfunction; alternatively, the same effect is reached when the neurotransmitters receive such constant electrical stimulation that they are overloaded and cause the muscles to seize up. The effect can be created by a different amplitude to the frequencies used in electro-convulsive therapy (ECT), which is at the 25 Hz or 40 Hz frequencies and creates a 'black-out' effect. Also, immobilization occurred in the subjects of Persinger and Ruttan's experiments. Field exposure evidently caused the unconsciousness and akinesia of the Aveley witnesses.

Andrew Collins mentions the close proximity of high-tension lines to the 'green fog' location. There seems to be little doubt that they contributed greatly to the ambient electrical fields associated with the 'fog'. Consider the following passage by Tom Graves, a researcher into geological energies:

> Basically, pylon lines split the energy-flow, allowing part of it to continue on its way, but sending the remainder down the pylon itself. The proportions 'stolen' by the pylons vary enormously, for no known reason. At each bend in the line of cables some of the energy that originally ran down the overground 'spins off', effectively forming a new low-powered

overground. The result is that in some areas ... the web of pylon lines, large and small, produces large numbers of unofficial 'overgrounds', allowing energy of the wrong kind to arrive at the wrong place at the wrong time and probably the wrong direction. The result, in other words, is not just a mess, it's absolute chaos. In some cases and areas it may be possible to divert the major overgrounds upwards so that they are above the powerlines ... the only satisfactory solution would be to put all the electrical power cables underground. Even given the enormous cost of doing so ... it would still be worthwhile ... because of the pylon's hidden effects on the health and fertility of the land.[37]

It would appear that this 'lost energy' would be instrumental in precipitating the extreme systemic effects in the Aveley witnesses.

Another more potent source of electronic pollution is the effect of attenuation, which has specific relevance for this case. Attenuation is a term which refers to the loss of signal between transmitting and receiving aerials:

Attenuation is that which creates a loss of signal power in a transmission path or electrical network. It is solely due to the resistive component of the path or circuit impedance for only in resistance can power be expended and lost as heat. This applies also to radio channels in which the signal is attenuated by contact with the ground (as we saw with the space-wave/ground-reflected propagation) or by its passage through the atmosphere ... In a transmission channel attenuation is usually unwanted and has to be overcome by amplification; i.e., an increase in power.[38]

Or, as electronic pollution consultant Anne Silk puts it:

Attenuation of radio frequency signals – this is when the signal strength sent, say 100 decibels, drops to say, 60 decibels at the receiving dish ... Where has the missing 40 decibels gone? Into thin air! Or rather water-laden air – there to produce odd effects.

These 'odd effects' included the creation of electrically charged water droplets that appeared as the 'green fog', which produced, in combination with the 'pylon effect', the tingling sensations, the shared altered state, the abduction scenario, which was a metaphor for the sudden systemic take-over by the fields, and other anomalous and 'freak' conditions.

Akinesia is a curious effect reported fairly frequently in UAP proximity, such as the Travis Walton case. The Plymouth/Denise Bishop case outlined earlier, where a young woman was zapped by a UAP as she put her hand on a metal door handle, showed how it can occur momentarily 'as if someone had stopped a film'. The Betty Andreasson 'abduction' case involved several members of a family who were seen by Betty to be 'frozen' like statues, while she herself 'recalled' under hypnosis a visionary experience with a meaningful, mythic-symbolic content of a religious nature. The Rowley Regis encounter also involved lengthy paralysis.

The Aveley scenario: a summary

To round off the Aveley encounter incident itself: we have a scenario where a family is driving home on a late autumn evening, and they enter the outer edges, and then mid-section, of a powerful ambient electrical field. During this period they gradually slip into a changed mode of perception, which, in combination with the direct effects of the field on their immediate surroundings within the car, brings on an accelerated decrease in external stimuli. This decrease had been noticed earlier, with the impression of an absence of traffic. This may indicate the introduction of the 'notional duplicate' process occurring in the early stages, but as it is the absence of *approaching* traffic that was so noticeable, another, more ominous factor suggests itself: drivers approaching from the other direction had already travelled into the outer edges of the field zone and may have already been affected and had lost consciousness after their cars had stalled due to electrical malfunction. They were having their 'time-lapses' already. If you think that this is not possible because everyone would know about it, remember John and Elaine kept their experience to themselves for three years, and then it only came to the attention of an investigator by accident. Also, not everyone realizes that they have had a time-loss. If they do, what do they do about it? Who do they tell?

The actual 'time-lapse' period evokes an image of drivers and passengers 'frozen' in their cars. This is an eerie scenario where stationary traffic either on the side of the Aveley road or on the road itself, embedded in thick green 'fog', contains travellers inside each vehicle apparently asleep. Perhaps they never got to this stage, and feeling odd and unwell they abandoned their journeys and turned off. Or perhaps their vehicles had just malfunctioned and an overview of the area would have shown isolated 'broken down' cars dotted about the approach roads, unable even to activate their hazard lights.

Our witnesses, however, encountering two UAPs – the overhead light and the electrical fog – found that their car's electrical system faltered, with the loss of noise from the engine, light from the headlamps and sound from the radio. However, the former fires intermittently, and eventually they reach the core of the field. Then the car stalls completely and rolls to a halt. They lose consciousness and become immobilized . . . for three hours.

It must be remembered that the situation was extraordinary in the literal sense of the word, and could certainly be called 'freak conditions'. In fact, a researcher named William Corliss has collected a wide range of reports of 'freak phenomena', such as slow lightning strikes; electrical 'spears' that stick into the ground for a few seconds before vanishing; instances of 'solid light' where luminous spheres project a beam of light with a flat, cut-off end; and all types of weird ball-lightning forms and behaviour. These are all UAPs of different types and have corresponding weird effects to go with them. One was a mini-lightning strike that entered a room and broke a pile of plates. It was found that each alternate plate was neatly broken into two even halves in the pile. Comparable oddities no doubt exist in relation to the effects of electrical phenomena on the human system.

A topographical field map

The Aveley case provides a model situation where we could plot an electrical/electromagnetic field on to a map and discern a centre and an outer edge. We could then plot the different effects and systemic responses according to UAP presence/proximity, and zonal areas, indicating field concentration. This is, of course, a simplification, for a number of reasons. For example, in terms of the effect upon the car occupants, the strength of the field is not so important as the frequency and the degree of coherence. We have already considered witnesses 'meeting their frequency', and that different individuals are triggered into a 'reality switch' or altered state by different specific frequencies; that is to say, zones of increasing concentration, according to how near the centre of the field they are, are not necessarily more able to induce an altered state. Some witnesses would 'trip' at a very low strength of field at its edge, but others would have to travel further into a more concentrated zone before it affected them. See Figure 9, a topographical map of the Aveley case:

1 The road on which the witnesses were travelling;
2 The field area divided into zones;
3 The observed trajectory of the overhead UAP;
4 Immobilized vehicles on roads leading to the electrical fog;
5 The linear positions of the pylons in relation to the road and the observed trajectory of the UAP, showing how the two coincide.

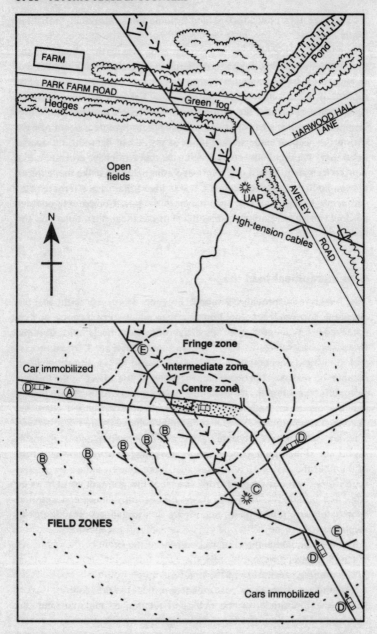

Fig. 9 A diagrammatic representation of the Aveley case location.

The map is produced as a useful method of visual analysis, and to indicate some of the main variables that may be plotted on maps generally.

Before the Aveley analysis is continued, the case should be put into context. It is part of a wider, discrete, 'vehicle at night' syndrome. There is clearly a reoccurring association of the close-encounter with the nocturnal car journey. To explain the reason for this association, we need to realize that it is significant that the car can be regarded as an extension of our own body and senses; that is to say, there is more than just an analogous parallel between headlights and eyes; wheels and legs; engine and metabolism; nerves and electrical wiring; ignition and consciousness. The connecting link between the two in the close-encounter situation is the sensory noise factor, as the same aspect acts upon them both, causing them to malfunction, which creates a sudden fall in sensory noise levels. That common aspect is, of course, field exposure.

The encounter core

The Aveley encounter experience functioned as a cathartic psycho-spiritual overhaul for the witnesses, which took place at a deep level. It was carried out by the unconscious utilizing a complex hallucinatory construct, where 'aliens' of two descriptions personified these unconscious processes. John was especially affected, as we shall see from the post-encounter analysis. It involved shared visionary material where both witnesses were 'examined' by two entity types depicted as using advanced technical/medical equipment. They felt that they had been levitated inside a pillar of light that ascended into a 'spaceship'. Initially, they were standing on a balcony-like platform at the base of the 'ship', but at the top of the pillar of light, where it was perceived as emerging from the underside.

With an overhead perspective of the car at this point, at the start of the experience, they reported under hypnosis that they could see themselves standing by it. Such hallucinations of Doppelgängers are commonly reported by those suffering from epileptiform conditions and are indicative of anomalous electrical activity in the brain of the witnesses. Such perceptions were evidently shared at this point, indicating mutual irradiation by specific frequencies. However, as would be expected, not all of their hallucinatory perceptions were so shared. Andrew Collins states that 'The similarities between her [Elaine's] account and John's are very noticeable although there do appear to be some marked differences.'

This mixture of shared and disparate perceptions is typical of such experiences, and it is indicative of an imperfect 'shared vision' process. This is to be expected, considering the internally produced nature of these experiences. A great deal of apparent interaction with aliens was perceived and it would be valuable material for an investigator compiling a 'content tracing' profile of the experiences. However, a detailed knowledge of the personal and psychological background would be needed. Much of the material that was remembered came as spontaneous 'flashbacks' induced by the hypnotic states carried out by qualified doctors, rather than successful 'regression'. This is the hypnosis/trance-matching effect described.

The full details are not provided here as this section is examining causative processes rather content analysis. (They can be found in a case-report from the now defunct Independent UFO Network.)

Post-encounter effects

Investigator Andrew Collins says:

> Soon after the incident John suffered a nervous breakdown for no apparent reason. He is not sure of the exact date but it was before Christmas. [The encounter took place on 27 October 1974.] Due to the breakdown, John had to give up his job and did not work again until September 1975. In September a job 'fell into his lap', a job which he had wanted to do for many years, this being working with the mentally handicapped. [Previously he had worked in the construction industry.] He now felt much more confident of himself, but this could quite well have been due to him recovering from the nervous breakdown . . . He is now working for himself and is hoping to launch a career in teaching arts and crafts. Since November John has written many poems about his life, all of which were written down on the spur of the moment.
>
> Elaine has also become more self-confident and since September has attended college . . . Kevin, who was backward in his reading at school, suddenly began to get better and now is way ahead of his reading age. At about the time of the encounter, John, Elaine, Kevin and Karen all gave up eating meat and now cannot even stand the smell of it. John and Elaine feel very strongly about this, pointing out that animals should not be killed so people can eat. They (particularly John) do their best to prevent other people around them from eating meat . . . both freely admit that the taste makes them feel ill. They are also very conscious of what they eat. No foods with any preservatives, colourings, flavouring or anything else unnatural are ever bought now . . . both feel very strongly about conservation of our environment . . . Whereas both John and Elaine liked

'a good drink' before the incident, they hardly touch alcohol at all now.

... John who had until then smoked up to 60–70 cigarettes a day, suddenly gave up smoking completely. Since then he has not wanted a cigarette and now hates the smell of them ... Several smaller changes can be seen in John, one of which I believe is a stronger personality and a more persuasive attitude. Also, John resents raising his voice to his children now.

Analysis

Obviously, all three witnesses have undergone a cathartic reorganization of their mental and physical processes. John, in particular, had re-integrated in terms of belief and metabolism, the former being influenced by changes to the latter to a large extent.

The principle behind electro-convulsive therapy is to send a jolt of electricity through the system in order to reorganize its electrical and chemical functioning. The witnesses appear to have undergone a parallel process of seizure involving akinesia or paralysis as a result of their exposure to the fields. Also, as we have seen from other encounters with a UAP and/or fields, acute electrical hypersensitivity was induced – demonstrated by their sudden sensitivity to food additives, alcohol, tobacco, and meat. We have noted that such multiple allergies (which Dr C. W. Smith defines as a failure of one or more regulatory systems in the body) are invariably associated with hypersensitivity to electrical and/or electromagnetic fields. Their field exposure, therefore, rearranged their body chemistry, lowering their ability to cope with a range of environmental chemicals. A comparable case was the encounter with the Subud Latihan (mentioned in Chapter One), where the percipient developed exactly the same type of mental and physical breakdown, also for a year, which was also resolved by eliminating certain food types from her diet, and a consequent reorganization of her life-style, which also included an avoidance of sugar, caffeine, tobacco, alcohol and, especially, food additives of the E variety. CH, after a close association with a field-emitting 'medium' and the experience with a BOL and field, also excluded tobacco, alcohol and meat, which he sees as part of a spiritual mission involving an alien intelligence.

This elimination of what became 'body pollutants' for these people, as well as the Aveley witnesses, is essential for their metabolic well-being; in fact, it now enables them to function more efficiently, physiologically speaking. This is because, before the field exposure finally undermined their systems, they were already coping to greater or lesser extents with the things that they eliminated after the encounter; as is the case so often, their allergies were at a sub-clinical level.

Everyone eats, drinks or takes in something that weakens their system to some degree, but they cope with it. They may notice that they feel slightly ill for a short period, or 'a bit down', when they come into contact with something to which they are allergic, sub-clinically. This can be anything from a personal computer to coffee. They are quite unaware that their system is fighting against its effects. While the allergenic substance is in their system, field exposure will trigger a full-blown allergic condition. Did John and Elaine eat meat, drink alcohol, smoke and take in food additives just before their fateful journey? The circumstances suggest that they did, or at least that the chemicals that constitute these things were still in their system. Alternatively, their metabolism just could not cope with these things after their irradiation.

Therefore, the attitudes that are found so repeatedly in witnesses after their encounter experience, that are preoccupied with a purity of food and environment, *are a simple projection of their own revised metabolic needs, fashioned into an ideology*. Their personal mental and physical regeneration is often expressed in quasi-spiritual contexts, and it is reflected in the adoption of a clean-living life-style, values and ideals concerning the environment. Their concern for environmental pollution comes about because of a dramatic and sudden change in their own personal sensitivity to polluting substances. As Karl Marx said: 'Personal circumstances give rise to ideology; not ideology then personal circumstances.'

As an ex-teacher, I would also venture a calculated guess that Kevin's developmental problems were partly due to a sub-clinical allergic reaction to the diet he shared with his family. This was evidently meat of some kind, but more potently, artificial food additives, because children are especially sensitive to these. They can cause emotional and behavioural problems that undermine performance in many areas. Another reason for Kevin's improved performance is related to the lower levels of family stress. If his parents were now metabolically well adjusted, they would be calmer and more stable, and they would be able to cope more efficiently, not having to combat a weakening and mood-altering factor of which they would have been totally unaware.

Extra-sensory perception in close encounters and investigation

In the light of the progressive normalization of what had previously been regarded as paranormal, we must approach labelling any phenomenon as extra-sensory with caution:

To be able to discuss extra-sensory perception it is first necessary to ascertain how far our senses could possibly take us before the fundamental limitations set by our present understanding of physics are reached. Anything beyond this must surely only provisionally be labelled extra-sensory unless, or until, it can be shown otherwise.[39]

For the most part, the lay person will more readily label a process paranormal than the scientist, because he or she is not fully aware of the options available that are 'normal' explanations, or explanations using conventional science. It is common sense that previously paranormal phenomena are 'normalized' by advances in knowledge. There is a generally held assumption that the paranormal is classified as such because no known scientific explanations exist. Instead, such assumptions reflect the uneven distribution of scientific knowledge, and until an individual catches up with current scientific boundaries, he or she will continue to regard something as ultimately mysterious or paranormal. This is especially the case among many UFO enthusiasts, who do not want their 'discoveries' to be stripped of their apparent mystery.

Moreover, to say that one is explaining one unknown in terms of another unknown usually indicates that the individual has not taken the trouble to get to know relevant information; that is to say, something will remain unknown until one gets to know it: it is the difference between 'unidentified' and 'unidentifiable'. Many do not seem to realize that they have to search actively for the scientific options that would explain a phenomenon; the fact that something is apparently mysterious does not mean that this should not be done. This is especially true with extra-sensory perception.

Rakovic's thesis provides a scientific basis for extra-sensory perception; it outlines the mechanisms and processes whereby information can be transferred between two neural systems. This information is frequently in the form of unconscious imagery, as we have noted from the imperfectly shared visionary material in the Aveley case. Rakovic also mentions that an altered state is not always required for this information transfer.

The link between ES individuals and psychic or mediumistic abilities occurs repeatedly in case after case of close-encounter experience; it points to the inescapable conclusion that, typically, these witnesses exhibit ESP, as part of these abilities. This conclusion has been arrived at from a case-file approach, which is a strategy that tackles the study of UFO CEs by examining a limited number of cases in depth, rather than many cases statistically. However, there has been a long-term study (Anamnesis Project) carried out by Dr Alex Keul and Kenneth Phillips into the personality profiles of CE witnesses. *This study is entirely compatible with the ESH,* and it comes to the same conclusion: these witnesses exhibit, first and foremost, extra-sensory perception abilities. Consider Kenneth Phillips's description of the project:

> The Anamnesis is a witness-based investigative tool which comprises a time-invariant, culture-free protocol which enables 'soft-science' researchers to study the life-profiles of close-encounter UFO percipients/experients, the principle components of these life-profiles being:
>
> **1** The subject's demographic whereabouts within his own society.
>
> **2** His/her belief systems.
>
> **3** His/her medical history.
>
> **4** His/her former anomalous experiences (if any).
>
> **5** His/her creative abilities.
>
> **6** His/her educational background.[40]

This study, like the ESH approach, concludes that these close-encounter witnesses/percipients have a high ESP profile. Consider Phillips's conclusions:

> From the point of view of Western Europe the Anamnesis studies *continue* to profile a witness who is, in order of strength of response:
>
> **a)** A self-reporter of ESP phenomena.
>
> **b)** A UFO-dream recaller.
>
> **c)** Socially inconsistent.

The ESH adds the important aspect of the electrical sensitivity (and therefore field-emission) link. Few investigators or researchers have acted upon the Anamnesis findings to draw any conclusions about the nature of the UFO phenomenon, or realized the implications involved. The most stunning implication surely must be that as the witness has a high propensity to extract information from the unconscious of others, it is possible for their unconscious to do this during the investigation period; that is to say, they could pick up material pertaining to other experiences that the investigators know, and use it in the construction of subsequent experiences. *Therefore, the witness can be 'contaminated' by the investigator(s).* Consider the following extract from C. W. Smith and S. Best's *Electromagnetic Man* on this interception of ESP information:

> An account of Russian and East European work on Extra-sensory perception (ESP) has been given by Ostrander and Schroeder (1970). They note a Russian experiment which suggests that ESP can be 'bugged'. When one subject, Kamensky, was attempting to send pictures telepathically from Leningrad to another subject, Nikolaiev, in Moscow, unknown to them was an interceptor, Milodan, in a different building in

Moscow. Nikolaiev got good images on three out of five images, Milodan also got good information on two of them. This raises the question as to whether one person can, through the interaction of the body's electromagnetic field on another person, read magnetic signals from that person's brain currents; or more importantly, is it possible for one person's field to access and scan another's memory locations? The magnetic field sensitivities of the human can be such that the magnetic fields due to the brain's currents are significant throughout the body, and thus strong enough for perception by a person close by.

In the UK, physicist Michael Shallis, at Oxford University, has carried out successful ESP experiments with some of Dr Jean Monro's allergy patients, who, *when in a highly reactive state, appear to exhibit enhanced ESP ability* [my italics].[41]

The fact that ES/allergic subjects exhibit ESP while emitting fields is an extremely significant finding. It confirms the proposal that the unconscious of an ES witness could scan the neural system, including the brain, of investigators for information, as, after all, it *is* the unconscious functions that are involved in ESP. This, of course, correlates well with the discovery that CE witnesses are 'psychic' generally, as we have found in case after case.

It also supports the early proposal that field exposure triggers these psychic abilities to construct CE realities; that is to say, the field triggers their allergies, which in turn produces the 'highly reactive state' mentioned above; and this produces field emission from the witness. The field emissions act as 'carrier waves' to be used in the encounter construction in order of tangibility:

1 by inducing a shared experience by influencing the other individuals with them during the encounter period;

2 organizing field particles to correspond with mental imagery to produce, for example, an apparition or a UFO-related entity: a 'physical hallucination';

3 organizing ambient materials by PK, just as we saw in the Phelps poltergeist case.

Of course, this last category would only apply if PK were part of the ESP process. Is there any evidence for this? For some years leading psychologists Hans J. Eysenck and Carl Sargent have been carrying out research into the paranormal. Here are their comments on their studies and how they view ESP and PK:

In deciding how to go about studying the paranormal scientifically, we might usefully take a strategic decision: we should concentrate our efforts, first, on phenomena which can be studied *easily*, and second on those which might have some common *linking principle*. Only if a common underlying factor can be discovered will we be obliged to change our thinking as scientists.

Two apparently paranormal human abilities stand out as being the best candidates for investigation. The first is extra-sensory perception (ESP). This category includes the apparent ability of human beings to *detect* information about people (*telepathy*, a familiar word), or events/objects (clairvoyance, a less familiar one) at distant places, by unknown means. The other is mind-over-matter, psychokinesis or PK, the apparent ability of human beings to *influence* other people, or events/objects, by an effort of will alone, without involving any known physical force. ESP and PK have been with us, as reported events, since antiquity, and surveys show that many people believe that they have had experience of one or the other . . . These four phenomena – precognition, telepathy, clairvoyance and PK – are the core of the paranormal . . . They should not necessarily be seen as four different things, although people often think of them as such. Very often it is difficult to separate instances of ESP from instances of PK.[42]

From the studies carried out by these leading figures in establishment psychology, we find an identification of ESP with PK. Therefore, we can state, with a reasonable degree of certainty, that if CE witnesses produce ESP effects in their experiences, then they also produce PK. However, other researchers have also come to this ESP/PK identification:

Decades of experimentation with PK led Rhine, if not to an understanding of the physics behind PK, at least to a conviction that it did exist . . . The work of Rhine and his many associates led to some significant speculations and observations. Foremost was the *a priori* deduction that ESP and PK were actually just different phases of a single mental process, or at least operating through the same energy medium.[43]

This is an extremely important correlation from mainstream parapsychology, for it lends support to the proposal that UFO realities are, in some cases, completely physical 'PK constructed' assemblies. It is clear that ESP is produced by these witnesses, and therefore so must PK be. It certainly occurs *after* their encounters as poltergeist effects, and this is an important indicator that it must be produced *during* them – how else but in the production of 'assembled' aliens and spaceships as part of the encounter dramatization?

John, of the Aveley 'abduction' case, made a strange remark to investigator Philip Mantle about his experience. He said that when he confronted the 'aliens', everything seemed very amateurish and staged, as if they were putting on a show for his benefit. Also, Ted Bloecher, an American investigator, stated:

> Falling back on my own experience of sixteen years as an actor, I think that a lot of these close-encounters, especially those involving occupants have the stagiest qualities about them I've ever seen. What the witnesses are describing may be true and they are telling the truth, but it doesn't mean necessarily that what they are describing is actually what is going on.[44]

Returning to the evidence for ES/psychic witnesses obtaining UFO-related imagery from investigators in an on-going and drawn-out investigation, it would seem that this can also occur in poltergeist outbreaks. In the investigation of the Enfield poltergeist, completely private information concerning the circumstances of the accidental death of the daughter of one of the investigators was obtained from the adolescent 'focus'. The author of a book on the case and one of the investigators commented on his investigator-colleague's daughter, and her posthumous involvement:

> If he believed his Janet had survived physical death and was somehow involved in our case, then he must have very good reasons to feel that way.
>
> I tried to put myself in Janet Grosse's [the deceased daughter] position. She had tried to 'get through' just after her death, and she had successfully steered her father to Enfield . . . How else could I account for the extraordinary involvement that Maurice had clearly felt in the Enfield case right from the first day he went there? He had certainly taken hold of it as if there had been some deep personal reason for his being there.[45]

Unexplained injections of information into the investigation situation that only the investigator would know, and his sense of personal involvement, are surely indicative of the transference of that information from investigator to 'focus'. It made the investigator reinterpret his role in the case and to consider seriously the existence of life after death. Without wishing to hurt the feelings of the investigator concerned, this is an extremely challenging hypothesis. A more likely answer is that the information was obtained from the investigator by ESP by the extremely 'psychic' 'focus'.

This 'focus' was, after all, producing PK effects constantly. As PK is identified with ESP, it follows logically that ESP must have been also occurring, possibly as frequently as the poltergeist phenomena he was investigating. We have seen the identification of PK processes with CE experiences, frequently to the extent of taking place *after* the encounter is over, as poltergeist phenomena. Once again, logically, we would expect the occurrence of ESP during the post-encounter investigation. It would explain how obviously 'UFO naïve' witnesses 'reveal' such imagery to investigators and it would also be consistent with the 'revelation' of private information in poltergeist investigation. The 'Jane Murphy' CE4 'abduction' case is a good example of witness/investigator ESP, and is described in detail in the case studies in the next chapter.

It concerns two seasoned, well-read figures in British ufology, who investigated a 'UFO naïve' witness in West Yorkshire. She telephoned a UFO 'hotline' to report that she had been interfered with by aliens over a period of 12 years. Both investigators regard her experiences as internally produced and perceived, but they were perplexed (just as the Enfield poltergeist investigators were) by the information that she gave during their five interviews with her. It corresponded with the 'abduction' cases they had read about in America, in books by artist Budd Hopkins. Although they felt that her experiences were intermingled with dreams (a potent source of ESP) they had no idea where the information came from. More gullible, fantasy-prone and less rigorous investigators would have attributed it to *real* abductions by *real* aliens. But the case revolved around the question as to where she obtained the information. It could only have been from the investigators themselves, although it may have been in combination with another option.

The entity experience

The alternative centres on the consistent characteristics of all entity types; basically put, it states that all of the different entity types – whether they are 'abduction aliens', guardian angels, men-in-black, incubi and succubi, Blessed Virgin Marys, devils, demons, goblins and so on – all have their own particular characteristics, which sometimes overlap.

Men-in-black are depicted as dressing and behaving in a particular way; Blessed Virgin Marys bestow faith-based religious messages and have a certain recognizable appearance; out-of-body-related entities and creatures are perceived during these experiences, and look and behave in particular ways, and so on. All of these are embodiments or personifications, *which also colour our dreams*, of the stresses, fears, obsessions, traumas, growth and rebirth developments, feelings of safety and stability, etc. that we all, as thinking and feeling human beings, possess. We are not usually aware of this inner life, and repress it as part of our way of looking at the world.

Furthermore, the unconscious, being eternally creative, will take material not only from the outside world and rearrange it for its own expressive needs, it will be aware of the inner workings of our nervous system, so it can produce images that embody unusual electrical activity or chemical imbalances or that express a newly acquired metabolic equilibrium that could have been acquired by the intrusion of electrical fields. 'Jane Murphy', from time to time, seems to have been perceiving imagery pushed up by her unconscious expressing an inner complex that revolves around sex and childbirth that other women evidently share. No doubt it has a psychoanalytic label, and a question that should be asked is: What would these experiences say about the witness if they were dreams? What would they reveal about the state of her psyche and/or bodily functioning? In fact, they *are* closely intertwined with her dream-life and, as we will see from the case details, she is not always too sure which are which.

Also, another important question that should be asked about 'abductions', is what function exactly does the experience fulfil for the witness? A series of 'abductions' usually means that the witness is being constantly exposed to fields from somewhere, and they could be seen as spontaneously occurring therapeutic 'doses' of psychodrama which act as a release valve for inner conflict. As a dramatic presentation, with the aliens symbolizing disassociated parts of the self induced by the effect of the field, the 'abduction' experience certainly *seems* to be an enactment of a monitoring of mind/body functions. The aliens are reported as capturing, examining, taking samples of sex cells to produce an alien/human hybrid (which is biologically impossible). This seems to be the self in the process of metamorphosis. On the functional level, the aliens are depicted as inserting probes in the nose, which appears to be a reference to the monitoring of atmospheric pollutants, because it is the nasal membranes that are the first to 'detect' allergenic airborne chemicals, etc. So, something of the 'alien' reality is left behind (none have ever been recovered)[46] when the aliens are gone, and it is reassuringly or threateningly there, according to the tone of the overall experience. It is this order of question that we should be asking to make sense of the 'abduction' experience: What function does it fulfil for the percipient?

Such enquiries about the mental state of these witnesses does not, of course, imply psychosis, but 'normal' levels of neurosis, which we all cope with to some degree. Developmental trauma exists within all of us, which affects our day-to-day functioning. The unconscious acts as the 'intelligence of the nervous system', as it were, and we have been aware of the existence of the unconscious in pre-Freudian times, but we have called it something else. In fact, every religion has its own name for that aspect of the human organism, such as 'soul' or 'spirit'.

Therefore, as I argued at the beginning of this book, the unconscious is using the perceptual apparatus to present dramas depicting aliens and their spaceships, and from sociological and psychological responses to them, these dramas can be regarded as seeds of future religions, potentially anyway; that is to say, such UFO-related experiences may give rise to religious movements, such as Subud, the Aetherius Society or the Pendragon Research movement established by Robert France. So, as well as psychological questions, we should be asking theological ones. The only trouble with this approach is that it is totally unscientific and faith-based, and there is already a surfeit of it in UFO-study circles.

The chemistry of the altered state in close encounters

For some time, respected researchers have repeatedly maintained that there is no evidence that the altered state exists. They have stated that we either have to make assumptions from the behaviour of those that we think are in altered states, or take their word that they perceive things differently. They claim that there is no detectable objective criteria to identify the altered state.

Yet, there are numerous scientific papers and studies on the chemistry of the altered state, which identify specific altered perceptual functioning with specific processes and organic brain chemicals that are responsible for such states. Research into the military and therapeutic uses of LSD 25 in the 1960s was a particularly potent source of such scientific material. Obviously, the two approaches are incompatible, and perhaps the former assumption was based on the inability of researchers to correlate specific electrical behaviour in the brain with the hypnotic or hypnoid state. However, even this limitation is dubious, because specific brain frequencies have been long identified with specific moods, thought patterns and habituation trances, and they have been labelled accordingly. This important aspect of brain chemistry in relation to the altered state in CE has been covered fairly recently in the books of Serena Roney-Dougal. Her rigorous material will not be duplicated here, apart from the following relevant extracts.

> The geomagnetic anomaly associated with the areas in which UFOs are most commonly found, affects our pineal gland which produces more beta-carboline which takes us into a psi-conducive dream state of consciousness where we are both psychic and 'think' at the collective unconscious level of our mind, in dream images, hallucinations, and archetypal primary process thought. It is at this level of our minds that we are most in touch with, or at one with, the world mind, which is

manifesting as UFO form. Thus the UFO energy will respond according to the prevailing conditions, such as how close one is, time of day, ambient electromagnetic conditions, psychic ability of the percipient, and so on.[47]

From this, it can be seen that field exposure produces an imbalance in the chemistry of the brain that is directly related to an unconscious-dominated state. We now have an understanding about how field-radiating UAPs affect specific areas of the brain (i.e., the pineal gland). This small peanut-sized nodule deep inside the centre of the brain's hemispheres can be regarded as its chemical factory. It is extremely sensitive to field exposure and, as we can see from the following extract, it is closely connected with psychic functions. Roney-Dougal continues:

> The link between psychic sensitivity and geophysical variation, is a very clear strong link between the Earth and our psychic spiritual sensitivity. I have noticed in my literature survey of research on the pineal gland that the pineal is also responsive to the EMF (Earth's Magnetic Field). The production of melatonin in the pineal gland, which is almost certainly the precursor for the possibly psi-conducive pinoline, is affected not only by light, but also by the EMF. The fact that the EMF affects the functioning of the pineal gland suggests a neuromechanism by which our psi ability is affected by the EMF.

This shows that both invisible and visible sections of the electromagnetic spectrum (the EMF and visible light) can affect the pineal gland to produce the chemical climate conducive to altered states. This corresponds with the two criteria that have to be managed during the CE experience in relation to sensory noise. It is also evident that magnetic anomalies can create consciousness anomalies, including, of course, CEs, but also a variety of strange perceptions. The following case provides an example.

The man who lives on a fault

Eric Howerd is a no-nonsense, tough-minded Yorkshireman who lives in Ossett, West Yorkshire. He has a large family and he has worked in a variety of challenging occupations, including coal mining. He is quite aware that his house is built over a fault-line, and a pylon carrying high-tension cables looms over his back garden. He reports that his garden shed is below these cables and if he is in there for a while he develops headaches. He also relates a wide range of psychic phenomena and perceptions in his house, including apparitions. The most startling hallucinatory and almost religious experience was also partially witnessed by one of his sons.

One winter's evening Eric went out into his conservatory to get away from the hustle and bustle of a large household. There he saw a huge orange full moon quite low down, with a few steel-grey clouds around it. After a few minutes everything went strangely silent – nothing was heard from the nearby pig-farm or busy motorway. To his astonishment, the clouds around the moon quickly formed themselves into an image of a huge angel with perfectly clear-cut features and huge wings. It had a sad, downcast expression on its face, and it was so clear that Eric could see the lines on the feathers on the wings. As Eric puts it: 'This was not a "could have been" or just some cloud formation that had a resemblance to an angel, but absolutely truly the form of an angel. I was astounded!'

He then called to his family and his young son joined him, but before he did this the angel had 'dismantled' itself and the clouds moved down to the 'base' of the moon's shape to form a 'stage', as Eric puts it, which was created by a line of clouds cutting off a chord at the bottom of the moon. He tells us that the clouds did not just blow away, but went in reverse order back into the 'stage'. Then, to Eric and his son's astonishment the steel-grey clouds rose up again and formed a 'classic mushroom cloud that follows a nuclear explosion'.

Afterwards, the clouds swirled up again into the form of a huge crucifix, standing taller than the moon. Eric relates: 'It was not a wispy, barely defined crucifix, but was well-defined with outlines and edges so sharp . . . its whole appearance was so solid.' This too disassembled and a battered eagle took its place: 'It looked as if it had a real good hiding, as if some great fox or dog had worried it.' Things returned to normal and the father and son were left with a great sense of awe.

Nobody else saw these forms; if they had been objectively real, they would have caused a furore in the population of Ossett. These perceptions were a good example of a shared hallucination and a non-UFO-related OZ factor silence. Both were caused by a magnetic field and/or seismic electricity from the fault below the house acting upon the brain. Ambient electrical fields from the pylons contributed to the EM conditions. The symbolic content was apocalyptic in theme and it was an attempt by the unconscious to induce religious belief.

It has been mentioned that ES people are able to emit fields themselves and sense the presence of other electrical fields in the environment. It was proposed that this ability was instrumental in their psychic perceptions and associated phenomena. It was also argued that these people can 'see' optically invisible UAPs or apparitional forms imprinted into a field by the unconscious, and fields act as a medium into which the unconscious can implement its imagery. Eric does perceive apparitions in his house fairly regularly, and when he was asked about a possible condition of electrical hypersensitivity, he casually mentioned that when he was in a friend's house he walked past a metal box mounted on the wall in the hallway and immediately felt a strong field presence. He mentioned this to his friend, who revealed that it was a transformer for the various power tools he used. This extra sense that ES people have is very closely linked with their psychic abilities and perceptions, and it can be detected, measured and generally investigated by conventional scientific/technical means. This alone should revolutionize the investigation procedures that UFO and psychic researchers employ.

The work of Michael Persinger

No discussion of altered states in the close-encounter experience would be complete without references to the findings and work of Michael Persinger. He is a professor of psychology and research science, and head of the Neuroscience Laboratory at Laurentian University in Sudbury, Ontario. He specializes in human behaviour and the physical mechanisms of the natural sciences. He has addressed the CE experience specifically, as we have already seen from extracts from his work, and his findings are entirely compatible with the major premises of the ESH.

For example, he too has come to the conclusion that the 'sense of presence' is a component of 'alien visitation', although he does not, of course, place it in the context of purposefully 'staged' encounter dramatizations. He also seems to limit its occurrence to 'bedroom visitations' rather than examining the broader context of the range of encounter situations that are found. Consider an extract from one of his papers:

> the 'visitor' experience is a more intense variant of the 'sense of presence'; a phenomenon frequently reported by normal people. (Approximately 30 per cent of 500 normal adults who have been assessed in the Neuroscience Laboratory over the last 15 years have reported this experience.) The 'presence' is felt most frequently in the early morning hours. If the person is asleep, he or she will suddenly awaken, often feeling some fear or even immobility.
>
> Such experiences are thought to be correlated with mesiobasal (amygdaloid-hippocampal) portions of the temporal lobes. These areas of the brain are associated *inter alia* with the experience of meaningfulness, the sense of self and its relationship to space-time (with its religious or 'cosmic' associations), fear, dreams, experiences of movements (like spinning or floating), smell, and memory storage and retrieval. Consequently, there should be (and there are) references to the sense of

presence, feelings of spinning or floating, or of vibrations; dreamlike sequences; and fear or irritability. Because an important part of the temporal lobe receives visual information from the edges of the visual field, flickering sensations can occur in the upper peripheral vision.[48]

Interestingly, the reference to 'irritability' describes CH's somewhat inappropriate response during the bedroom BOL experience described earlier. It is these seemingly trivial, but highly specific, correlations that repeatedly occur when exploring encounter experiences that tend to confirm the validity of the field exposure 'diagnosis'. Relatively few ufologists have actually absorbed Persinger's highly important work into their view of UFO-related phenomena, and this is partly due to the entrenched positions of the ETH fraternity. It is also due to the absence of Persinger's work in a popular format in Britain, as most of his publications appear to be either scientific papers or tucked away in the specialist journals not easily accessible to the general public.

Returning to the extract from the 'visitor' experience, we can identify numerous systemic effects that are repeatedly reported in encounter experiences outside the 'bedroom visitor environment'. Also, in addition to this 'sense of presence' utilized to make an entity hallucination 'more real', immobility (which occurs to an enhanced degree with ES witnesses) is an especially well-reported symptom. Elements such as this are manipulated by the unconscious to establish and maintain a sensory noise-free state. Therefore, in the ESH, Persinger's work has been extended, in that the systemic effects he describes are *managed* by the UI to create and maintain, once more, an altered state.

Another important extension relates to the field source that precipitates the effects Persinger found. Consider his statements on this:

> The specific trigger for the 'visitor' experience, particularly the type that is associated with UFO phenomena, has been hypothesized to involve direct exposure to tectonic strain fields. People whose houses are built over susceptible areas (e.g., fault-lines) may be exposed frequently to the displays of these fields, which, while thought to be very focused and of brief duration, are very intense. Because of the intense electrical lability of the temporal lobes, their stimulation would generate the electrochemical changes that could promote the 'visitor' experience. Short pulses of energetic stimuli would be optimal for facilitating the normal burst firing pattern of the human amygdala . . . We have found that exposure to low-intensity, extremely low-frequency brain frequency fields evoke partial amnesia, exacerbate vestibular images, and alter suggestibility.[49]

Part of the ESH's supporting structure extends the identification of the seismic/tectonic field sources to include artificially produced fields. That Persinger has not done this is somewhat puzzling, as it was artificial fields that *he* used in his experiments in the laboratory. This absence of the correlation of natural and artificial field sources is probably due to a general lack of information about the effects of electronic communication systems on the human organism and environment; that is to say, an absence of public information and public awareness on electronic pollution. Without being conspiratorial about this aspect, organizations which operate multi-billion-pound/dollar communications systems *are* reluctant to reveal information about their equipment's possible side-effects and safety levels. Public awareness could limit the systems' usage, thereby jeopardizing current investment and future profits.

Returning specifically to the information in the last extract, it is evident that periods of amnesia *can* be induced by field exposure. This is, of course, highly relevant to the 'time-lapse' or 'missing time' of UFO lore. In fact, the Aveley case is a good example of this. In other papers by Persinger produced subsequently, he notes that the symptoms produced at the time of the pulsed-field exposures can reoccur several days afterwards. Such post-encounter effects have been found and interpreted by those favouring alien intervention, as further proof of such alien involvement. Needless to say, this is a misinterpretation.

In the Ossett case, two witnesses were subjected to fault-line radiation and hallucinated, which resulted in a shared experience. It was detailed how the fault-line experience closely parallels the CE experience in many ways, and this provides much needed practical confirmation, from a spontaneous case, for the scenario implied by Persinger's findings.

Persinger *does* go on, however, to identify other triggers to the 'visitor' experience that he identifies with encounters. Predictably, these relate to developmental trauma (described by Janov), in addition to stress associated with life-crises; that is to say, those who have a high level of stress/trauma would be more likely to be triggered into producing the 'visitor' experience. This cross-refers exactly with the conditions found in poltergeist-active households, where an unhappy or disturbed individual becomes the 'focus' for PK effects. This is, of course, Jung's 'exterior-ization' theory that was earlier correlated with encounter reality-producing witnesses.

In terms of investigation, these aspects highlight the need for in-depth exploration of witnesses' current life patterns and preoccupations. This 'status report' is comparable with a quasi-psychoanalytic approach that would be undertaken to determine the reasons for, and significance of, specific dream contents. However, having stated the approach with reference to dreams, it is evident that other sources, such as the physiological conditions within the nervous system and other systemic areas, can be symbolically represented in encounters: for example, physiological reactions to field exposure. As a general rule, the intrusion and effect of fields are symbolically represented as alien, for that is how the nervous system apprehends them. As the human nervous system reacts more or less consistently to fields from person to person, a similarly consistent set of dramatizations, themes, symbols, physical effects and entity types will occur. This *key* aspect in the understanding of 'abduction' experiences, for example, was touched upon in the section on the issue of consistency, in Chapter Two. Therefore, it can be said that encounter material derives from parallel but distinctly different levels in the unconscious – from dream origins. That is to say, the symbolism of dreams relates to the life-flow of the individual, whereas encounter imagery consists of scenarios which contain urgent systemic information about the state of the body in relation to allergens in the environment. Persinger continues his comments on personal trauma as a trigger for the 'visitor' experience:

> A more common but more mundane form of the experience associated with grief is the apparition following bereavement, which appears to be promoted by sudden increases in geomagnetic activity.

Persinger is referring to the close cousin of the 'crisis apparition' which the SPR have also documented countless times, which need not be associated with death, but danger, stress and/or isolation. There have been reports of figures of friends or relatives who have appeared 'in the nick of time' in desperate situations and given the witness some information that solves their predicament in some way. Uncle Bill appearing bizarrely misplaced on the roadside with a cheerful demeanour, while the witness is out driving in dangerous snow-bound and icy conditions, to direct the car to safety or a short-cut, etc., is the sort of 'crisis apparition' that the unconscious can produce. In such a case, it is clear that the unconscious of the traveller has obtained practical information by clairvoyance and presented it to the conscious mind in the form of cheerful and helpful Uncle Bill.

Surely then, if UFOs or sightings of 'alien craft' are sometimes apparitional, we should find examples of 'crisis alien craft' or 'crisis UFOs' which fulfil the same survival function? If this were the case, the witness would have to be someone with such imagery in their 'picture library' for the unconscious to use. Consider an example of *precisely* this:

> It happened some years ago in the Mojave Desert of California, a hell on earth where temperatures can soar to such levels that you cannot survive for long unprotected.

It was 130° F as the sun beat down relentlessly. He had ridden out on a motorcycle along with four friends, and they were in the middle of nowhere, at the mercy of the elements. Stopping for respite and a very necessary drink of water, he let his friends ride on into the distance. Their machines glinted in the sun as they vanished over the roadless horizon.

With his thirst quenched he decided it was time to catch them up. His heart missed a beat when he realized that the motorcycle engine was not turning over. It was totally dead – as he would be himself if he did not find a way out of this mess very soon. He hoped that his friends would return, but they probably knew better than to get themselves lost by turning back. Besides they had no immediate reason to think he was in danger.

After many frustrating minutes of trying to fix the machine, during which his canteen of water soon disappeared, he knew that he had to start moving. He pushed the heavy motorcycle, blindly trusting to luck that he was heading towards civilization rather than away from it, but the heat and exhaustion soon got the better of him. Strong as he was, this was just too much, and he collapsed on to the ground, with concern rapidly turning into despair.

Then something flickered in the sky above. It was streamlined and made of shiny metal. It looked for all the world like a UFO.

As it moved away, he felt an urge in his mind that he should set off walking in a different direction. What was happening? It was as if some kind of telepathic voice was telling him softly inside his head and encouraging him to keep going and to take a certain path. Perhaps, he thought, foolishly, this was some alien intelligence connected with the UFO, and it was trying to rescue him.

. . . Then after a while, to his intense relief, a petrol station loomed up ahead . . . he returned home without ill-effect.[50]

The witness in the above encounter experience was William Shatner, Captain of the Starship Enterprise of *Star Trek* . . .

7 Case-Studies

Trance machines and spirit ships,
Land during total eclipse,
In the evening, after dark,
Quietly landing in the park,
Trance machines and spirit ships,
Inner space and inner trips.

The following case-studies have been chosen to illustrate the central principles of the ESH, namely that the human unconscious, in response to specific field exposure that produces altered states of consciousness, can present dramatically 'staged' perceptions of interaction with 'aliens and their spacecraft', and that these perceptions overlap with such psychic experiences as apparitions, poltergeists and visions.

These examples present three cases of encounters with an 'earthlight' UAP, which provided the radiation-trigger, and four where such radiation emanated from artificial sources.

Essington Canal, Birmingham, England

Location: By the towpath of the Essington Canal, near the disused Sneyd Canal basin, between Bloxwich and Short Heath
Witness: Mr A. M. living at Walsall
Investigator: Stephen Banks
Date: 27 January 1983

The investigator describes the sighting as: 'A night sighting of a cigar-shaped object of some size and altitude, akin to a mirror in effect, plus subsequent contact with alleged beings of humanoid appearance in archetypal costume. Brief conversation and disappearance.'

217

One winter's evening, the witness decided to walk to a friend's house alongside a disused network of canals. It was cold and the towpath was wet underfoot, with occasional marshy areas. The journey took the witness along the length of the Essington Canal. After he had been walking for about 20 minutes, his attention was caught by an elongated mirror-like object in the sky above him, which blinked out almost immediately. Puzzled, he continued for a short distance until he noticed two figures standing in a grassy area to his right (canal to his left). They spoke to him 'in an educated tone above his level of speech, but with a sort of mechanical sound associated with robots . . . The speech was in English and they used their arms as if to express themselves.' They asked him if he would go on a journey with them and he replied he would not. Then, after AM had explained that he wanted to see his wife and children again, they reassured him on this point and said that he would get a reward if he did agree to go. He still refused and tensed himself for the use of force. It did not come and the figures turned and silently glided away together over the rough grass 'like ice-skaters', and when they were about ten yards away, faded from view.

AM relates that they were definitely waiting for him, and that he was more stunned by the encounter than disturbed. He returned home rather than continue on his walk and he described his encounter to his disbelieving wife. The figures were not tall, at about five feet six inches, and were good-looking, with dark curly hair. They had a composite of features of many racial types: oriental-shaped cheek-bones, blue eyes, red lips, negroid nose but with a very white complexion. They were identical and had perfectly proportioned muscular bodies with sleek waists, all covered with a tight, grey one-piece body suit. They spoke in unison through a permanently open, gaping mouth which did not move. There was a logo on the top corner area of their chests and they were both self-luminous.

Post-encounter effects
AM had a series of 'super-real' dreams about a king-like authority figure whom he associated with his experience.

The witness
AM was long-term unemployed, with a history of psychic experiences which included sightings of apparitions. His beliefs include witchcraft and they are an amalgam of spiritual Von Daniken ideas and personal philosophy of a left-wing nature. He is ES and electrical equipment malfunctions in his presence.

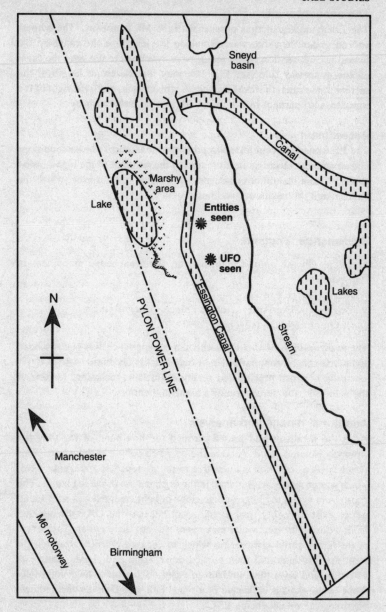

Fig. 10 A diagrammatic representation of the Essington Canal incident location.

The encounter site

The Essington Canal runs parallel with the M6 motorway. The witness walked under the motorway and along the length of the canal on the towpath. High-tension cables mounted on pylons were just over the canal on the motorway side (see Fig. 10); they run the entire length of the section of the canal that AM walked. A stream runs just to the right of the towpath, also parallel with it, and ends in a reservoir near by.

Assessment

The ES witness was subjected to prolonged low-sensory noise conditions and an ambient electrical field created by the presence of the high-tension cables. These conditions induced an altered state during which he hallucinated the encounter realities.

Stonehenge, England

Location: On the approach to, and at, the Stonehenge monument in Wiltshire
Witnesses: Dorne and Lee
Investigators: Clive Potter, Robert France, Albert Budden
Date: On or about 18 November 1990

The main outline of this close-encounter experience has already been given and can be summarized as a duel-witness encounter with a UAP/ 'earth light' which precipitated reality distortions, including, for one of the witnesses, the perception of a humanoid entity.

Additional details and analysis

After the witnesses had passed through the first band of fog they felt strangely isolated, 'as if we were the only two people in the world'. This typically silent isolation is indicative of the presence of a magnetic field, which was probably instrumental in the organization of the fog bands. The copse from which the huge orange globe of light emerged was later found not to exist in reality, just as the small hill that the UAP disappeared behind during its spectacular movement was not there either. The period of the light's aerial manoeuvres which so engaged Dorne's attention ('it went up very high and then hurtled down again and zipped along just above ground level then straight up again tracing out a huge rectangle-shape in the sky') is indicative of a signal link with Dorne's unconscious/ physiological system (being ES).

The hallucination of the trees and hill were to control sensory noise, that is to say, her system would have detected the invisible part of the field emission from the UAP as they approached, but the visible light that emanated from the globe would have created a sensory noise level that would have undermined the maintenance of the altered state, so it had to be controlled. This was accomplished by inducing an 'apparitional' type of hallucination of the copse and the hill to obscure the light when it threatened the stability of the altered state. We have seen that apparitions can act like physical objects in that they can obscure a line of vision or other objects.[1] The unconscious used these apparitional objects as a cut-out mechanism to control the visible light emissions when required, as it monitored the altered state that Dorne was subject to. It was stated earlier that sensory noise control was an intregal aspect of the 'stage management' of encounters. The rapid movement of the globe also served to reduce the amount of exposure to the light upon the retina, as a stationary light would have exceeded this and acted as a source of interfering sensory noise, which would have undermined the altered state.

Oddly, Lee refused to look at the luminous globe, and actually stood with his back to it, facing the monument. It may be that this in-appropriate behaviour was subliminally induced and related to a higher level of instability of his altered state (i.e., he had a lower sensory noise tolerance). However, both were irradiated, as evidenced by the 'cooked' banana in the car. Also, Lee's perception of the huge dark entity, which reflected his anxiety regarding the security guards, was another product of this state. The 'staging' depicted it as meanacing as he hallucinated its noisy 'leaf-stamping' approach, despite the fact that there were few leaves around the windswept monument. This depiction made the witnesses flee the scene. This 'stage management' strategy, utilized by Lee's unconscious, reflects the transient nature of this apparition, with a limited visual life.

At one point, Dorne touched the heel-stone and received a tingling shock from it, or so she believed. It was later found that this would have been impossible due to the security fence. This was evidently a systemic field effect incorporated into the encounter drama which left a lasting circulatory symptom as periodic 'pins and needles'. Dorne and Lee had visited the monument a few weeks previously. Therefore, they had a fairly fresh 'stock' of Stonehenge imagery in their 'picture library' that the unconscious would have been able to draw upon in the construction of this experience; that is to say, Dorne's experience consisted of a large proportion of internal memory-based perceptions into which her uncon-scious could introduce 'reality replacements' and 'memory loops'.

The witnesses and the post-encounter effects
Dorne, predictably, has a history of dramatic psychic experiences, including UFOs that she regarded as illusory. She is an intelligent and

articulate young woman who takes a balanced view of her experiences and rejects suggestions of such things as spirits and aliens. She is ES, and relates: 'I first noticed it when I was 16. I thought it was coincidence; in particular, electric kettles kept coming on by themselves. Also, Lee sometimes says I seem to give off something that makes him feel uncomfortable. I get migraines from fluorescent light in shops, but the only allergy I have noticed is hay fever.'

Lee suddenly developed strong psychic abilities after the encounter, which is the 'over-run' effect of a field-activated unconscious function. However, he has blocked the memory of the encounter, and apart from acknowledging its existence, he will not speak about it. Limited space restricts comment on numerous other aspects of this case that serve to confirm the ESH's involvement in the understanding of cases like this.

Central Promenade, Blackpool, England

Location: Grasmere Road, near the sea-front
Date: 6 July 1989
Witness: Andrew Billing
Investigators: Joseph Dormer and June Reynolds

This case is comparable, in some respects, with the sighting of a UAP/'earthlight' by Kevin Cunningham from the Central Pier. We have seen in case after case how witnesses involved in close-encounter experiences almost always have a history of psychic phenomena and ES, and this witness conforms to this pattern.

This case provides another example of an individual affected by an earthlight UAP to the extent of undergoing a 'reality replacement' experience. I am indebted to Joseph Dormer of the Fylde UFO Investigation Group for the following material taken from the case-study entitled 'Glowing Object with Tornado in Pursuit'.

The encounter experience

'At 11.10 pm Mr Billing was driving down Grasmere Road, towards Central Drive (on the sea-front), when he noticed, through an open window of his cab (he is a cab-driver), a large orange-red, brightly glowing, round-shaped object "about the size of a two-pence piece held at arm's length". He had been watching it for little more than a couple of seconds when it moved "at fantastic speed", "faster than the eye could see" to another part of the sky further away. Here it hovered for a further couple of seconds before repeating the manoeuvre, finally disappearing out of sight in the north-west.

Within no more than five seconds after the object went out of sight, an RAF Tornado fighter plane, flying very low, 400–500 feet (somewhat lower than the Blackpool Tower at 519 feet) and very fast, with its wings swept right back shot across the sky from over the sea, in the direction of the UFO, as if in pursuit of it. "It had no lights on at all," said Mr Billing, "which was unusual because it was dusk, though not completely dark. As it came across I saw smoke in front of the aircraft and also behind, with a dull flash in the middle." This, the witness believes, could only have been an air-to-air missile being fired at the object.'

The idea of a military plane firing a missile at *anything*, let alone a UFO, in a popular seaside resort at the height of the holiday season, is ridiculous. Nevertheless, the slim possibility that this took place was checked by the investigators. They found that there was nothing in that air-space at all at that time. The radar was not switched on at Blackpool airport, but British Aerospace also confirmed the negative findings.

The witness reports that there was no noise whatsoever from the Tornado, and the absence of any lights and the 'dull flash' of the purported missile firing is indicative of the low-sensory noise conditions imposed by the unconscious harnessing ambient field effects, in its hallucinatory production of this 'Earth vs Flying Saucers' theme drama. Not surprisingly, nobody else came forward to report the Tornado, which is further evidence of the personalized reality of the encounter. A fast-moving orange light over the sea may have been missed, but a jet circling the Blackpool Tower . . .

The witness has a long history of psychic experiences, including apparitions and, like Jean Hingley, the fairy being shaken from a Christmas tree. Years earlier he had experienced a similar scenario where a Lightning fighter had chased a black cylinder-like UFO, causing the latter 'to become invisible'. This 1989 version is obviously a more dramatic remake of this recurrent symbolism, just as dreams reflect an inner complex. In terms of the function of the symbolism, it is difficult not to notice that the names of both types of plane correspond with powerful and energetic natural phenomena – a tornado and lightning. The choice of these planes from his 'picture library' reflects a thematic response by his unconscious. It is as if the UFO is regarded as an alien element which has to be destroyed by powerful Earth-originating forces. This is archetypal conflict symbolism that represents aspects of the witness's psyche and inner life that perhaps only he could identify.

The movement of the earthlight UAP

The behaviour of the earthlight was covered in Chapter Five, and it is proposed that its movement in 'instalments' relates to a radar sweep from the BBC weather survey radar dish on Blackpool Tower, pulling it through the atmosphere 'faster than the eye could see' and then releasing it as it revolved away. The area is evidently earthlight prone, with numerous sightings over the years. Whether they are produced by offshore submarine geology or elsewhere (e.g., a Bacup quarry) and are then attracted to the area presents two options that are not necessarily exclusive. The area of Fylde is faulted with deep saline caverns throughout, and there is evidence from Kevin Cunningham's observations that earthlights emerge just offshore from the sea; that is to say, *both* may be origins for the high incidence of these UAPs.

'Jane Murphy' alien abduction experiences

Location: Yorkshire
Date(s): The experiences began in 1975 when the witness was sixteen years old and they have occurred sporadically throughout a twelve-year period to the present day.
Witness: 'Jane Murphy'
Investigators: Philip Mantle and Andrew Roberts

I am indebted to Philip Mantle of the Independent UFO Network for the following information on this case, taken from interview transcripts and a case-file compiled by him and Andrew Roberts, editor of the well-known UFO study periodical *UFO Brigantia* (now defunct). This extended case consists of numerous events, beginning in 1975. It contains material which corresponds with what has come to be regarded as 'alien abduction' experiences. Much of the material is undated and unsequenced owing partly to the educational restrictions of the witness, but also to a distinct blurring of memory on her part. The witness's bizarre experiences are events which have a sense of temporal isolation about them. They are recounted with a tantalizing vagueness at times, and at others seem to arise spontaneously during the interviews she gave, *as if* the memories had just 'popped into her head': for example, during the fifth interview (there were over a dozen) Mantle states ' "Jane" immediately told us she had remembered the exact date of her "abduction" experience . . . many of the things raised by "Jane" have occurred in this way – suddenly remembered, even though the same topic had been covered in previous interviews.'

The trigger and the response

When 'Jane' was 16 and living at home (in the same area of the town where the experiences happened), she was awoken one night by a red light flooding through the curtains of her bedroom, accompanied by a 'spinning' sound. From her mother's testimony, this was not the first time that an unexplained light circled the house and a field at the rear. For the next five years, 'Jane' regularly had strange vivid dreams which changed into 'reality' after she moved into a house with her common-law husband to have a child. One very real dream amounted to what is known as an 'abduction by aliens'.

After going to bed one night, she 'awoke' to find herself in a field at the back of her house. In this field there was an enormous 'spaceship' that she could not describe, and some aliens were leading her towards it. They put something over her mouth to make her sleep and she pretended to be unconscious, but they were aware of this and gave her an injection. However, 'Jane' did not see the needle. She 'awoke' and found herself presumably inside the 'craft' and realized that the aliens wanted her to wash in a bath shaped just like the human body. Here she was somehow cleaned without water and then led to a table on which she lay down. After an alien communicated with her telepathically, she was examined in the genital area. The alien then had sex with her and during this she noticed that he had a 'bad smell'.

After intercourse, 'Jane' sat down at the table and saw some coloured pills, one of which she ate. It had no taste. Shortly after this, she suddenly found herself back in bed at home. She looked at her arm and saw a mark that looked like an injection site. Over the following weeks, she developed a vaginal infection which treatment from the doctor could not clear up, and she had to spend some time as an out-patient of a hospital, which eventually did eradicate the infection.

Comment

This is a typical 'abduction' experience, although the 'sex with an alien' aspect is uncommon, although not unique. Like so many of these accounts, many aspects have been left out (that the astute investigators included in their report, incidentally) to make the story flow and appear fantastic but feasible. Such 'narrative packaging' is a media requirement, where detail and shades of grey are stripped away, thereby rounding off the account. Like all accounts of this nature, once a balanced picture is sought, the credibility of much detail collapses; that which remains was caused by prolonged field exposure after a major electrical event in combination with 'contamination' from UFO literature of from those around the witness who had read more widely than she had. There is also the possibility that the witness obtained information about 'abductions' by electromagnetically scanning the investigators. Let us look at the evidence for these statements. It can be summarized as follows:

1 The UAP exposure at an early age, which was witnessed by her brother and sister who also were affected to some extent, triggered her unconscious into an activated state of increased imaging. Many witnesses like 'Jane' have had an experience with some kind of electrical phenomenon early in life. This increased imaging took the form of vivid dreams.

2 The area in which she lived all her life is overlooked by a major BBC and NTL transmitting antenna mounted on a hill – a situation which is comparable to Jean Hingley's (described in the next case-study).

3 When she moved to her present address, the phenomena increased noticeably. A row of pylons run across the fields at the back of her garden. From this it is possible to construct a picture of early UAP-induced field sensitivity combined with prolonged radio-wave exposure, to which was finally added electrical field exposure from pylon-mounted, high-tension cables.

4 The vaginal infection is the first field-induced systemic symptom noted. There is considerable scientific literature on the adverse effects of field exposure on the immune system, and the increased growth of bacteria and fungal infections in animals and humans when exposed to specific (but common) 'frequency windows'. This effect was incorporated into the internally perceived 'abduction' vision as 'alien intrusion'. This is consistent with this process in other encounter experiences.

5 *Acquired allergy* – 'Jane's' eventual electrically hypersensitive condition is confirmed by her description of a puzzlingly sudden and violent nauseous reaction to coffee which she herself notes appears particularly 'after something has happened', meaning a field-induced hallucination.

6 The witness describes the experience of electrical field exposure precisely, albeit unwittingly:

> Like I say, sometimes my mind blanks. It's as if I've started having these things more as well within the last three months . . . where I've woke M [husband] up, haven't I? . . . I've been that frightened. I've had this thing, like er, a force pulling me from my brain and my body. And I can feel, it's like a right loud noise through my head and in my body. It's like it's somebody's drawing [pulling] my body and my brain, and that's only started happening within the last few months.

The witness moved to her present home a few months before this report.

7 *Scratched pimples* – The witness called in the investigators to see one of the 'injection marks' which appeared suddenly. They both identified it as a pimple with the skin scratched off the top. Most allergies cause dermal irritation and rashes.

8 *Hyperaesthesia* – Minute amounts of domestic gas make 'Jane' feel ill. ES and associated allergy sufferers are hypersensitive to many stimuli that would not bother others.

9 *Radar hearing* – 'Jane' reported that she could hear a Morse-code-like 'signalling' at times. This phenomenon is 'radar hearing'.[2] It can be reproduced at specific frequencies in ES subjects and it is caused by electromagnetic waves setting up vibrations in the tiny bones in the inner ear, which resonate and send sound waves across the tympanic membrane (ear-drum).

10 *Anomalous sexual feelings* – These have been described by Blakemore (1988) and Ruttan (1990). They found that sexual feelings can be induced if the septal region of the brain (below the corpus callosum which joins the two hemispheres) is electrically stimulated. The maximum sensations were found to have been induced between 20–40Hz.

This is an abbreviated catalogue of 'Jane's' clearly recognizable and reproducible phenomena and symptoms, which have been 'identified' as alien activity by the ETH fraternity. It is clear that they are unquestionably and undeniably wrong in their assumptions.

Investigator 'scanning'

As a post-encounter effect, many reports include an incidence of what can only be described as 'information exchange' between the witness and those around her/him: a two-way flow can be identified, where the witness becomes aware of the private information of others, and others find that the perceptions of the witness intrude into their lives. Rakovic's work has shown that this is within scientific boundaries and Dr C. W. Smith's comments also support the existence of this effect. It occurred in the Rowley Regis case with the investigators and also in the Stonehenge event between the witnesses and others. In the Enfield poltergeist case, it was common and the investigators often found their private details (such as a family death and a car malfunction due to a racing engine) spoken through the adolescent 'focus'. The 'Jane Murphy' case could be boiled down to the question: Where did the witness get the details of the 'abduction' phenomenon from? I would suggest partly from the investigators themselves, although the human system reacts to fields consistently.

Concluding comments

In order to identify the specific aspects of this case, a lengthy analysis would be needed; space allows us only to consider the following:

1 The human-shaped bath reflects an unconscious response to the witness's perception of *a disturbed body-image*. Monroe's earlier comments indicate that this can be affected by field exposure.

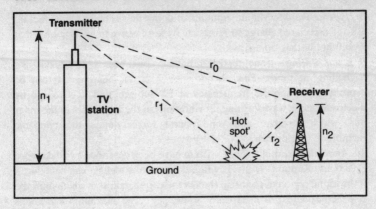

Fig. 11 Typical overland microwave communications circuit for AM, FM or TV.

2 The field presence that the witness is exposed to is personified as an alien presence, and, depending on the part of the body or brain that is affected by it, the alien activity will be depicted accordingly: field-induced sexual feelings were dramatized as intercourse with an alien.

Electronic pollution profile

Figure 11 shows a typical overland microwave communications circuit for AM, FM or TV frequencies. From such diagrams, which can be found in any reference book on electronics and/or radio-wave propagation, the location of the 'hot spot', at which on-going anomalous perceptions often occur, can be determined by simple geometry. Instead of waiting for cases to be reported, investigators can actually calculate where they should occur, and go out and look for them there. This would be case-prospecting!

Fig. 12 Plan of the ground floor of Jean Hingley's house and garden. (*Courtesy of Andrew Collins*)

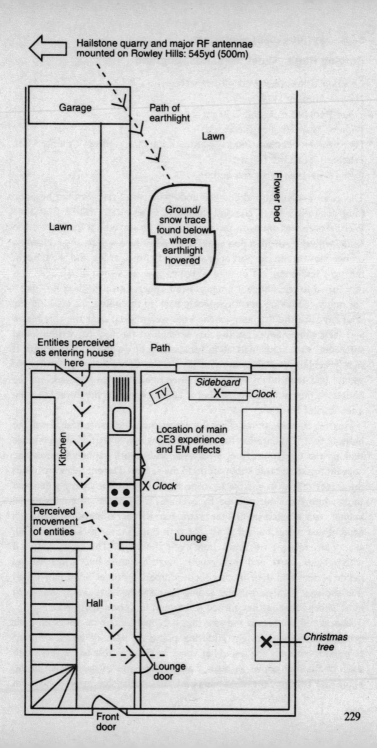

Hailstone quarry and major RF antennae mounted on Rowley Hills: 545yd (500m)

Garage

Path of earthlight

Lawn

Lawn

Flower bed

Ground/ snow trace found below where earthlight hovered

Entities perceived as entering house here

Path

TV

Sideboard
X — Clock

Location of main CE3 experience and EM effects

Kitchen

X Clock

Perceived movement of entities

Lounge

Hall

Christmas tree

Lounge door

Front door

Rowley Regis, West Midlands, England

Location: Bluestone Walk, Rowley Regis
Date: 4 January 1979
Time: Between 6.30 and 7.30 am
Witness: Jean Hingley (deceased)
Investigators: Stephen Banks, Martin Keatman, Andrew Collins, Mark Pritchard, Richard Tolley
Case re-investigated by the author

This case involved a middle-aged housewife who lived with her husband (and dog) on a small crescent-shaped housing estate, called Bluestone Walk. There was snow on the ground as Jean waved her husband off to work, with the Alsatian dog at her side. After he had left, she noticed an orange glow in the car-port area at the end of the garden and she thought the light had been left on. On walking down to switch it off, Jean was astonished to see a huge, orange glowing sphere hovering over it – 'like a big orange'. Making her way quickly back to the house she stood in the doorway with the dog and watched the sphere float over the small lawn and turn white. Suddenly the dog seemed to throw a fit, writhing and stiffening into a statue with all its fur standing up on end in spiky points. It rigidly keeled over sideways and lay on the floor, its eyes staring. No sooner had Jean taken this in than three beings rushed past her into the house. As they did this, she felt herself float away from the floor, hovering a few inches from it.

Hearing a commotion from the living-room, Jean drifted down the hallway to it. On entering the room, she saw two bizarre-looking entities shaking the Christmas tree. Eyes wide and mouth gaping, she saw the fairy on top of the tree shoot off on to the carpet. The entities were about three feet tall, with narrow tapering limbs coloured a silvery-green and snow-white faces surrounded by a close-fitting hood. A goldfish-bowl helmet, which had a small light on top like a miner's lamp, covered each head. Each wore a silver waistcoat with buttons down the front. Thin silvery streamers hung down from their shoulders. Their eyes glittered with a black lustre and their mouths were a simple line. They had no hands or feet and their limbs ended in tapering points. Jean now found that she was paralysed in the gaping pose she had struck and was even more shocked when they turned to her and in unison said, 'Nice?'

Jean could not speak and saw that they had large oval wings on their backs covered with bright glittering points of light of many different colours. Eventually she found her voice, so she was able to converse with them about such topics as Jesus, babies, the place of the woman in the home and Tommy Steele. At one point, the entities flew around the room

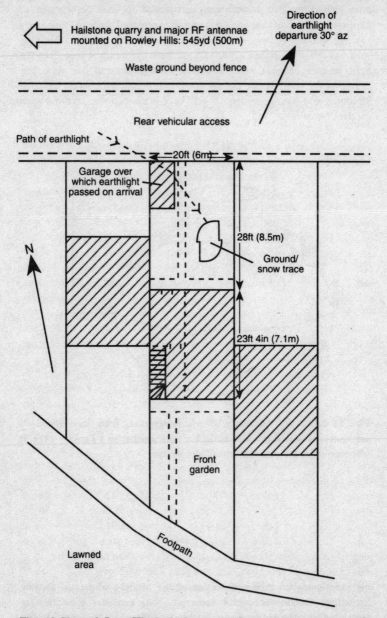

Hailstone quarry and major RF antennae mounted on Rowley Hills: 545yd (500m)

Direction of earthlight departure 30° az

Waste ground beyond fence

Rear vehicular access

Path of earthlight

20ft (6m)

Garage over which earthlight passed on arrival

28ft (8.5m)

Ground/ snow trace

N

23ft 4in (7.1m)

Front garden

Footpath

Lawned area

Fig. 13 Plan of Jean Hingley's house, garden and rear access road. (*Courtesy of Andrew Collins*)

after a third one had joined them, and picked up small objects such as Christmas cards and tape-cassettes and then replaced them. At times they would touch the buttons on their waistcoats which gave out a bleeping tone. At other times they would shoot a laser-like beam at Jean from the lights on their helmets, which struck her on the forehead, just above the bridge of the nose. It had the effect of both dazzling her to the point of blindness and paralysing her. It felt very hot when she received such sudden 'blasts'.

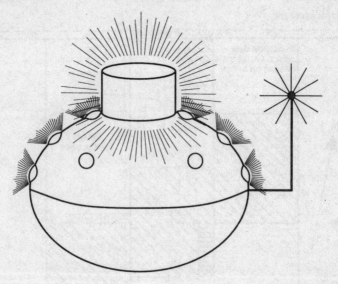

Fig. 14 Based on Andrew Collins's impression, with Jean Hingley's assistance, of the vehicle she saw in her back garden on 4 January 1979. It was seen from the rear window of the lounge.

Fig. 15 Geological map and section of the location where the Rowley Regis/Jean Hingley encounter occurred. Note extensive local faulting associated with the production of earthlights. (Based on *British Geological Survey, Technical Report: WA/91/55 by C. N. Waters, 1991*)

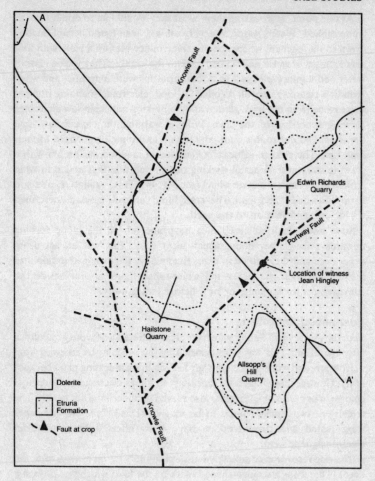

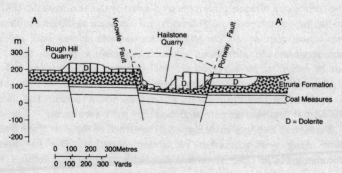

At one point, after asking them what they would like to drink, they all three replied 'Water, water, water' in unison. Jean found herself floating down to the kitchen, where she put some mince-pies on a plate with four small glasses of water and floated back to the lounge. They took a glass of water and a mince-pie each as if their arm-tips were magnetic, and when Jean lit a cigarette they all recoiled. A loud, electronic-sounding trumpet noise came from the back garden and on looking out, Jean saw an orange glowing 'spaceship' on the lawn. Without warning, the entities flew from the room and out to this craft, still with a mince-pie magnetized to their limb-tips. The strange vehicle looked like an inverted mushroom with a glowing stalk and an aerial sticking out of one side that ended in what looked like a rimless bicycle wheel (see Fig. 14). This began to revolve and lit up with a bright blue light. The 'craft' lifted vertically upwards, described a wide arc, and shot off to the north.

Soon after, Jean collapsed in a heap and felt all the blood rushing upwards through her body, which went cold. This was an agonizing experience and she writhed in pain. Eventually, she managed to flop into a chair and then she saw a tall white-robed figure appear beside the television set for a minute or two, before fading away.

Post-encounter effects

Like the Aveley and Subud witnesses, Jean suffered a nervous breakdown after the event. This was partly caused by the ridicule she received from neighbours and work-mates (she left her job in a car-sealing plant because of it). However, her increased sensitivity to things electrical and a distinct change in her physiological state also served to undermine her health. The television, two clocks (found to be magnetic) and some cassette tapes were tested and discovered to have been affected by a powerful electromagnetic field.

The dog recovered completely but slept soundly for many days after the event. There was a strange-shaped mark on the lawn which was probably the outline of a filled-in garden pond revealed by the heat from the UAP. In the light of the geophysical aspects and electronic pollution profile, it was almost certainly an 'earthlight'. Jean was also able to 'scan' others and obtain private information at times. Incredible as this may seem, it can be facilitated by increased personal electrical field emissions and is fairly common among ES subjects (Lee, in the Stonehenge case, was able to do this). The investigators were amazed when Jean suddenly told them the central details of an unrelated case they were working on.

There was a five-inch circle seemingly scratched on the glass of the front door along with a number of random scratches. This has been documented as an effect associated with fields that lightning produces. A similar effect was the whitening of Jean's gold wedding-ring after the encounter.[3] Smaller incised circles have occurred on the human body also which have been interpreted as 'alien tissue-sampling', but they are undoubtedly another field effect.

Jean also began having 'black-outs', which can be induced as a response to field exposure. Judging from the high electronic pollution profile, this was a response to on-going exposure that she had previously coped with at a sub-clinical level, but which now affected her more overtly.

The witness

Jean was quite a large lady with forthright views and a lot of down-to-earth common sense, despite her poor education. She was deeply religious and had psychic experiences throughout her life which were enhanced after the encounter.

The area of Rowley Regis (see Figures 15 and 16)

'Earthlights' have been correlated with the position of fault-lines and the area is five miles from the major Birmingham fault. Two large faults, Hodnett and Church Stretton, run directly through the area. The aero-magnetic map shows a major ridge of buried magnetic rocks. These include the naturally magnetic 'lodestone', or magnetite, and an abundance of ironstone, plus a widespread stratum of basalt, which becomes magnetic when struck by lightning.[4] The extension of the Birmingham Canal, fed by a reservoir, is close to the River Stour, near to Jean's area. The huge Hailstone quarry is about a quarter of a mile from Jean's rear garden, and it has been excavated from the highly mineralized Rowley Hills which loom over the area at the back of the car port where Jean first saw the hovering 'earthlight' (see the plate section between pages 112 and 113). In all, the area is a model geophysical type conducive to the production of earthlights.

Electronic pollution profile

Sited on the top of the Rowley Hills are two large transmitting radio masts (see the photographs) used by the minicab services in the area. One such mast in this 'ideal' location could certainly have created Jean's highly ES/'psychic' condition, but two, in conjunction with the unusually extreme geomagnetic aspects, would push this condition to a chronic level.

The UAP/'earthlight'

'Earthlights' have been consistently associated with quarries by investigators, and it is a safe deduction to identify the nearby Hailstone quarry as the origin of the one that Jean encountered. One of the radio masts would

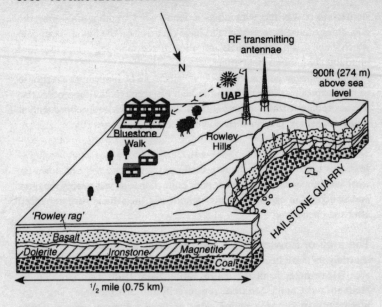

Fig. 16 Geophysical representation of the Hailstone Quarry area, Rowley Regis, showing the radio antennae and the trajectory of an earthlight UAP to Jean Hingley's house in Bluestone Walk.

have acted as a conductor from ground to air, and a transmission would have propelled it through the atmosphere. It is strange to think that someone ordering an early-morning cab would have unknowingly been instrumental in sending the huge globe of electromagnetic energy into Jean Hingley's 'lap' . . .

The encounter

Limited space does not allow for an exhaustive analysis of what exactly happened in Jean's house and garden. The UAP evidently irradiated both extremely powerfully, inducing the hallucinatory encounter that overlaps with so many other 'classic' cases.

'Terror in the House of Dolls'

Location: Gateshead, Strathclyde
Date: Events began in August 1979
Witnesses: 'Steve', 'Carol' and their family
Investigator: John Watson

This extremely bizarre case began in August 1979 and continued for almost a year. A family of four was affected by chronic field exposure, although the mother, 'Carol', was affected most severely due to her home-centred life-style (as was the case with 'Jane Murphy' and Jean Hingley). A number of standard effects resulting from field exposure can be identified, in conjunction with apparitional imagery of dwarfed alien figures and a tiny 'flying saucer' to match. Like the 'Jane Murphy' case, the field is transposed into 'alien' imagery, which is somewhat apt. Gateshead is surrounded by several powerful transmitting antennae, and should be an area of bizarre undiscovered cases. The reason for the sudden onset of phenomena is probably associated with a cumulative effect. This case represents a multiple exposure situation.

The events
In the early hours of 16 August, the husband, 'Steve', was on a nightshift, and 'Carol' could not sleep because she was suffering from toothache. She made some coffee and, while she was drinking it, she saw a red light flooding through the curtains. Looking out, she saw a dome-shaped object with red and white lights hovering over the houses opposite. It suddenly spiralled upwards and vanished. 'Carol' went back to bed and she was astonished to see a small, flattened bell-shape hovering at the top of the curtains, similar to the one she had seen outside. This one, however, was only 18 inches across and lit by a pale-grey light. Behind the 'saucer' was a 'swarm' of tiny glittering particles, which moved to the light-shade in the middle of the ceiling and hovered there. Then, the swarm descended on 'Carol'. She felt a tingling sensation accompanied by a heavy feeling which seemed to push her down. She felt subdued by this as if her senses had been dulled, and she could hear a loud buzzing and droning noise. Suddenly the swarm returned to the disc and she slowly returned to normal. Like 'Jane', she could hear a loud 'signalling' effect. She could also hear a strange 'lawn-mower' noise that seemed to circle the house. This went on all night.

Three hours later, 'Carol' was awoken by the intense tingling sensation, which she tried to shake off. When 'Steve' came home from work, he found her crying and in a state of shock. She felt hot and flushed and wax was running out of her ears. During the next few days she felt a pain in her left cheek and jaw and she developed a rash on her neck. Also, her young daughter, 'Nicola', would run into their room at night, which was atypical. She appeared frightened or apprehensive.

The next incident occurred two weeks later, once again in the early hours of the morning. 'Nicola' woke her mother up in a state of fear and 'Carol' had to go into her room to settle her. She suddenly felt the tingling and saw the 'saucer' tilted over on its side, looking brighter than before. It suddenly vanished, and 'Carol' was going to scream when it appeared again and she was overcome by the tingling. It vanished and reappeared near the light-fitting and then flew through the closed window. 'Carol' screamed and 'Steve' came in and saw a flash outside the window. The street lights were flickering too.

'Carol' went to her doctor, who prescribed tranquillizers. That night she and 'Steve' heard the 'mowing noise circling the house in all directions'. The next night, too frightened to stay at home, 'Carol' and 'Nicola' stayed at her mother's house, which was only a hundred yards away. At 4 am she felt the tingling very strongly in bed. She was completely paralysed and could only turn her head slightly, even with the greatest of effort. The 'saucer' appeared with a tube-like projection coming from its top. The tingling abruptly stopped and was replaced with a floating and relaxing feeling, although 'Carol' was still paralysed. Turning her head with difficulty, she saw a group of small beings right beside the bed.

Some were standing and others kneeling, with more approaching from the bedroom doorway. They all came up to the bed where 'Carol' was lying, until there was a group of about a dozen or more around her. Her glasses were on the floor so she could not see them clearly. They were about 30 inches in height and their heads seemed too large for their bodies, like babies. They all had tall foreheads, large pale eyes and full lips. Their faces were strangely beautiful and feminine, and she could not determine their sex. Their skin was pale and they wore white clothing. One was wearing a white cloak. 'Carol' described their hair as being close-cropped and artificial, like a doll's hair.

The cloaked being reached over to her and touched her eyes, but 'Carol' felt nothing. It seemed interested in her eyes and her glasses on the floor. In fact, it seemed to be examining them. This cloaked individual then 'said', 'She's just like any other Earthling.' But 'Carol' was not sure if the words were in her head or if she actually heard them. There was no movement on the being's face. Suddenly, after turning her head away for a moment, 'Carol' looked back and all the beings had vanished, along with the 'saucer'. Just before this, she had heard the beings making frequent clicking noises and the mowing noise all around her. She found that she was not paralysed but totally bemused. She went to the window:

outside the street-lights were flickering . . .

In the early hours of the following morning, 'Carol's' father felt the tingling sensation slightly, and her brother felt it strongly. He also heard the mowing noise at a deafening pitch. He began sweating and shaking and felt as though he was 'burning up'. He too developed a rash on his neck. Then 'Carol' heard the mowing noise very loudly, but her mother could hear it very faintly as if it were far away. There were many other incidents similar to these, including another sighting of a being. The investigator, John Watson, reported: 'The family is now on the verge of collapse and only wishes the bizarre series of events would stop.' In fact, over the next few months, they gradually tailed off.

'Staging' and field effects

The alien-theme perceptions created unconsciously by 'Carol' took on all of the erratically 'objective' characteristics of apparitions, and they could be perceived by others in her family. The encounter dramatizations were a scaled-down version of 'outdoor' encounters, complete, absurdly enough, with tiny 'spaceship'. This demonstrates the hallucinatory nature of 'structured craft', although some have more physical characteristics due to their UAP basis. (It makes one realize how easily such perception would become official if they were experienced by military personnel, especially if they were high-ranking officers.)

Many of the systemic effects in this case have already been covered and by now readers should be able to make their own identifications. For example, the secretion of wax from the ear of the main witness is indicative of a diathermal reaction of the tissue within the inner ear to the field presence causing the 'radar hearing' effect; the rashes, hot flushes due to hypothalamus stimulation, tingling and floating sensations (discovered by Persinger) are all systemic reactions to field exposure that can be found in the medical literature. The 'mowing noise' has been associated with radar hearing. The 'clicking' also occurred in the Rowley Regis (see the plate section between pages 112 and 113) and Aveley cases and it was no doubt the Page Effect of magnetostrictive acoustic phenomena, described earlier.

Cynthia Appleton

In 1957 a Birmingham housewife was astonished to see a 'spaceman' materializing in her front room. She felt a pre-thunderstorm-like atmosphere, then 'he appeared just like a TV picture on a screen, a blurred image and then suddenly everything was clear'. At the moment of his appearance, a whistle exactly like the old wireless sets used to make when tuning into a station could be heard.

The man was tall and fair. He was wearing a tight-fitting garment like a silvery plastic macintosh. He made a sweeping lateral movement with his hands, and there appeared between his outstretched fingers what Cynthia could only describe as a TV picture. She could clearly see a spaceship. It was circular with the top half like a transparent dome. Two smaller ships appeared. Eventually Cynthia blacked out.

Notes

Chapter One

1 John Spencer, Vice-Chairman of BUFORA.

2 *Man and His Symbols*.

3 *Heaven and Hell*, Aldous Huxley.

4 *The Intensive Journal*, Ira Progoff (Dialogue House Library, New York, 1975).

5 *Other Worlds*, Paul Davies (Abacus/Sphere, 1982).

6 *Visions, Apparitions, Alien Visitors*, Hilary Evans (1984).

7 Wilder Penfield.

8 *Space Time Transients and Unusual Events*, M. A. Persinger and G. F. Lafrenière (Nelson Hall, Chicago, 1977).

9 *Earthlights Revelation*, Paul Devereux (Blandford, 1989).

10 ibid.

11 *Electromagnetic Man*, C. W. Smith and S. Best (Dent, 1989).

12 *Hauntings and Apparitions*, A. MacKenzie (Heinemann, 1982).

13 *Invitation to Sociology*, Peter Berger (1970).

14 *The Naturalistic Fallacy*, Karl Popper.

15 *The Social Reality of Religion*, Peter Berger (1971).

16 *Witness*, J. G. Bennett (1955).

17 *Hauntings and Apparitions*, op. cit.

18 *Explaining the Unexplained*, Carl Sargent and Hans J. Eysenck (1982).

19 *The Primal Revolution*, Arthur Janov (Abacus, 1975).

20 ibid.

21 ibid.

22 'Dreams That Do as They're Told', *New Scientist* (6 January 1990).

23 *The Pennine UFO Mystery*, Jenny Randles (Granada, 1983).

24 'Non-Ionizing Radiation Protection', World Health Organization (WHO), Geneva (1989).

25 ibid; 'The Electromagnetic Spectrum: Influence on the Pineal: Melatonin Production and Potential Health Effects', R. J. Reiter, Symposium: Man and Environment, Texas (1991).

26 *Earthlights Revelation*, op. cit.

27 'Ghosts, Outgassing and Seismic Energy', Anne Silk, BUFORA lecture (5 September 1992).

28 *Oxford Companion to the Mind*, R. Gregory (Oxford University Press, 1989).

29 ibid; 'Analysis of Microwaves for Barrier Warfare', K. Oscar, US Army R&D Center, Fort Belvoir; declassifed 1991 (1972).

30 R. J. Reiter (1991), op. cit.

31 *Where Science and Magic Meet*, S. Roney-Dougal (Element, 1991).

Chapter Two

1 *Psychokinesis*, John Randall (Souvenir Press, 1982).

2 *Passport to Magonia*, Jacques Vallée (Neville Spearman, 1970).

3 *Hauntings and Apparitions*, op. cit.

4 *UFO Reality*, Jenny Randles (Hale, 1983).

5 *Lightning*, National Meteorological Library (1990).

6 *Superhealth*, Mark Payne (1992).

7 *This House is Haunted*, Guy Lyon Playfair (Sphere, 1981).

8 *Flying Saucer Review*, Vol. 27, No. 1 (June 1980).

9 Geological survey, USA.

10 'Experiments, Discussions and Problems of Biophysics of the Cerebrum', *Quaderni Di Psichiatria* (1929).

11 'The Microwave Auditory Phenomenon', J. Lin, Institution of Electrical Engineers (IEE) conference (1980); WHO (1989), op. cit.

12 *Poltergeist!*, Colin Wilson (New English Library, 1982).

13 *Alien World*, Hilary Evans (Orbis Publishing, 1983).

14 ibid.

15 *The Dyfed Enigma*, R. J. Pugh and F. W. Holiday (Faber & Faber, 1979).

16 *UFO Reality*, op. cit.

17 *The Mothman Prophecies*, J. Keel (Illuminet Press, USA, 1991).

18 *Electrohealing*, R. Coghill (Thorsons, 1992).

19 *Poltergeist!*, op. cit.

20 *The Sunday Times* (21 August 1983).

21 *Earthlights Revelation*, op. cit.

22 *Dreams and Dreaming*, Norman MacKenzie (Aldus Books, 1965).

23 ibid.

24 *Poltergeist!*, op. cit.

Chapter Three

1 *Cyber-Biological Studies of the Imaginal Component in the UFO Contact Experience*, edited by Dennis Stillings, article by Hilary Evans (Archaeus Project, 1989).

2 *Psychokinesis*, op. cit.

3 *Mind Over Matter*, Kit Pedler (Thames Methuen, 1981).

4 *This House is Haunted*, op. cit.

5 *Psychical Research*, I. Gratton-Guiness (Aquarian Press, 1982).

6 *Poltergeist!*, op. cit.

7 *The Roswell Incident*, C. Berlitz and W. Moore (Granada, 1980).

8 *The Welsh Triangle*, Peter Paget (Granada, 1979).

9 *Handbook of Magnetic Phenomena*, A. E. Burke (Van Nostrand Scientific, 1986).

10 *Electromagnetic Man*, op. cit.

11 *Resonance*, No. 24 (May 1992).

12 *The Flight of the Thunderbolts*, Sir Basil Schonland (Clarendon, 1964).

13 'Enhancement of Temporal Lobe-Related Experiences During Brief

Exposures to Milligauss Intensity ELF Magnetic Fields', M. A. Persinger, L. A. Ruttan and S. Koren, *Journal of Bioelectricity,* Vol. 9, No. 1, pp. 33–45 (1990).

14 *Encyclopedia of Science and Technology* (McGraw-Hill, 1987).

15 *The Flight of the Thunderbolts,* op. cit.

16 *Oxford Companion to the Mind,* op. cit.

17 *Earthlights Revelation,* op. cit.

18 *Electromagnetic Man,* op. cit.

19 ibid.

20 ibid.

21 ibid.

22 ibid.

23 ibid.

24 ibid.

25 *Poltergeist!,* op. cit.

26 *Electromagnetic Man,* op. cit.

27 ibid.

28 *Body, Mind and Sugar,* Abrahamson and Pezet (1977).

29 *Electropollution,* R. Coghill (Thorsons, 1990).

30 *Electromagnetic Man,* op. cit.

31 *Poltergeist!,* op. cit.

32 ibid.

33 *Electromagnetic Man,* op. cit.

34 ibid.

35 ibid.

36 *Alien Contact,* Jenny Randles and Paul Whetnall (Spearman, 1981).

37 ibid.

38 *Electropollution,* op. cit.

39 *Explaining the Unexplained,* op. cit.

40 'Flicker as a Helicopter Pilot Problem', L. Johnson, *Aerospace Medicine* (1963).

41 *UFOs Over Plymouth,* Bob Boyd, Plymouth UFO Research Group (1981).

42 *Electromagnetic Man*, op. cit.

43 *UFO Study*, Jenny Randles (Robert Hale, 1981).

44 *ELF Electromagnetic Fields: The Question of Cancer* (Battelle Pacific NW Laboratories, 1990).

45 *UFO Reality*, op. cit.

46 *Electromagnetic Man*, op. cit.

47 ibid.

48 *Progress in Psycho-Biology*, Thompson (Freeman, 1976).

49 *Science and the UFOs*, Jenny Randles and Peter Warrington (Blackwell, 1985).

50 ibid.

51 *Where Science and Magic Meet*, op. cit.

52 ibid.

53 *Handbook of Magnetic Phenomena*, op. cit.

54 *Poltergeist!*, op. cit.

55 *This House is Haunted*, op. cit.

56 Persinger, Ruttan and Koren (1990), op. cit.

57 *This House is Haunted*, op. cit.

58 ibid.

59 *Electromagnetic Man*, op. cit.

60 J. Lin (1980), op. cit.; *Superminds*, John Taylor (Macmillan, 1975).

61 *Electromagnetic Man*, op. cit.

62 *UFO Study*, op. cit.

63 *Electromagnetic Man*, op. cit.

64 *Daily Mirror* (October 1983).

65 *Electromagnetic Man*, op. cit.

66 *This House is Haunted*, op. cit.

67 *Intruders*, Budd Hopkins (Sphere, 1988).

68 *Psychical Research*, op. cit.

69 *Superhealth*, op. cit.

70 *Electromagnetic Man*, op. cit.

71 ibid.

72 *Journeys Out of the Body*, Robert A. Monroe (Souvenir, 1992).

73 *Superhealth*, op. cit.

74 *Northern UFO News*, Ed. Jenny Randles No. 106.

75 *Biological Effects of Environmental Electromagnetism,* H. Konig et al. (Springer Verlag, Berlin, 1981).

76 *Where Science and Magic Meet*, op. cit.

77 The 'Jane Murphy' case in case-studies in the final chapter; investigated by Philip Mantle and Andrew Roberts.

Chapter Four

1 The *Observer* magazine (1990).

2 *Poltergeist!*, op. cit.

3 *Alien Contact*, op. cit.

4 'Medical Device Electromagnetic Interference Problems', W. Midgette, Center for Devices and Radiological Health, Rockville, Maryland (IEEE Conference, Paris, November 1992).

5 Persinger, Ruttan and Koren, op. cit.

6 *Alien Contact*, op. cit.

7 ibid.

8 ibid.

9 'Ghosts, Outgassing and Seismic Energy', Anne Silk, BUFORA lecture (5 September 1992).

10 *This House is Haunted*, op. cit.

11 ibid.

12 ibid.

13 Lionel Beer, *BUFORA Journal* (1980).

14 *The Welsh Triangle*, op. cit.

15 'Resonance', Bioelectromagnetics Special Interest Group (May 1992).

16 *The Welsh Triangle*, op. cit.

17 *This House is Haunted*, op. cit.

18 *The Dyfed Engima*, op. cit.

19 *Alien Contact*, op. cit.

20 *This House is Haunted*, op. cit.

21 ibid.

22 *Electrohealing*, Roger Coghill (Thorsons, 1992).

23 'Mental Phenomena Evoked by Electrical Stimulation of the Human Hippocampal Formation and Amygdala', E. Halgren et al., *Brain*, No. 101, pp. 83–117 (1978).

24 *The Nervous System*, Peter Nathan (Oxford University Press, 1988).

25 *Electromagnetic Man*, op. cit.

26 *This House is Haunted*, op. cit.

27 *The Welsh Triangle*, op. cit.

28 ibid.

29 ibid.

30 ibid.

31 ibid.

32 ibid.

33 ibid.

34 ibid.

35 *Radio Systems Technology*, P. C. Green (Pitman, 1979).

36 *Electromagnetic Man*, op. cit.

37 'Environmental Health Criteria 137: Electromagnetic Fields (300 Hz to 300 Ghz)', World Health Organization (1993).

Chapter Five

1 *Operation Earth*, Brinsley Le Poer Trench (Neville Spearman, 1969).

2 *Phenomenon*, edited by J. Spencer and H. Evans, chapter by David W. Clarke (Futura, 1988).

3 Kevin Cunningham, Security Officer, Blackpool Pier (February 1979).

4 'Geosound arel Nanoearthguake', Zheng Zhizhen, Adv. in Geophysical Res. Vol. 2, Pergamon Press, 1991.

5 *Earthlights Revelation*, op. cit.

6 ibid.

7 *Global Seismology*, British Geological Survey (1985).

8 Mercalli table.

9 'On the Facts and Theory of Earthquake Phenomena', R. Mallett, Report of the British Association, p. 133 (1858).

10 *New Scientist* (March 1993).

11 *The Welsh Triangle*, op. cit.

12 *Northern UFO News*, Ed. Jenny Randles (April 1990).

13 Vol. 126, No. 6 (1981).

14 *This House is Haunted*, op. cit.

15 *UFOs – The Final Solution?*, chapter by K. Phillips (Blandford, 1993).

16 *Fate* (April 1951).

17 *Mysteries of Time and Space*, B. Steiger (Prentice Hall, 1974).

18 *Handbook of Magnetic Phenomena*, op. cit.

19 ibid.

20 *Hauntings and Apparitions*, op. cit.

21 *Earthlights Revelation*, op. cit.

Chapter Six

1 *Trance*, Brian Inglis (Grafton, 1990).

2 *Epilepsy – The Facts*, A. Hopkins (Oxford University Press, 1981).

3 Courtesy of Pendragon Research, Robert France, Reading, UK.

4 'Artificial Electromagnetic Fields and Illness', S. Perry, *Royal College General Practitioners' Reference Book* (1990).

5 ibid.

6 *Man and His Symbols*, op. cit.

7 *Earthlights Revelation*, op. cit.

8 *Anomaly*, John Keel (USA, 1970).

9 *Earthlights Revelation*, op. cit.

10 *Hauntings and Apparitions*, op. cit.

11 ibid.

12 BUFORA *Bulletin* (August 1984).

13 *Hauntings and Apparitions*, op. cit.

14 Mercalli table; *Chinese and Japanese Reports*, W. Corliss (Sourcebook Project, MD, USA, 1990).

15 M. A. Persinger, *Journal of Bioelectricity* (1990).

16 *Dreams and Dreaming*, op. cit.

17 *Superminds*, J. Taylor (Macmillan, 1975).

18 *Earthlights Revelation*, op. cit.

19 Oscar (1972), op. cit.; *Oxford Companion to the Mind*, op. cit.

20 *Earthlights Revelation*, op. cit.

21 Persinger, Ruttan and Koren, op. cit.

22 *Intruders*, op. cit.

23 'The Winchester Encounters', Lionel Beer, *BUFORA Bulletin* (1978).

24 *Superminds*, op. cit.

25 *Superhealth*, op. cit.

26 *Explaining the Unexplained*, op. cit.

27 ibid.

28 *Hauntings and Apparitions*, op. cit.

29 *Superminds*, op. cit.

30 *This House is Haunted*, op. cit.

31 Rakovic (1992), op. cit.

32 ibid.

33 *Black's Medical Dictionary*, edited by C. W. H. Havard (Black, 1990).

34 Rakovic (1992), op. cit.

35 Andrew Collins, Independent UFO Network/UFOIN (1991).

36 *Superminds*, op. cit.

37 *Needles of Stone*, T. Graves (Turnstone, 1978).

38 *A Reference Guide to Basic Electronics Terms*, F. A. Wilson (Babani, 1992).

39 *Superminds*, op. cit.

40 *UFO Times*, BUFORA (July 1990).

41 *Electromagnetic Man*, op. cit.

42 *Explaining the Unexplained*, op. cit.

43 *PK*, Michael H. Brown (Steiner Books, 1976).

44 *The Ufonauts*, H. Holzer (Granada, 1979).

45 *This House is Haunted*, op. cit.

46 *Earthlights Revelation*, op. cit.

47 *Where Science and Magic Meet*, op. cit.

48 'The "Visitor" Experience and the Personality: The Temporal Factor', *Archaeus* 5 (1989).

49 ibid.

50 *Phantoms of Soap Operas*, Jenny Randles (Hale, 1989).

Chapter Seven

1 *Hauntings and Apparitions*, op. cit.

2 J. Lin (1980), op. cit.; *Superminds*, op. cit.

3 *Lightning Pranks*, W. Corliss (Sourcebook Project, MD, USA, 1988).

4 *Electromagnetic Man*, op. cit.

Sources of Further Information

British UFO Research Association (BUFORA), Suite 1, The Leys, 2c Leyton Road, Harpenden, Hertfordshire AL5 2TL, England

Allergies and Aliens: The Visitation Experience: An Environmental Health Issue, Albert Budden, Discovery Times, 270 Sandycombe Road, Kew, Surrey TW9 3NP, England

Index

INDEX